PREACHING TO
POSTMODERNS

Robert Kysar *and* Joseph M. Webb

PREACHING TO POSTMODERNS

New Perspectives for Proclaiming the Message

HENDRICKSON
PUBLISHERS

Preaching to Postmoderns
© 2006 by Hendrickson Publishers, Inc.
P. O. Box 3473
Peabody, Massachusetts 01961-3473

ISBN-13: 978-1-56563-400-8
ISBN-10: 1-56563-400-4

Printed in the United States of America

First Printing — August 2006

Except where otherwise noted, Scripture quotations are from the New Revised Standard Version of the Bible, copyright © 1989 by the Division of Christian Education of the National Council of the Churches of Christ in the United States of America, and are used by permission.

Cover Photo: *Coffee Shop, New York, USA.* Digital Vision Collection. Getty Images. Used with Permission.

Library of Congress Cataloging-in-Publication Data

Kysar, Robert.
    Preaching to postmoderns : new perspectives for proclaiming the message / Robert Kysar, Joseph M. Webb.
       p. cm.
    Includes bibliographical references and indexes.
    ISBN-13: 978-1-56563-400-8 (alk. paper)
    ISBN-10: 1-56563-400-4 (alk. paper)
    1. Preaching. 2. Bible—Homiletical use. 3. Bible—Hermeneutics.
  I. Webb, Joseph M., 1942– II. Title.
    BV4211.3.K97 2006
    251—dc22
                        2006005592

Table of Contents

Preface

Our interest in biblical interpretation for preaching is founded, in both our cases, on experience as parish pastors and the task of preaching frequently, if not every Sunday, to one congregation. The memories of our personal struggles to find something in a Scripture passage that "would preach" are always fresh and unforgettable. In particular, we know the responsibility of faithful biblical interpretation and its importance for the formation of a sermon. However, our involvement in the question of biblical interpretation for preaching also entails our years as professors of preaching in seminaries, and our effort to help students find profitable ways of studying a passage and then making legitimate application of it to the life of a congregation.

As both pastors/preachers and as homiletics professors, we know the frustration of seeking assistance from one's training in biblical studies when preparing to preach. Sometimes it is not easy to cross the gap between seminary biblical studies and preaching, and sometimes it seems nearly impossible. How does a method for biblical interpretation help us as preachers? Fortunately, seminary departments of biblical studies are becoming more and more concerned with bridging that gap. At one seminary we know, students take their first course in preaching at the same time they are enrolled in an introduction to the Gospels course, and both a biblical and a homiletics professor team-teach the preaching course. In another, a New Testament professor gives his students the option of writing and submitting sermons rather than research papers. Still, once out of seminary it is difficult for preachers to integrate their preaching with sound biblical interpretation. On the one hand, it is sometimes difficult to find commentaries and other helps that aid in solid biblical preaching. Commentaries are often too technical and not meaningful for today's congregations. On the other hand, some modern preaching demonstrates little interest in sound biblical interpretation.

However, our writing this book is also motivated by the almost endless appearance of new forms of biblical interpretation. Scholarly journals are filled with a variety of new methods for reading and understanding Scripture, and those who are not privy to the inner workings of biblical scholarly groups today are easily brought to despair by the multiplicity of interpretative methods, some of which are unbelievably obscure and technical. One may feel that there is no way to understand all that has been taking place in biblical studies in the last several decades and may even decide that it is all irrelevant to the task of preaching.

Our conviction is that faithful biblical interpretation today does require at least a cursory knowledge of what is going on in the studies of Scripture. Furthermore, it occurred to us that preachers might welcome a book that surveys in broad strokes the movements afoot in biblical studies and tries to find something of value in each of them for exegeting texts for preaching. There are, in fact, books aplenty that present surveys of the methods, but there are few dedicated to communicating with actively preaching pastors by analyzing these methods for their potential role in homiletical biblical study.

Having enjoyed working together on *Greek for Preachers,* we decided to undertake the book you hold in your hands. Webb is trained in communication, rhetoric, and language studies, as well as in theology, while Kysar's specialty is New Testament studies. Both of us became professors of homiletics, in part because we believe preaching is so important in the life of the church. As you might well imagine, it has not been an easy task to write this volume together. Although the two of us share a great many views on the major methods of biblical interpretation advocated today, we each have special interests and commitments, each of which had to be negotiated to produce a book that had both integrity and clarity. The final test, of course, will be "in the field" where preachers can read and evaluate our work.

Understandably we are deeply indebted to many people in our lives who, at one time or another, have shaped our thinking on this matter. We most certainly cannot name each and every one of them. However, we do want to acknowledge key figures in our training and express our gratitude for their great minds and effective teaching. We do this because studying and understanding interpretative methods have forced each of us to draw on his primary intellectual roots. Webb in particular is indebted to the work of Kenneth Burke in symbolic interaction, while Kysar is increasingly aware of how important his study of Bultmann and his existential thought has been to Kysar's own thinking and writing.

Of course, everything either of us writes is undertaken for the benefit of the church and is an expression of what we understand to be our ministries.

We seek by our efforts to aid clergy in their task of interpreting Scripture for preaching and thus to enhance the church's ministry in this crucial period of its life.

Robert Kysar
Joseph M. Webb

Abbreviations

AB	Anchor Bible
ABD	*Anchor Bible Dictionary*
ACNT	Augsburg Commentary on the New Testament
GBS	Guides to Biblical Scholarship
Int	*Interpretation*
IBC	Interpretation: A Bible Commentary for Teaching and Preaching
JAAR	*Journal of the American Academy of Religion*
JBL	*Journal of Biblical Literature*
LCL	Loeb Classical Library
LEC	Library of Early Christianity
NCB	New Century Bible
NIB	*New Interpreter's Bible*
NICNT	New International Commentary on the New Testament
OBT	Overtures in Biblical Theology
SBLDS	Society of Biblical Literature Dissertation Series
SBLSymS	Society of Biblical Literature Symposium Series
SNTSMS	Society for the New Testament Studies Monograph Series
StABH	Studies in American Biblical Hermeneutics
WBC	World Biblical Commentary

Introduction: Living at the Epicenter

We preachers may sometimes feel that the earth is quaking beneath us![1] At the beginning of the twenty-first century, we stand at the epicenter of a hermeneutical earthquake in biblical studies. We are committed to sound biblical interpretation as the basis of our preaching. However, biblical interpretation is being redefined, refocused, and reconstructed. We want to find the meaning of a biblical passage from which we can discern its message for contemporary Christian life and faith today, but biblical interpreters are advancing a multitude of new forms of criticism and even debating the meaning of meaning! How do we go about the homiletical task with faithfulness when the tectonic plates of how we interpret the Bible, upon which we stand, are shifting?

It is odd that the earth should shift now! Preachers have, for the most part, been trained—and many are still being trained—in the classical historical critical methods of Bible study. Many of us who have taught biblical hermeneutics, the interpretation of texts for preaching, have been adamant that one must first determine what the text meant in its original context before attempting to decide what it means now.[2] The historical inquiry into the origin

---

[1] Kysar first wrote portions of this introduction for the 1998 Yost Lectures at the Lutheran Theological Southern Seminary in Columbus, South Carolina, which were later published under the title, "Living at the Epicenter: Preaching and Contemporary Biblical Interpretation," in "Ethics and Preaching at the Turn of the Millennium: Essays in Honor of Paul T. Jersild," *Taproot: The Journal of Lutheran Theological Southern Seminary* 14 (1999–2000): 114–53.

[2] See Krister Stendahl, "Biblical Theology, Contemporary," *IDB* 1:418–32. The article was reprinted in a revised form under the title "Biblical Theology: A Program" in Stendahl's collection of essays, *Meanings: The Bible as Document and as Guide* (Philadelphia: Fortress, 1984), 11–44.

of the text and its meaning for the first readers must precede attempts to discern anything like a contemporary meaning. Moreover, we have just about convinced our congregations that historical questions are important for interpretation. The laity are asking about the original setting of passages. In many cases, they crave historical knowledge. Popular magazines and television programs regularly explore the historical context out of which the Bible emerged.

Now, however, the whole historical critical enterprise is under assault. In some circles, the distinction between what a passage meant and what it means is denounced. Indeed, for some, the whole assumption that we should be interested in meaning at all is up for grabs.[3] What a time for an earthquake!

INTERPRETATION AT THE EPICENTER

How does the preacher live at the epicenter of an earthquake in biblical interpretation? We certainly cannot still the shaking. In fact, it is safe to say that the shifting plates of biblical interpretation will probably not settle down into some new configuration for at least several decades. Nor should we act as if nothing has happened, stick our heads in the sand, and go on reading and interpreting the Bible as we have always done. Instead, perhaps we can find some survival techniques—not escape routes, but ways of coping in the midst of shifting paradigms. Even better, we may be able to discern some ways of turning the shifting of biblical interpretation to our advantage in our preaching ministries.

An example will help us understand how this earthquake intrudes into pastors' studies as we investigate a text for the sake of preaching. For a century or more most of the so-called "mainline theological seminaries" have

---

[3] Your authors have each contributed to various degrees in challenging the historical critical method we inherited from the nineteenth century and questioning the traditional meaning of meaning. Therefore, we do not pretend to be disinterested observers of developments in biblical interpretation. However, we do hope to describe fairly those developments for the sake of preachers. Among Webb's writings, his volumes, *Old Texts, New Sermons: The Quiet Revolution in Biblical Preaching* (St. Louis: Chalice, 2000), and *Preaching and the Challenge of Pluralism* (St. Louis: Chalice, 1998) best exemplify his challenge to traditional historical criticism. Kysar's contribution has been mostly confined to several articles, one of which is "The Dismantling of Decisional Faith: A Reading of John 6:25–71," in *Critical Readings of John 6* (ed. R. Alan Culpepper, Biblical Interpretation Series, 22; Leiden: Brill, 1997), 161–82, but see also, *Stumbling in the Light* (St. Louis: Chalice: 1999).

taught students to be sensitive to the composite nature of the book of Isaiah.[4] The first thirty-nine chapters, we learned, are the work of "Isaiah of Jerusalem" in the eighth century B.C.E.[5] Chapters 40–55, however, were composed at a later time and for a different audience. The intended audience of these chapters were Israelites in exile in Babylonia and elsewhere, and the prophet (whom we designate with the horrid title "deutero-Isaiah") brought a message of hope and assurance to those who had suffered dislocation. Finally, the last eleven chapters of the book of Isaiah, as we know them today, were the work of still a third prophet (sometimes called "trito-Isaiah") who lived in resettled Jerusalem and directed a message toward those who had repopulated the Israelite homeland.[6]

Many preachers have taken this hypothetical reconstruction of the composition of Isaiah seriously and carefully treated passages from various parts of Isaiah in accord with the historical thesis regarding that portion of the book. Indeed, some powerful messages arise from the idea that Second Isaiah is speaking to an exiled people.[7] What happens, however, to our preaching when the composite nature of the book is challenged by contemporary literary critics—at least insofar as a sharp delineation of the three portions is concerned? For instance, Christopher R. Seitz insists that the editing of the book of Isaiah was carefully done so that the book has a unity which defies partition theories. Seitz asks,

> Have the indications of historical, literary, and sociological cleavage between chapters 40–55 and 56–66 been overplayed in the interest of pursuing one

---

[4] The question of the authorship of Isaiah rose to prominence in the eighteenth century, and the suggestion that chapters 40–66 were written by a different prophet than the first thirty-nine was first proposed by J. C. Döderlein, *Esais* (Norimbergae et Altdorfi: Apud Georg. Petr. Monath, 1789) and J. G. Eichhorn, *Introduction to the Study of the Old Testament* (London: Spottiswoode, 1888; trans. of *Einleitung ins Alte Testament,* 1780). A third "Isaiah" was first advanced as the author of chapters 56–66 in the commentary by Bernhard Duhm, *Das Buch Jesaia* (Göttingen: Vandenhoeck & Ruprecht, 1892).

[5] Some of us were also taught to treat chapters 24–27 as still another independent section, sometimes called "The Little Apocalypse" of Isaiah and most often dated in the post-exilic period.

[6] The fact that the *Anchor Bible Dictionary* (*ABD*) published in 1992, includes separate articles on the "three Isaiahs" is evidence of how deeply embedded this composite view of the book is in the minds of biblical scholars. See *ABD* 3:472–506, as well as Claus Westermann's classic commentary, *Isaiah 40–66* (OTL; Philadelphia: Westminster, 1969).

[7] For example, the stimulating study by Walter Brueggemann, *Hopeful Imagination: Prophetic Voices in Exile* (Philadelphia: Fortress, 1986).

type of diachronic analysis? Are the differences between chapters 40–55 and 56–66 explicable on other grounds? Are there indications of clear linkage between these two sections which do not depend upon a Babylonian prophet and Palestinian disciple model of interpretation but are rather the consequence of a far greater common purpose in authorial, redactional, and theological intention?[8]

By reading Isaiah as a single unity, some of our older pet ideas of preaching these chapters are seriously threatened, or at least need to be drastically revised. What does it mean for preaching, for instance, to link the whole of chapters 50–66? It is a question to which we shall return later in this book.

PURPOSE AND METHOD

The purpose of this book is to answer the question, Why it is important for preachers to be equipped with a variety of critical methods in order to read biblical passages most effectively? This book asks "so what" to the field of biblical hermeneutics. We have therefore entitled the chapters "What Difference Do _____ Criticisms Make?" While we will not pretend to be entirely objective and admit to having our own opinions about these methods, our purpose is not to advocate one critical approach over another but to explore the possibility that preachers can use a variety of interpretative methods to their advantage. As authors of this study and as preachers we find ourselves thinking our way through some of the very issues about which we will write, trying to see more clearly how various methods of interpretation impact the preacher's work.

In the chapters that follow, we ask what difference each of the following critical methods make: Historical, Social-Scientific, Literary, Liberation, and Deconstruction. The final chapter wrestles with the impact of theories of meaning, or the idea of meaning itself as it is understood by the various critical approaches. We will discuss how these theories of meaning impact an interpretation of a passage for preaching. We select what seems to us to be some of the most significant movements afoot in biblical studies, describe them briefly, and offer a few suggestions as to how they might impact our homiletic study of texts. We try to identify the plates that are in motion—in particular the ones which are the most likely to perplex us.

Readers should be aware of a number of things about this discussion. We cannot pretend to discuss every sort of criticism that has been proposed in the last several decades, nor shall we try to elucidate every subdivision within the

---

[8] Christopher R. Seitz, "Isaiah, Book of (Third Isaiah)," *ABD* 3:506.

broader rubrics we have used. There are so many of these that this book would become an encyclopedia of biblical interpretation, and there are already such books available.[9] Moreover, we have collapsed some critical methods under one title for the sake of clarity, and we ask you to allow us to describe these movements in broad and general strokes. Some critical methods relate to several of the types we propose and are not necessarily always in one or the other of our broad and convenient topics. Some forms of rhetorical criticism, for instance, belong with those under the rubric of historical criticisms, while others are best treated in connection with the newer literary movements.

It is difficult to answer the question, "What difference do these critical methods make to the preacher?" without showing samples of sermons built on some aspect of each particular method. We have, therefore, included a number of complete sermons and fragments of sermons in each of the chapters and sometimes in subdivisions of the chapters. These samples are not necessarily to be taken as examples of the very best sermons. All we hope to demonstrate is how a particular critical method yields an interpretation on which a sermon can be constructed.

DEFINING INTERPRETATION

Before beginning our discussions of the various methods of interpretation available to preachers today we should address a number of matters. First, we need a working understanding of the terms "interpret" and "interpretation." An initial attempt to develop such an understanding, however, leads almost immediately to the question of "meaning," a topic to which we shall devote an entire chapter later in this book. The meaning of meaning is one of those plates that we feel moving underneath our hermeneutical feet and is for many the most troubling of all. For now we must attempt to define interpretation in such a way as to leave open the question of its relation to the concept of meaning.

"Interpretation" is simply the effort to seek understanding. To interpret means to consider how an experience of some sort can be comprehended in ways that approximate "truth" (that is, "truth" either in the sense of what

---

[9] For example, see Robert Morgan and John Barton, *Biblical Interpretation* (Oxford Bible Series; Oxford: Oxford University Press, 1988); Donald K. McKim, ed., *A Guide to Contemporary Hermeneutic: Major Trends in Biblical Interpretation* (Grand Rapids: Eerdmans, 1986); and Steven L. McKenzie and Stephen R. Haynes, eds., *To Each Its Own Meaning: Biblical Criticism and Their Application* (rev. and exp.; Louisville: Westminster John Knox, 1999).

some understand to be universal, or more narrowly in the sense simply of what a passage proposes). For many the concept of truth itself has been radically refashioned in the course of the last several decades. Suppose someone says to you, "You are indeed a wise man." At the most fundamental level, you would wish to understand exactly what the statement means. How is the word "wise" used in this sentence? Why does the adverb "indeed" appear in the statement? Does it imply that you have proved something that was heretofore uncertain, or is the function of "indeed" simply to emphasize "wise"? To interpret this sentence, you will need to consider the sense of the individual words, how they are linked in this particular sentence, and how the sentence relates to its immediate context.[10] If the statement were, "You're a cool cat," the process of interpretation would be no different, with the exception that "cool cat" would require understanding contemporary jargon.

Actually the interpretation of linguistic statements is only one kind of interpretation and the process of interpretation is much more complicated and comprehensive than our simplistic examples. All our lives, we seek to understand the world around us and how we experience it. Webb calls this process "defining." Everything one looks at, one defines. We humans must define everything, first of all, in order to talk about it. Whatever one says about something—anything—is an interpretation of it. Therefore we must interpret, but no two definitions or interpretations of anything are ever quite alike and probably cannot be.[11]

Hence, we almost instinctively interpret or define all of our experiences. A car suddenly swerves in front of us, and we barely avoid a deadly accident. We may pray, "Thank you, Lord!" and thereby imply that we understand the event involved some sort of divine intervention. Or, we may tell others how "lucky" we were, which assumes the categories of fortune—good luck and bad luck. Or, we may understand the near-miss as evidence of our skill as a driver. Ultimately, of course, our basic understanding of life in this world is the result of interpreting experience. The way we "read" life's experiences based upon our view of life becomes a fundamental assumption for our understanding. We develop our view of life by means of the consistent use of interpretation, and in turn that interpretative stance becomes the basis on which we understand all experience. (This is a form of what has been called "the hermeneutical circle.")

---

[10] We have discussed the relationship among these elements of interpretation in Joseph M. Webb and Robert Kysar, *Greek for Preachers* (St. Louis: Chalice, 2001).

[11] See Chapter Two in Joseph M. Webb, *Preaching and the Challenge of Pluralism* (St. Louis: Chalice, 1998). He writes, "Life, in short, is a continuous definitional stream" (36).

Sometimes that interpretation assumes there is an objective "truth" to which a statement or an experience refers or in the light of which it is to be understood. In a later chapter we will ask what happens to the process of interpretation when, on the one hand, interpreters assume such a view of "objective truth" and, on the other hand, what happens to the process of interpretation when they do *not* assume there to be a body of "objective truth." Some contemporary philosophical shifts in the understanding of truth have direct impact on biblical interpretation. If, for instance, there is no one single body of truth to which a statement or experience directs us, then interpretation must redefine what is meant by "understanding" and "meaning."

Biblical interpretation, then, is but one instance of the broader human effort to understand. It is a specific form of linguistic interpretation, of course, which for some people (including preachers) is far more important than the interpretation of the newspaper. For some the Bible is a sacred book, for others a literary classic, and for still others an ancient document that contributes to our understanding of the past. Hence, the interpretation of the Bible is based on, and determined in large part by, the preunderstandings we bring to interpretation.[12] Any act of understanding depends on earlier "understandings," including our "symbolic hub," whether we suppose it is discerned, created, or inherited. As Webb has written elsewhere, "'hub symbols' [are] those unique symbols that, by their placement within us, provide the key to human behavior in all of its often-terrifying volatility." That is, the hub symbol embodies the emotionally-charged "truth" that we take for granted and which provides a structure within which we understand all experience.[13] Our concern in this book is with exactly how our presuppositions shape interpretation, and that concern is addressed several times in the following chapters. Needless to say, for Christians the interpretation of Scripture is especially shaped by one's faith perspective and doctrinal posture.[14] Recent biblical interpretation (and theological reflection) stresses that social location and ideological commitments are also part of the cluster

---

[12] See the articles in Part III, "How the Bible Is Read, Interpreted, and Used," in *NIB* 1:33–212.

[13] Joseph M. Webb, *Preaching and the Challenge of Pluralism* (St. Louis, Mo.: Chalice, 1998), 49. See a full exposition and application of Webb's concept in Andrew Carl Wisdom, *Preaching to a Multi-Generational Assembly* (Collegeville, Minn.: Liturgical, 2004). This book won first place in the liturgical category of the Catholic Press Association for 2005.

[14] Donald K. McKim surveys different understandings of biblical authority and the impact they have on preaching in *The Bible in Theology and Preaching: How Preachers Use Scripture* (rev. ed.; Nashville: Abingdon, 1994).

of presuppositions which influence interpretation and are perhaps the most powerful of all our presuppositions.

In summary, we use the words "interpret" and "interpretation" to speak of that process by which readers seek to understand a portion of Scripture. When we speak of a "*critical*" interpretation, we mean simply that the process of seeking understanding entails careful questioning of and interaction with a text. Critical scholars ask questions of the text and in turn are themselves questioned by it. The interpretation of Jesus' statement, "If your right hand causes you to sin, cut it off and throw it away" (Matt 5:30), for instance, becomes critical when we realize we cannot take the text at face value and need to ask just what sort of language this is. Is it possible that the statement is hyperbole? Further, we might ask what the sentence is "intended" to accomplish. Simply put, criticism involves *the rational interrogation of a passage.* This makes such a search for understanding "critical" as opposed to one which accepts the text in terms of what it first seems to say and assumes that it should not be properly subjected to rational interrogation and interaction. An "uncritical" approach takes for granted that rational query is not necessary to understand the text.

What then do we mean when we call a process of interpreting Scripture a "method?" In general a method is any systematic way of going about something. That process may be mapped out in advance, or it may evolve as it is used. Some methods are complex and highly structured, while others are freer and flexible. Over time, most interpretative methods become very deliberately planned and highly intentional. The interpretative "methods" we explore in this book have each evolved under intense scrutiny by those who use them and by others who criticize them. In our discussion the word "method" means little more than a way of reading and interpreting that has been practiced by a significant number of scholars over a period of time.

WHOSE BIBLE IS IT?

In addition to proposing a working definition of "interpretation," it is helpful at this point to sketch very briefly the history of biblical criticism that has brought us to where we are today. In the final two or three decades of the past century, the number of methods for biblical interpretation has greatly multiplied until now they comprise a virtual flood.

The history of biblical studies provides us a context within which to read the present situation. Moreover, even a cursory awareness of that history helps us realize that there have been numerous periods in which radical changes occurred in widely accepted ways of reading Scripture. This historical perspective may help us see the current situation as much more "normal" than we might at first experience it.

One way of structuring the history of interpretation is to ask the question, "Whose Bible is it?" Through the centuries that question has been asked and answered in various ways.

Christians Claim the Hebrew Scriptures

Biblical interpretation had its beginnings in the Bible itself. Insofar as we find biblical authors and/or communities interpreting one portion of Scripture in their composition of another part, biblical interpretation was one of the sources for certain biblical books. The clearest example of biblical writers interpreting (what was to become) the Bible is found in the use of the historical books of 1 and 2 Samuel and 1 and 2 Kings in the composition of 1 and 2 Chronicles. While the dates for the Chronicles and the historical occasion for their production are debated, the chroniclers' use of these other biblical books is clear. An example of the manner in which those authors and their communities interpreted the work of their predecessors is clear from a comparison of 1 Chr 21:1 with 2 Sam 24:1. The latter states that God inspired David to take a census of the nation, while the former attributes the inspiration not to Yahweh, but to Satan. This reinterpretation of the earlier text demonstrates the influence of a different understanding both of God and of the source of evil.

Likewise, the theory that those responsible for the Gospels of Matthew and Luke made ample use of the Gospel of Mark in their writings suggests the interpretation of a New Testament book by the authors of two other books. For example Mark claims that Jesus "could do no deed of power" in Nazareth because of their unbelief (Mark 6:5). The author of Matthew interpreted Mark's statement carefully, saying, "And he did not do *many deeds of power* there, because of their unbelief" (Matt 13:58). Luke, on the other hand, does not bother even to mention the question of Jesus' ability to do wonders in Nazareth. Instead, the Gospel repositions the story of Jesus' rejection at Nazareth by putting it immediately after the story of his temptation in the wilderness. Additionally, in Luke the reaction of those in the synagogue is so radical (and fostered by Jesus' own words) that Jesus must avoid their effort to throw him off a cliff (Luke 4:22–30).

However, among the clearest acts of interpretation in the New Testament are those which involve the Hebrew Scriptures (frequently called by Christians the Old Testament or the First Testament) and the Christians' claim that those Scriptures were also theirs. Within the scope of the New Testament itself there is no evidence that the earliest Christians had any hesitancy in laying claim to the Hebrew Scriptures as their Bible, even though they engaged in a variety of interpretations that (it often seems) drastically altered the message of the Hebrew Scriptures. Paul used a christological framework within which to interpret the First Testament and thereby drastically changed what would appear to have been the message of a particular passage (e.g., 1 Cor 10:1–4), and Matthew did much the same in the form of "prophecies" (e.g., Matt 2:13–15). There also emerged a "typological interpretation" of Hebrew Scriptures especially evident in the New Testament book of Hebrews. Old Testament passages are used there to suggest prefigurations of Christ—"types" that are fulfilled in Christ. Some would say that the radical re-reading of the Hebrew Scriptures found in Hebrews essentially eliminates any meaning the texts of the Old Testament may have had in themselves. The Christians claimed the Old Testament as their own, even though they so re-interpreted it that it is sometimes hardly recognizable. (Of course, the same may be said of some Jewish interpreters.)

The interpretation of ancient literature, like that which we find in the New Testament's use of Hebrew Scriptures, assumes a very different understanding of meaning than the one western culture devised and eventually canonized in the Enlightenment. For the most part, our ancient ancestors believed the meaning of a written passage was open to re-interpretation. There was no presumption that an author's original meaning determined what the written text meant when it was read at a later time. Especially in the case of sacred literature, such as what we now call our Bible, the texts were presumed to be endlessly open to the construction of meaning. We find evidence of this practice most easily in the "deuterocanonical" books that were included in the translation of the Hebrew Scriptures into Greek in the period between the third and first centuries B.C.E. In these apocryphal or deuterocanonical writings one finds a number of documents which were additions to biblical books, especially Jeremiah, Esther, and Daniel. The authors of these "additions" felt free to attach their writings to those that were gradually becoming more and more authoritative for Jewish people. Jeremiah 29:1–23 is reportedly the prophet's letter to the exiles of 597 B.C.E. The deuterocanonical "Letter of Jeremiah" imitates the prophet's letter, perhaps in an effort to address the threat to Jewish monotheism in the author's own day (probably between the fourth and second century B.C.E.) in which Jewish people living in Egypt, Syria, and Greece were tempted to worship foreign gods. In a similar way 1 Enoch 6 and 7 freely interprets Gen 6:1–4. The biblical literature was open to various interpretations, sometimes with little regard for the original sense of the documents. It is precisely this understanding of what a text means that allowed the early Christians to re-interpret the Hebrew Scriptures in the light of the Christ event.

The belief that texts are susceptible to re-interpretation time and again is also the basis of the rabbinic method of reading Scripture. Like the early Christians, the rabbis continued to read Scripture in the light of contemporary needs in their communities. The same kind of interpretative freedom is also found in the evidence of scribal changes and additions in the texts of both the first and the second Testaments. For instance, some unknown scribe felt at liberty to add the so-called "Johannine Comma" between 1 John 5:7 and 8. Moreover, a number of scribes tried their hand at completing what they regarded to be an inappropriate conclusion to the Gospel of Mark.[15] The difference implicit in the ancient and the modern understandings of a written text will occupy us later on.

The Church Claims the Bible

The creation of the categories "heresy" and "orthodoxy" may have occasioned another of the early claims to ownership of the Bible. In the early third century, Tertullian (ca. 160–230 C.E.) denied the use of the Bible to any who did not teach what had become the faith advocated by the church, and with that decision the orthodox church in effect claimed exclusive authority to read and interpret Scripture. Officials of the church interpreted the Bible for the masses, and the church's word held sole authority. In that setting, for the most part, dogma determined meaning. The church was interested in bolstering its own position without regard for other issues. In the simplest of terms, the church claimed that the Bible was *its* book and could only be interpreted properly within and for the sake of the church.

To enable the Bible to speak more helpfully to the church, allegorizing became a common interpretative technique, along with the division of a passage's literal and spiritual meanings (e.g., the Alexandrian School and Origen in the third century). The freedom to read a passage as an allegory made it possible to ascribe ecclesiological relevance to any portion of Scripture. However, the church centered in Antioch continued to argue that the deeper truth of Scripture was always based on its literal meaning. One discovered a text's spiritual meaning through its material or literal meaning.

The Middle Ages brought an important shift in the primacy of the literal sense of the Bible and effectively split theology and biblical interpretation. In Robert Grant's view, the Middle Ages (and particularly the work of Thomas Aquinas) marks a step toward the future:

---

[15] On 1 John 5:7–8 see Raymond E. Brown, *The Epistles of John* (AB 30; Garden City, N.Y.: Doubleday, 1982), 775–87. On Mark see Lamar Williamson Jr., *Mark* (Interpretation; Atlanta: John Knox, 1983), 286–88.

xxiv   PREACHING TO POSTMODERNS

No longer could the interpreter claim to be directly inspired by God in the setting forth of his exegesis. All knowledge comes through the senses, and the interpretation of scripture requires no special inner grace. . . . In the medieval claim to objectivity we find the beginning of modern scientific study of the scriptures. Reason is set up as an autonomous agent.[16]

The Laity Claims the Bible

The Bible remained the church's book, and for the most part the rise of humanism and the Reformation were the crucial events that began to break the church's hold on the Bible. The impact of these two movements was significantly increased by Gutenberg's invention of the printing press in the fifteenth century, which made possible the distribution of the Bible to the common people. When the invention of the printing press was combined with translations into the vernacular, common folk could claim the Bible as their own.

In a sense Luther encouraged the laity to claim ownership of the Bible but he also opened the way for critics to assert that it was theirs to interpret for the laity. Luther supplied the German-speaking church with one of the first translations into the language of the common folk. He also insisted on the literal sense of Scripture and devalued allegorical interpretation. Moreover, his biblical studies enabled him to recognize and stress the historical setting of the authors. Still further, his simple claim that the Bible's authority resided in its proclamation of Jesus as the Christ/Messiah reconnected biblical interpretation once again with theology, albeit a different theological theme. For Luther the revelation in and through Christ was the standard or criterion for judging what was, or was not, God's revelation. This christological assessment of the authority of a passage also introduced a "subjective" element into exegesis (what is the proclamation of Christ?), although Luther claimed that Scripture was clear in and of itself. John Calvin tried to preserve the absolute objectivity of biblical truth, and the reformed church eventually insisted on theories of verbal inspiration and infallibility. In doing so, it denied Luther's view that the Bible's authority arises exclusively from its proclamation of Christ.[17]

---

[16] For the history of interpretation, see Robert M. Grant, *A Short History of the Interpretation of the Bible: An Introduction to the History of the Methods Used to Interpret Scripture* (rev. ed.; New York: Macmillan Company, 1963), 126–27. For the history of interpretation see pp. 75–90. This small and older book is still very useful in gaining an overview of the history of interpretation.

[17] See D. C. Steinmetz, "Luther, Martin," *Dictionary of Biblical Interpretation* 2:96–98.

The Critics Claim the Bible

Humanism set in motion a new way of studying the Bible, namely, to treat it as one would treat any other classical literature. Desiderius Erasmus (1466/69–1536) tried to stand with one foot in the church and the other in humanism, contending that learning "enhanced by piety could renew theology and restore both church and society."[18] He linked classical studies with biblical studies, and as a result was maliciously attacked by both the Roman Church and the reformers. However critical the reformers were of Erasmus, his work combined with the efforts to make Scripture accessible to lay people were effective in beginning to free the Bible from its captivity within the church.

Still, that liberation was far from complete in the sixteenth century, and the interpretation of the Bible remained dominated by Christian leaders. The impact of the Enlightenment, however, dramatically changed the place of the Bible in society. The superiority of reason over biblical authority, the importance of history, and the splitting of philosophy and theology led some to recognize the importance of the historical setting of biblical passages and how the setting shaped a biblical author's meaning.

During the eighteenth century the distinction between "lower" and "higher" criticisms emerged. The term lower criticism was used of the scholarly effort to study and analyze ancient biblical manuscripts, and from such study to construct texts in their original languages which scholars believed approximated the originals (the "autographs"). This enterprise was distinguished from "higher criticism," which is the analysis of the reconstructed texts in terms of their historical setting, date, composition, authorship, and related issues. The spatial terminology (lower and higher) refers only to the fact that an original language text must first be established before other scholarly questions can be raised regarding it.

The nineteenth century saw a gradual shift from the authority of the church to interpret the Scriptures to the development and adoption of historical critical methods by those who claimed to be Christian and stood within the church. Such methods stressed the importance of knowing the historical context of the Scriptures in order to guide readers in discerning the meaning of the biblical text. Far more important, however, is the fact that in the middle decades of the nineteenth century this historical criticism gave birth to "modernism" and all that term came to mean for the western world for nearly three centuries. At the center of the movement was a new sense of history. Darwin

---

[18] Manfred Hoffmann, "Erasmus, Desiderius," *Dictionary of Biblical Interpretation* 1:341.

demonstrated that everything had a history and that the origins of everything became crucial to understanding the present. There emerged a fascination with chronology and learning history for the sake of history.[19]

In the nineteenth century rationalism came to reign in many quarters of biblical interpretation. This rationalism meant that philosophical views became the guiding assumptions in biblical studies,[20] that historical investigations were valued as a means of critiquing Scripture, and that an early form of "liberal theology" arose in the place of biblical thought. An example is surely D. F. Strauss who sought to demolish the New Testament view of Jesus and to substitute for it a spiritual and "eternal Christ."[21] The nineteenth century set in place a strongly rationalistic and historical view of Scripture and a theological liberalism characterized by a bold optimism. Both this view of the Bible and its related theology were decisively challenged in the twentieth century, but modernism once and for all claimed the Bible was no longer the exclusive property of the church. Another question, however, lurked nearby. Do scholars alone own the Bible?

The Scholars' Bible

The answer to the question of who owns the Bible is not yet clear. In the nineteenth and the first half of the twentieth centuries, the historical critical methods became more complex even as they were becoming more dominant. Scholars devised elaborate historical structures behind the text, all of which had to be utilized if an interpreter hoped to understand a passage (see Chapter One). In one way or the other, the historical criticisms all assume that the meaning of a text is anchored in past history, and in particular the historical setting in which the text was written. Therefore, to understand a text one must understand its historical setting as scholars have described it.

Yet in the second half of the last century those historical-critical structures gradually began to crumble. Censure of the established historical methods came from several different directions at once. In the early stages of this onslaught, the rational and liberal theological assumptions of the historical-

---

[19] A. K. M. Adam, *Making Sense of New Testament Theology: "Modern" Problems and Prospects* (StABH 11; Macon: Mercer University Press, 1995), 7–47.

[20] Robert Grant writes, "One of the most striking features of the development of biblical interpretation during the nineteenth century was the way in which philosphical presuppositions implicitly guided it." *A Short History of the Interpretation of the Bible,* 154.

[21] David Friedrich Strauss, *The Christ of Faith and the Jesus of History: A Critique of Schleiermacher's* The Life of Christ (trans. Leander E. Keck; Philadelphia: Fortress, 1977).

critical methods were both unmasked and called into question. Further scrutiny of those methods challenged the entire modernistic understanding of history on which historical critical methods are based. Critics began asking difficult questions: Do such methods suppose more than we can know? Is the sense of the text lost in the elaborate methods of historical reconstruction? Many preachers, too, began to feel betrayed by historical criticism because it often left them with complicated historical and literary theories but without a clear sense of how a passage might speak to our age.

Among the first pillars of historical criticism to tumble was the pretense of objectivity.[22] The historical critical method assumed that one could investigate history in a detached and objective manner, free of presuppositions and prejudice. As the presumption of objectivity was weakened, historical critical investigations of Scripture began to take a turn.[23] Into the vacuum created by doubts about historical criticism came what has become a parade of new methods. Some are aimed at renewing historical criticism; some seek to supplement its limitations; and some aspire to replace it entirely.[24] In later chapters we will exam the distinctions among these methods in greater detail. Certainly historical methods are still practiced and even practiced with a new

---

[22] See the 1957 classic essay by Rudolf Bultmann, "Is Exegesis Without Presuppositions Possible?" *Existence and Faith: Shorter Writings of Rudolf Bultmann* (trans. and ed. Schubert M. Ogden; New York: Meridian Books, 1960), 289–96. In some ways, Bultmann represents a figure on the threshold between nineteenth-century liberal rationalism and its critique by newer methods. His training was classical nineteenth century, his use of existential philosophy is reminiscent of the dominance of philosophical presuppositions in early historical criticism, and his "demythologization" method highly rational. On the other hand, Bultmann's enterprise moved biblical studies in a new direction, not least of all because of the radicality of his existentialist challenge to idealism. Moreover, his existential perspective led him to stress "self-understanding" and thus to introduce a strong subjective element into the interpretative process.

[23] In retrospect Karl Barth's assault on biblical criticism seems to have foreshadowed more than we could have imagined at the time. Karl Barth, *The Epistle to the Romans* (trans. E. C. Hoskyns; London: Oxford, 1963). Unlike Bultmann, however, he stressed the absolute objectivity of the biblical message, which supersedes all else including all philosophical perspectives. See also Walter Wink, *The Bible in Human Transformation: Toward a new Paradigm for Biblical Study* (Philadelphia: Fortress, 1973).

[24] A useful summary of a number of different methods is found in Janice Capel Anderson and Stephen D. Moore, eds., *Mark and Method: New Approaches in Biblical Studies* (Minneapolis: Fortress Press, 1992). Among the methods exemplified in this collection are narrative, reader-response, deconstruction, feminist, and social criticisms, each of which is applied to interpret a Markan passage.

vigor. While they may be weakened by recent challenges, they have also become more self-critical and in some circles show little evidence of having suffered mortal wounds.

Another movement within the field of biblical studies has implications for the question of who owns the Bible. Within the last quarter or third of the twentieth century a form of biblical studies has arisen that makes no claims whatsoever for the faith value of Scripture or its authority for today. The efforts to establish an objective historical study of the Bible made it possible for such an investigation to be done without regard to the truth or falsehood of the religious views contained in Scripture. As a result, departments of religion grew up within state universities and purely secular colleges. In such departments the Bible is treated as an interesting historical document that traces the origins and developments of both Judaism and Christianity (and to a lesser degree, Islam). In other courses the literary quality of the Bible in and of itself may be the subject of study. In both cases, the Bible is treated as a religious book without advocating the religious views contained within it. This phenomenon of faith-free or "neutral" studies of the Bible has surely helped to free the Bible from the grasp of the church (and more particularly the grasp of the churches that practice a biblical literalism), and to some degree has addressed the new biblical illiteracy in our society. However, it raises questions which the twentieth century never answered. For example, is it possible to read and understand the biblical documents without sharing its faith perspective and to do so outside a community that embraces its faith perspective?

Whose Bible Is It Today?

The historical critical study of Scripture sometimes tends to assume that the Bible belongs to the scholar, and only with the help of scholarship can it be properly interpreted. One of the results of "modernism" is the creation of "a gap between expert and public."[25] With their complexities and inscrutable analyses, many of the newer methods also assume that biblical interpretation requires extensive scholarly credentials. Secular studies of Scripture have claimed that the Bible belongs to Western culture and hence to the whole of society. The church, however, has persistently clung to the Bible, claiming it even when interpreters and those beyond the church's faith have applied their critical methods. Moreover, in some of the newer methods we will examine the church has made efforts to reclaim the Bible as its own—to wrest it away from the scholars and critics. In a sense, then, the answer to the question, "whose book is it today?" remains up for grabs.

---

[25] Adam, *Making Sense of New Testament Theology,* 45.

In recent years we have seen a concerted effort on the part of the church's laity to reclaim the Bible for themselves. For better or for worse, Luther and Gutenburg made it possible for lay people to read and interpret the Bible for themselves; they do not have to depend on the church to interpret it for them. Scripture in one sense was demystified when it was freed from its Latin tomb and placed in the hands of common people. That move, of course, has resulted in the endless accumulation of interpretations of nearly every biblical passage. To some degree, too, it has nurtured the rise of literalism, since the ordinary lay person is inclined to take the Bible on its word and to read it as one would read the newspaper. No critical questions are required; no elaborate methodologies are necessary. As one woman said, "My church studies what the Bible itself says and not some interpretation of the Bible!"

Notwithstanding literalism and its influence, there is evidence of a revival of interest in the Bible among lay people.[26] The Bible remains a best seller and its publication in sundry forms (e.g., "The Man's Bible") evidences its popularity. Home Bible studies have cropped up everywhere. Yet it is important to note, too, that there are more and more Christians in the so-called "mainline" churches whose attention to the Bible has led them to deny its value. Actually reading the Bible (which many had never done) has convinced some that it is fatally outdated and cannot be used in any helpful way today. The revival of interest in the Bible—whether it leads to literalism or denunciation—makes one point clear: lay people are trying to claw the Bible out of the hands of the scholars and claim it as their own.

If there is such a renewed interest in the Bible, laity understandably look to their clergy for leadership in the interpretation of Scripture. Clergy are asked to explain how lay people can read and understand the Bible without extensive historical knowledge. Particularly in our preaching ministries, pastors are rightfully expected to offer insights into Scripture both in terms of what it says and what it "means" for contemporary Christian life. All the more reason, then, that clergy understand how biblical interpretation is changing today.

WHAT DIFFERENCE DOES IT MAKE TO THE PREACHER?

Amid the critical methods of historical study and the mass of new interpretative methods—some of which are obscure and confusing—many

---

[26] In part Kysar designed his book *Opening the Bible: What It Is, Where It Came From, What It Means for You* (Minneapolis: Augsburg, 1999) to encourage laity to reclaim the Bible as their own and to provide them guidance in understanding the Scriptures.

preachers have despaired of formal biblical interpretative methods. It may not be an accident that, coinciding with the hermenteutical earthquake we are describing, conservative biblical literalism has gained enormous support. It may seem to some in the church that biblical scholars have abandoned the Christian community. Some preachers have also become content with their own interpretations without recourse to formal methodology, or they have come to rely on the publication of sundry "preaching helps" (many of which offer interpretations of the lectionary texts) without feeling a compulsion to understand the interpretative moves that are made to come to some of the authors' conclusions.

The authors of this book know the feeling of despair when faced with the multiplicity of methods for biblical interpretation and the tendency to limp on without the help of biblical scholars. However, we are convinced that the issues involved in the multiplication of interpretative methods and the resulting methods themselves are important for preachers. If you believe that Scripture remains essential to the life of faith and to preaching, then you are—we believe—obliged to understand what is happening in biblical interpretation today. Understanding these contemporary movements equips you to deal more effectively with individual texts and hence to remain faithful to your calling. Simply put, we believe that the variety of interpretative methods matters to preachers because it gives us new tools for our reading and study of texts for preaching.

Therefore, our study begins in chapter one with an examination of the critical methods that arose between the nineteenth and early twentieth centuries and still hold sway in many quarters today, that is, those rooted in modernism. We proceed in chapter two to newer methods that go beyond the traditional historical critical tools while still assuming that history plays a crucial role in biblical interpretation. Chapters three through six focus on methods that abandon the essential structure of modernism in biblical style and come finally to the question of what might be a postmodern biblical interpretation.

Earthquakes always change the landscape before they subside. The hermeneutical earthquake of which we speak is no different. The landscape of biblical interpretation will be drastically different after the shaking has ceased. Our task together with you, the reader, is to explore what the new landscape will look like, and to find useful ways to mine it for the improvement of our preaching.

Chapter 1

What Difference Do Historical Criticisms Make?

Suppose we were to discover a note, tucked away among the books on a musty, old used bookstore shelf. Scribbled in pencil on the back of an envelope, the note reads:

> I can no longer contain myself! The anguish and torment is too much to bear. You know that I care deeply about you and the children, but my patience has worn thin. If what I am about to do seems cruel and heartless, then so be it. But I must be true to myself and to my values. If what I am about to do brings you shame and embarrassment, you will have to deal with that. For my part, this is my only honest way out. God help me if I am wrong.

The note stimulates our curiosity, but we find it impossible to interpret. What was the crisis facing the author? Why did it so agitate him or her? What was the source of her or his "anguish and torment?" Is it a suicide note? Perhaps a note from a spouse who is leaving her or his family. Or, is the author about to start a revolution? How would the event cause others shame and embarrassment? Is it a note of a "real" person, or a part of a fictional story?

Is there a way of knowing what the note "meant" at the time it was composed? We wonder when it was written, who wrote it, and for whom it was written. If our curiosity is sufficient, we might undertake an investigation of the possible sources of this note. The setting—historical, social, personal, etc.—in which it was written would most likely hold the clues to its meaning. Perhaps too there is an historical event that might "match" the situation described in the note.

This hypothetical situation is not all that different from those in which we find ourselves when reading the Bible. Our curiosity is very much like the curiosity about the Bible that began to compel scholars in and after the

Enlightenment. The emergence of a "consistent historical" approach to Scripture is complicated and gradual, and the intricacies of that development need not concern us here. Still, a historical sketch of the rise of historical-critical studies will help us in our exploration of how these studies are applied to the Bible.

THE RISE OF HISTORICAL CRITICISMS

In a sense, this idea of seeking the historical setting for a document in order to understand it is so taken for granted today that its relatively recent development may not be fully appreciated. Nor can we quite imagine a world in which it is was not commonplace to think this kind of problem-solving is natural. We take for granted today that the historical background of a document or an event explains its meaning. The "historical" questioning of the background of an important document, like our biblical documents, is, in large measure, a product of what we will call the "modern world." It is a world in which we are fully self-conscious of history and historical change. It was not until the great post-Medieval skeptical age that history would become the primary means of solving problems.

To call the fifteenth century the watershed century may seem to some an overstatement, but we think not. The coming of mechanical printing in the mid-fifteenth century replaced once and for all the laboriously handwritten manuscripts and revolutionized everything in the Western world. The church-state monopolies on information and education were broken. Over the next two hundred years there arose out of the innovations of the fifteenth century movements which would become the defining characteristics of the modern world.

The widespread availability of printed material set mass education in motion, and it could not be stopped. With the explosion of literary works and education came a profound human curiosity. This, in turn, led directly to wonder about the world. Global explorations began in the late fifteenth century and continued throughout the sixteenth. Wonder about the world also led directly to questions about the heavens—the planets, the sun, moon, and stars, gravity, the movement of air, and so on. The result was the beginnings of modern science with its endless question-asking and devising of ways to find answers without relying on old authorities. In fact, all of the old authorities were repudiated, and the power of the human reasoning took their places.

The natural sciences found order and predictability in the universe, and, by extension, in human affairs. In time the dominance of traditional institutions such as the state and the church gave way to the emergence and the dominance of the individual in a new and emphatic form. Individuals were gifted with reason to solve problems for themselves. Descartes' understanding of the individual person as the one and only undoubtable truth became one of the cornerstones of modernity.[1] In and through it all, the Renaissance, the Enlightenment, and the idea of human progress were born. Humanity assumed we were embarking on an upward journey which seemed almost endless. The past would continually be superseded by a new future. Everything had a history and nothing would remain the same.

All of this had a profound effect, of course, on religion. Whereas the Bible as it was interpreted by the church had been the absolute authority, now both the Bible and the church were to be constantly scrutinized. Like everything else, it was subjected to reason and critical examination. Now the study of Scripture for the first time became "scientific" and "historical."[2]

The fifteenth century replaced a static worldview with a dynamic one. In the static view, God had presided over everything; and God was unchanging. Historians could keep records, of course; and their records could have value over time to understand God's workings. But there was no such thing as "opening up the past," or trying to understand historical roots or causes. The Bible, for example, was an ahistorical book, like all sacred books. God gave the Bible, and one did not ask questions about it. Not, that is, until the fifteenth century broke the world open, and questioning spouted forth. A search for truth began as what aptly has been called by the twin names of "historical" and "critical" began to take hold.

The critique of religion mounted in England by the Deists paved the way for a more thorough historical and critical approach to Scripture. Their critique established a way to investigate Scripture without adherence to ecclesiastical dogma and it enthroned reason in the place of dogma. Moreover, the Deists' approach to Scripture treated passages contextually, that is, in their historical and literary settings, rather than as scattered independent pieces, each of which was to be interpreted on the basis of its content alone.[3]

Robert M. Grant offers a succinct summary of the forces which united to bring about the period of rationalism and thoroughgoing historical methods.

---

[1] For example, see A. K. M. Adam, ed., *What is Postmodern Biblical Criticism?* (GBS/NT; Minneapolis: Fortress, 1995), 5–6.

[2] Carl R. Holladay makes a helpful distinction between "the divine oracle" and the "historical" paradigms of the Bible, noting the features of both. "Contemporary Methods of Reading the Bible," *NIB* 1:125–36. Holladay goes on in this same article to describe "the literary paradigm" and its methods and approaches (136–49).

[3] For example, John Locke's 1695 work, *The Reasonableness of Christianity: as delivered in the Scriptures* (ed. John C. Higgins-Biddle: Oxford: Clarendon, 1999).

The recovery of classical literature and the higher value placed on it by the Renaissance undoubtedly encouraged a critical attitude toward the Bible. Moreover, the rise of philosophy as an autonomous science and its gradual divorce from theology made possible and indeed made necessary a fresh evaluation of the meaning and interpretation of the Bible. At the same time, Protestant bibliolatry raised questions in the thinking men's [sic] minds.[4]

BASIC ASSUMPTIONS

The marvelous transformation of the world by the Enlightenment produced a legacy to which we are indebted and which is the foundation of the historical-critical methods of Bible study. This book will have to explore the nature of the historical approach to Scripture in some detail and at different points in our discussion. Without some understanding of the historical method we cannot fully comprehend the new movements in biblical interpretation that have arisen as the older methods have lost their grip on scholarship. We will begin by exploring at least some of the basic assumptions of historical criticism of the Bible.

A Scientific Undertaking

The study of history is a scientific undertaking. The past can be discovered and known through careful and objective (that is, scientific) study of evidence. This entails study by one who is personally detached from the "facts," so that individual bias, presuppositions, and opinions are not allowed to distort the evidence. Such an understanding of the study of history is just a part of the larger appreciation of human reason as a means of discerning "truth." It represents the dominance of the rationality of which we spoke earlier. This view of history underlying the "consistent historical" methods entails a preoccupation with empirical, verifiable data. The discovery of that evidence and its use to construct a past event is based entirely on the idea of historical "fact." The study of history which arose early in the modern period assumed both the reality of "facts" and their knowability.

The Historical Occasion

The historical occasion of the writing of any and every part of the Bible is absolutely necessary to understanding its meaning. Any meaning derived

---

[4] Robert M. Grant, *A Short History of the Interpretation of the Bible* (rev. ed.; New York: Macmillan, 1963), 144.

from a passage without sufficient historical knowledge is tenuous at best and subject to distortion by the interpreter. One of the expressions of the supremacy of history was and is the assumption that historical context "determines" meaning. This entails breaking both the Old and the New Testaments into disparate parts and treating each individually, because each passage may spring from a different and unique historical setting. "Meaning" cannot be determined by a passage's place in the Scripture nor by its relationship with other canonical writings.

Carl Holladay suggests that the features of historical-critical studies include these three understandings of Scripture. First, the Bible is understood to be a "historical narrative." If studied carefully and critically, one can construct from it a history of the origins of both Judaism and Christianity. Secondly, because it is a historical narrative, it is also a "historical artifact," meaning that it provides evidence for the construction of biblical history. Finally, Holladay writes, "the text is seen as a historical product that has grown and developed through time." Hence, each text has its own history while it also contributes to the broader biblical historical narrative.

> The interpreter is now able to think of the history *in* the text—the story it tells, the official, canonical version; the history *behind* the text—the story to which it bears witness; the history *of* the text—the story of its origin, formation, and development.[5]

The Original Meaning

From the first there is (or was) only one "true" and original meaning in written passages. This view signaled the absolute end of what we spoke of earlier as the "ancient understanding of Scripture" evident both in early Judaism and Christianity. Rather than understanding writings as producing many meanings, each of which is appropriate to a particular time and place, what arose as the modern or scientific view in the sixteenth century insisted that only a passage's *original* meaning (the one intended by the author) is the true interpretation. In this sense, "true" means that which is identical to what was in the author's mind or consciousness when the text was written.

A Human Book

Whatever else it might be, the Bible is a human book which arose in specific historical contexts and as a result of human endeavors. Where does God fit into such a human book? For some historical critics, God does not fit

---

[5] Holladay, "Contemporary Methods of Reading the Bible," 128.

into the picture at all. But for other historical critics, it was possible, even probable, that God worked through the historical forces and currents out of which the human authors wrote. So, for instance, there was no hesitancy in crediting biblical ideas to sources beyond the biblical religions. For such critics the idea that Yahweh is lord of the seasons and of weather arose in large part as a result of Israel's struggle to become an agricultural people, as the Elijah cycle of stories suggests. Therefore, biblical material could arise entirely from natural and human sources without direct divine intervention.

THE CONTRIBUTIONS OF TRADITIONAL MODERN HISTORICAL CRITICISMS

Equipped with these assumptions, we might undertake a search for the meaning of the note we found in the shelves of the library, much as biblical scholars would undertake a study of any canonical book. However critical one might be of the assumptions of the enterprise, the historical study of Scripture has made uncountable contributions to our understanding of the Bible and the history of Jewish and Christian origins. The most important of them is simply the fact that our interpretation of Scripture is no longer dictated by the doctrines of most Christian churches.[6] To describe the historical-critical methods that developed since the sixteenth century is a formidable task. However, we can best summarize them by pointing to the key questions that have occupied historical biblical scholarship. Each of the following concerns reflects both a critical approach to Scripture, questioning the biblical book and its claims, and also a historical approach to Scripture, suggesting that the answers to the questions about the meaning of the texts are found in history.

Authorship, Date, and Canon

Authorship and date of a biblical text usually lead the list of topics addressed in a commentary (or an introductory textbook) written from a historical-critical perspective. The assumption is that knowing both the authorship and date of writing is important to the interpretation of a passage as well as to our general knowledge of the biblical period. For instance, critical investigation of authorship has taught us to be cautious about taking the word of the document itself when it names its author. Historical investiga-

---

[6]The Second Vatican Council of the Roman Catholic Church (1962–65) opened the way for historical-critical scholarship among scholars of that expression of the church.

tions of authorship, for example, have demonstrated that pseudonyms were often used in ancient documents as a way of honoring and extending another person's thought.[7] In this way, the contributions of a great leader in the past would be augmented by what that leader might say in the "present time" of the actual author. The historical paradigm also questions the apostolic authenticity of some of the New Testament books, such as the Gospel of John and the Revelation of John.

The fascination with authorship at first glance may seem strange. How the naming of an author changes the interpretation of his or her writing is not clear (unless one can argue that that person is the author of other literature). It, however, has to do with the reliability of a text. It is the equivalent of knowing whether a quotation about freedom came from John F. Kennedy or Adolf Hitler. The earliest interest in authorship in the Christian church arose from the effort to preserve an apostolic witness and the leaders of the early church sought to discover whether or not the author of a given text was among the first disciples (for example, James and John, the sons of Zebedee) or closely related to some one of them (such as Mark or Luke). Thus one task of the historical concern for authorship is to examine whether these associations between text and author are "true" to history. The issue is a matter of reliability. A good deal of effort has been exerted, for example, to try to prove whether the author of the Pastoral Epistles was or was not Paul, though the documents *clearly claim* to be Pauline.

The historical pursuit of the identity and personality of authors implies a concern to show that the biblical authors were heroic, genius personalities. Preoccupation with authorship was the result of the importance modernists placed on the individual. Since modernism began to be challenged, scholars have become far more interested in the religious *communities* responsible for biblical documents than in an individual author. This is especially true of studies of the four Gospels. There was a time when scholars concentrated attention on exactly who the four persons (Matthew, Mark, Luke, and John) were. Now, however, they are far more concerned to learn something about the Christian communities out of which a gospel was written and to which it was addressed.

In addition to these studies into authorship, studies into the date of a text's writing have yielded other kinds of important insights for interpretation. Imagine, for instance, the difference between dating the book of Jonah according to the setting of its story, that is, the eighth or seventh centuries B.C.E., and setting it in the sixth or fifth centuries, as do some critical scholars. Jonah stands in the canon between the books of Amos and Micah both

---

[7] See James H. Charlesworth's article, "Pseudonymity and Pseudepigraphy," in *ABD* 5:540–41.

written at the earlier date. Does Jonah share the issues that concern these writers? When critical scholarship first dated the origin of the book later in post-exilic Israel, entirely new and different interpretative results emerged.

A careful reading of the historically-oriented studies of Jonah (or of any biblical book) soon betrays the difficulties in establishing the date of any portion of Scripture. To be sure, there is some empirical evidence that may help, such as the Aramaic character of some of the language of Jonah suggesting the later date. Nevertheless, precise dating is most difficult and tenuous. As another example, the dating of any one of the synoptic gospels hinges on determining whether that evangelist seems to assume that the Jerusalem Temple had already been destroyed at the time of writing. Given the determination by scholars to interpret any piece of biblical literature in its original historical setting, scholarship has strived to propose at least general dates for each of the biblical documents.

These concerns for date and authorship have taken priority over concern about a text's placement in the canon. As a matter of fact, historical-critical scholarship will not allow a book's place in the canon to influence interpretation.[8] So, the Mosaic authorship of the Pentateuch was widely denounced in historical-critical studies (in this case, following insights that were gained in the Middle Ages[9]), and the gulf between David and the "author" of the Psalms widened. In a more general way, the canon came to be regarded as a "historical phenomenon," giving raise to the notion that investigations of extra-canonical books is as necessary as the study of those included in the canon. This view later expanded into the "history of religions" movement, to which we will turn later. Today, we can see this broader interest in the efforts to understand the Gospel of Thomas as representative of a genuine early Christian tradition that was never canonized.[10]

---

[8] The recent movement called *canonical criticism* directly contradicts this historical-critical view. Although canonical criticism is a broad term that is applied to a number of different views, it is essentially the effort to take the canon seriously in interpretation. A passage needs to be read in the light of the whole canon and how it is related to other canonical views. As an example of the views of the most influential canonical critic, see Brevard S. Childs, *Introduction to the Old Testament as Scripture* (Philadelphia: Fortress, 1979).

[9] See Otto Eissfeldt, *The Old Testament: An Introduction* (trans. P. R. Ackroyd; New York: Harper & Row, 1965), 158–60.

[10] For instance, note the use of the Gospel of Thomas in Bernard Brandon Scott's *Hear Then the Parable: A Commentary on the Parables of Jesus* (Minneapolis: Fortress, 1989). For a different assessment of the role of the Gospel of Thomas in the interpretation of the parables, see Arland J. Hultgren, *The Parables of Jesus: A Commentary* (Grand Rapids: Eerdmans, 2000), 430–49.

Historical and Religious Settings

Scholars in the historical-critical mode are interested in discerning the occasion and historical setting for the writing of a biblical document. What was the impulse for the composition of the book? Historical research seeks to look through the biblical text to see the concrete social situation behind the book. What was going on in the faith community that led someone or some group to compose and circulate a particular biblical document? The text becomes what has been called "a window" into the past.[11] While the division is rather arbitrary, there has developed two different subjects of the historical investigation of a text. We will call one the historical occasion and the other the religious setting.

The Historical Occasion. Historical critics seek to construct what might have been the immediate and concrete situation that evoked the writing of any biblical document. In this case, the interest is not in the wider religious and intellectual influences which might have shaped the author's mind and the community to which the writing is directed. The interest is rather the political and social events which necessitated some leader or leaders to compose the document at hand. In the case of the imaginary note discovered in the library at the start of this chapter, knowing what occasioned the author to write would be most helpful in interpreting it. One example of the historical occasion for a portion of Scripture entails the destruction of the city of Samaria and the subsequent exile of its people in 721 B.C.E.. According to some, these two events motivated a prophetic circle to preserve the traditions of the southern kingdom and support Hezekiel's unsuccessful reform movement (2 Kgs 18:4, 16, 22). The rule of Manasseh (ca. 687–642 B.C.E.) further encouraged the formulation of these traditions. The result was the Deuteronomistic History.[12]

Another example of the importance of determining the historical occasion is the theory that the Revelation of John was occasioned by the

---

[11] According to R. Alan Culpepper, Murray Krieger first used the image of "window" to designate the approach which seeks the history behind the text by discerning what a text suggests about its setting. *A Window To Criticism: Shakespeare's Sonnets and Modern Poetics* (Princeton: Princeton University Press, 1964), 3–4. Cited in Culpepper's *Anatomy of the Fourth Gospel: A Study in Literary Design* (Foundations and Facets: New Testament; Philadelphia: Fortress, 1983), 3. See Joseph M. Webb, *Old Texts, New Sermons: The Quiet Revolution in Biblical Preaching* (St. Louis: Chalice, 2000). Also see Chapter Three of this volume.

[12] The Deuteronomic History refers to that view of events suggested by Deuteronomy, Joshua, Judges, 1–2 Samuel, and 1–2 Kings and regards these books as a single unit. See Steven L. McKenzie, "Deuteronomistic History," *ABD* 2:160–68.

aggressive persecution of the Christians in Asia Minor by the Roman emperor Domitian (ca. 51–96 C.E.). This view gradually gained wide acceptance until it became nearly a truism among historical critics of Revelation. However, more recently this popular understanding of the occasion for the writing of Revelation has been severely and successfully challenged, in part by the reassessment of the historical evidence for such a persecution.[13]

The hypothetical occasion for Revelation suggests the way in which historical-critical theories of the setting of a biblical book enlighten it and may be an interpretative key to understand some writings. However, such theories are often highly speculative, even while some views seem to have become canonized in historical-critical circles. There is little doubt that searches for an event that explains the writing of a biblical document can be extremely helpful. Yet the historical evidence discernible through the text is often slim and, therefore, conclusions are frequently faulty.

The Religious Setting. The historical approach to biblical interpretation assumes that religious communities are vulnerable to the influence of other religious and philosophical movements at the time a document was written. For example, in our own day we are not surprised that books on Christian spirituality reflect the influence of meditative practices in other religious traditions, such as Buddhism. The human mind or the religious community never operates in a vacuum but always closely in association with a culture and all that comprises it.

More to the point, the culture in which one lives is bound to pass on certain assumptions and perspectives which are simply taken for granted. Often it is only when we encounter persons from other cultures that we become aware of our own cultural assumptions. The biblical scholar is interested in delineating what cultural (particularly religious and philosophical) influences impacted the lives of both the authors and recipients of biblical material. The meaning of certain words, for instance, may be shaped by the cultural influences on the author.

An example of this is the use of the Greek word *logos* in the early verses of the Gospel of John. Historians have tried to detect the cultural influences

---

[13] See for example the rather careful examination of the evidence for the dating of Revelation in David E. Aune, *Revelation 1–5* (WBC 52a; Dallas: Word, 1997), lvi–lxx. Adela Yarbro Collins argues that the "perceived crisis" of the readers of Revelation was social and not the result of Roman violence. *Crisis and Catharsis: The Power of the Apocalypse* (Philadelphia: Westminster, 1984), 84–110. Charles H. Talbert rejects the notion that John wrote during a Roman persecution and speaks instead of an "anticipated persecution" and the dangers of assimilation. *The Apocalypse: A Reading of the Revelation of John* (Louisville: Westminster John Knox, 1994), 9–12.

behind this word. Was the author swayed by the word's use in Hellenistic culture of the first century? Or was the author's intent to speak of or in Hebraic and Jewish concepts? One can readily see how supposing a specific setting for words and phrases can effect interpretation. How a word comes to mean something depends on the context out of which it comes. However, the determination of the specific setting out of which a document is written requires a thorough knowledge of the cultures of another day.

For example, historical critics for years drew a sharp distinction between Hellenism and Judaism in the first century C.E.—a distinction which more recent investigations have called into question. Little is still known, however, about the Judaism of this period before the destruction of the Temple in 70 C.E. and the rise of rabbinic Judaism later in the century. The discovery and subsequent study of the Dead Sea Scrolls in the last half of the twentieth century has shed precious light on the factionalism of Judaism during the period. Nevertheless, the sketchy knowledge of the Jewish faith in this crucial time continues to plague us. It hampers our interpretations of passages that represent Jesus and his ministry, and our understandings of the relationship between Christianity and Judaism in the New Testament period.

One of the contributions of historical criticism to our present understanding of Hebraic and early Christian thought is the emergence of an interest in the *history of religions* as applied to biblical studies. In Old Testament studies, for instance, there was a concerted effort by scholars of the history of religions to learn about the evidence of the worship of the Canaanite deity Baal found in both Ugaritic and Phoenician texts. Such evidence might help historians better to understand the conflict of cultures to which some of the Hebrew Scriptures witness and how that conflict influenced Hebraic thought.[14] An example of interest in the history of religions in New Testament studies is the study of Hellenism and in particular the religion of Mithra. In whatever form this religion was employed, historians of the religions of the biblical era and locale hope to shed light on the meaning of biblical passages by understanding how other religions and philosophical movements influenced the thought of the author of a given passage.

A specific example of the way the history of religions has been used can also be seen in the great theologian and New Testament scholar Rudolf Bultmann's discussion of baptism in the early Christian community. Bultmann

---

[14]The first scholar to study literary discoveries in the ancient Near East as a means of understanding the Hebrew Scriptures was Johannes Heinrich Hermann Gunkel (1862–1932). Gunkel also launched a study of the literary forms of the Bible that shaped the method of form criticism. See J. J. Scullion's article on Gunkel in *Dictionary of Biblical Interpretation* 1:472–73.

claimed the idea that "Baptism imparts participation in the death and resurrection of Christ . . . [and] undoubtedly originated in the Hellenistic Church, which understood this traditional initiation-sacrament on analogy with the initiation-sacraments of the mystery religions." He cites Romans 6:2–14 as evidence of how Paul was influenced by both the mystery religions of his day and by Gnosticism.[15] In the twentieth century Bultmann demonstrated that historical criticism regarded nothing too sacred to be studied and rooted in non-Christian religious tradition.

The history of religions produced a massive literature which has drastically changed our understanding of the origins of both Judaism and Christianity. Largely as a result of the search for connections between the biblical religions and the other religions of the time, there arose an entire field of study which is sometimes called *backgrounds,* meaning the historical settings out of which the biblical material emerged.[16]

HISTORICAL-LITERARY CRITICISMS

Literary concerns have always been a part of the historical-critical methods, although in a different way than the newer literary criticism which we will discuss in chapter three. As one example, the historical-critical studies have drawn our attention to the matter of *genre* and its importance. The study of the different types of Psalms, for instance, helps us read those poems with greater insight.[17]

Genre criticism has for the most part been devoted to studying the literature of the ancient Near East and Greco-Roman worlds. In New Testament studies there has been a great deal of attention focused on the gospel genre. Scholars seek to understand the Gospels better by trying to identify a Hellenistic or early Jewish antecedent to them. While much has been written, there is still no consensus on the sort of literature which might have been

---

[15] Rudolf Bultmann, *Theology of the New Testament* (2 vols.; New York: Charles Scribner's Sons, 1951), 1:140. See also Bultmann's *Primitive Christian in Its Contemporary Setting* (New York: Meridian, 1957).

[16] For example, C. K. Barrett, *The New Testament Background: Selected Documents* (rev. and exp. ed.; New York: Harper & Row, 1987) puts the student in touch with bits of the original documents that might parallel New Testament thought. Now a commentary seeks to do the same thing: M. Eugene Boring, Klaus Berger, Carston Colpe, eds. *Hellenistic Commentary to the New Testament* (Nashville: Abingdon, 1995).

[17] For instance, Sigmund Mowinckel, *The Psalms in Israel's Worship* (2 vols.; Oxford: Basil Blackwell, 1962).

a model for the gospel genre.[18] Another instance of genre study is found in the work of Richard I. Pervo, who argues that the closest Greco-Roman parallel to Acts is not works of history but the historical novel. Hence, Acts is filled with fast moving adventure stories.[19] Such a view of the genre of Acts has far-reaching impact on how we interpret the book.

The nineteenth and twentieth centuries saw the rise of *form criticism,* which sought to identify different textual forms and to locate them in the religious life of the community for which they were written. A "hymn," for example, is a particular form. Forms can be incorporated into a larger narrative text. The first eighteen verses of the Gospel of John are thought to have originally been a hymn that is now a part of a larger gospel story. The same is true of aphorisms, or parables, and creeds. Form criticism is the art of identifying these various forms.

As a historical method form criticism played an important part in biblical study, even though it was never able to produce anything like certainty. Perhaps its most lasting contribution is the identification of different forms within the synoptic Gospels, such as the conflict stories in which Jesus is reported to have clashed with the religious leaders of his day. However, form criticism goes further than the identification of forms; it makes suggestions as to how these various forms aided Christian communities. It might be, for instance, that the stories in the synoptic gospels about fasting (Matt 9:14–17; Mark 2:18–22; Luke 5:33–39; and possibly John 3:29–30) and paying taxes (Matt 22:15–22; Mark 12:13–17; Luke 20:20–26) arose and were preserved because both of these were issues that confronted the early church and they sought some teaching of Jesus to guide them.

Form criticism also established with some certainty that much biblical material had a pre-written or oral stage. The gospel pericopes, for instance, were likely transmitted by word of mouth. Hence form criticism led scholars to find the roots of much biblical literature in something close to what we call folklore and storytelling. For all of its rich benefits, however, form criticism often exemplifies the kind of speculation that became typical of a number of historical methods.

By searching for the roots of biblical material in oral form before it was written, form criticism emphasized the fact that historical and literary studies

---

[18] See Philip L. Shuler, *A Genre for the Gospels: The Biographical Character of Matthew* (Philadelphia: Fortress, 1982) and William S. Vorster, "Gospel Genre," *ABD* 2:1077–79.

[19] Richard I. Pervo, *Profit with Delight: The Literary Genre of the Acts of the Apostles* (Philadelphia: Fortress, 1987). See also Pervo's marvelous little book, *Luke's Story of Paul* (Minneapolis: Fortress, 1990).

are, as Holladay notes, also interested in *the history of the document under study.* The integrity of a document is a major concern of the historical critic. Does the current document as it appears in our Bible truly represent the original, and, if not, what kind of changes, deletions, and expansions has it undergone? Our mention of the book of Isaiah in the Introduction illustrates this view, but so, too, do theories concerning the whole of Paul's correspondence with the Corinthian church. Those theories often suggest that Paul wrote as many as four letters to the Corinthian Christians, one of which is lost and two of which are joined together in our 2 Corinthians.[20]

Integrity of the Document

Consequently the literary analysis in which historical criticism engages is generally comprised of two parts: the integrity of the document and the history of its composition. As for the integrity of a document, theories that a document was composed of different parts, only some of which originated with the first author, are often based on at least three criteria. The first is *style*. Can one see a single style of writing throughout the document, or are there points at which the style seems to change? An example is Mark 13 which seems to some to be written in a different style than the whole of the Gospel. This stylistic difference, among other things, has led some scholars to think the evangelist or a later editor inserted an "apocalyptic tract" at this point in Mark.

The second criterion for testing the integrity of a document is its *content*. Is there a consistent perspective advocated by the author of this document, or can we find ideas expressed in one section that contradict those expressed elsewhere? A comparison of the first two chapters of Genesis convinces many that there are significant and fundamentally different perspectives between 1:1–2:4a and 2:4b–25. On the basis of content criticism (among other matters) many suggest that in these two chapters we have two different stories of creation brought together from two different sources. So wide-spread is this view that the New Revised Standard Version leaves a space between the two halves of 2:4.

In New Testament studies some scholars think that 1 Cor 14:33b–36 is an addition to Paul's letter from a later source. One of the reasons for this view is that these words seem to contradict some of what Paul says in chapter 11 of the same letter. Moreover, the advice that women should remain silent in church is more like 1 Tim 2:11–12 and Titus 2:5 (held by most scholars to

---

[20] See the discussion of this question in Victor Paul Furnish's *II Corinthians* (AB; Garden City, N.Y.: Doubleday, 1984), 22–55.

be non-Pauline writings) than Paul. As a result, the New Revised Standard Version even puts these verses in parentheses.

The third criterion for identifying a source incorporated within a passage is its presumed *historical-social setting*. In this case, setting means the prevailing circumstances under which a passage was written. Does the whole of the document imply one single setting, or are there some passages which seem to imply another set of circumstances? It is not uncommon to find commentators on Jeremiah proposing that some of the materials found in the book were later additions to the document penned by "Deuteronomic redactors" who wrote in the exilic and post-exilic periods in hope of addressing Jeremiah's words to later generations. It is the distinction among the historical settings of pre-exilic, exilic, and post-exilic which determines the isolation of later material.[21] Of course, much the same is true of the view that Isaiah is composed of material written out of and for at least three different settings.

On the basis of these three criteria (content, style, and historical-social setting), further examples of composite structure are frequently cited in the work of historical-critical scholars. Several theories of the composition of the Pentateuch have held sway for many years. The traditional assumption of Mosaic authorship was challenged and in its place a complex theory, the Documentary Hypothesis, was postulated which assumed the integration of at least four different components or sources, the Yahwist (J), the Elohist (E), the Deuteronomist (D), and Priestly Writer (P). With time the proposal was expanded with still additional components, such as two deuteronomic strands—D[1] and D[2]. Other theories involved speculation about the source of the Psalm found in Jonah 2 and the suspiciously optimistic conclusion of Amos (9:11–15). In terms of interpretation, these theories encouraged one to seek an understanding of any one passage only after discerning and placing it in its "original" setting and not the setting out of which the whole document came. One cannot help but sometimes be suspicious that scholars are prone to call any passage that does not suit their own conceptions of what the document was saying an interpolation.

The History of Composition of a Document

The other ambitious literary effort of historical-critical scholars has been to construct a narrative of how a document developed from its origin to its incorporation in Scripture, what is sometimes called "writing a history of

---

[21] For an exhaustive discussion of the composite nature of Jeremiah, see William L. Holladay, *Jeremiah 2* (Hermeneia; Minneapolis: Fortress, 1989).

the tradition."[22] The same work is termed *tradition criticism,* especially in Old Testament studies. In most cases, the effort to reconstruct the history of the composition of a document was in part the result of identifying the document's composite nature. So, for instance, the elaborate Documentary Hypothesis for the composition of the Pentateuch arose from the sense that there were various strands of material. The question then became how to account for those strands and their place in the received text of the Pentateuch.

Historical studies developed a number of different sub-disciplines designed to assist us in understanding how a biblical book reached its present form. We have already mentioned *form criticism* and its importance, but should now point out again that it was instrumental in convincing scholars that parts of the Bible were first of all transmitted orally before being written down. That is surely the case, scholars thought, in the Pentateuch, the prophetic literature, and the Gospels of the New Testament. During the period of oral transmission, the materials were shaped into the forms which are still identifiable even after they have been integrated into a whole document (for example, stories of Jesus' healings in the synoptic gospels). So, in many cases the first step in writing the history of a passage would begin with the oral form of the story and its place in the life of a religious community, that is, it would begin with a form critical analysis of a passage.

Source criticism arose from the effort to discover what *literary* sources lay behind a passage and differs from form criticism in that it deals with what are thought to be written sources, rather than oral sources, used by a document's author. Again, the JEDP hypothesis was first conceived by some as written sources which were incorporated into the Pentateuch. Easier examples, however, are the theories that sought to solve the so-called "synoptic problem." The problem is the relationship among the first three Gospels and how to account both for *their similarities and their differences.* The "two-source" theory assumes that one Gospel was written before the other two and was used as a source for the later two. Such a theory provides a way to understand the similarities among the three synoptics. It was first supposed that Matthew was written first and used by Luke and Mark in writing their Gospels. In the first quarter of the twentieth century, however, the priority of

---

[22] The German titles for these critical methods actually speak of "history" rather than "criticism." For instance, form criticism originated with the German title, *Formgeschichte.* Redaction criticism was called *Recaktionsgeschichte* and composition criticism, *Kompositionsgeschichte.* The advantage of these titles is, of course, the fact that the methods concentrate on the history of the material at some point in its preservation and transmission. The German titles also demonstrate the importance of history as the fundamental theme of all such critical methods.

Mark was adopted, along with Matthew's and Luke's use of a "sayings source" called Q. Eventually the two-source theory (Mark and Q) was expanded by assuming the existence of written and oral sources which supplied the material unique to Matthew (called M) and another source peculiar to Luke (called L).

In more recent years there has been a rejection of the priority of Mark in favor of the older view of Johann Jakob Griesbach who thought Matthew was written first and used by Luke, while Mark was the last gospel written and used both Matthew and Luke as sources. Hence, the supposition of a Q document proves unnecessary.[23] Those who embrace the priority of Matthew remain a small minority among scholars and have been unable to marshal persuasive evidence against the theory of the priority of Mark.

One result of the popularity of the two-source hypothesis has been extensive studies of the hypothetical Q. There have been laborious reconstructions of Q, some of which suppose several editions of Q and describe the occasion for the creation of the sayings source.[24] The history of the synoptic source question demonstrates several of the features of historical-critical methods. First, it is highly speculative but elaborate in its imaginative constructions. Second, theories in historical-critical studies tend to become so popular that they are taken not so much as hypotheses but proven facts. Third, there is no historical-critical question that is settled once and for all. Instead, questions are reassessed and different answers are frequently suggested.

The writing of the history of composition includes a third critical method which seeks to identify and study the contributions of those who edited sources to produce a single document. For example, study of the four evangelists seeks evidence for the way in which each handled the Gospel's sources. This was first known simply as compositional criticism but was elaborated and strengthened in what came to be known as *redaction criticism* (from the Latin word *redactio,* a verb that means "to reduce to order"). For preachers, redaction criticism would become an important movement in

---

[23] As part of his synopsis of the Gospels (a Gospel parallel), Griesbach first published his theory in 1774. It was first entitled *Libri historici Novi Testamenti Graece,* and latter editions appeared under a number of different titles. A major figure in the revival of this view in North America is William Farmer. See *The Synoptic Problem: A Critical Review of the Problem of the Literary Relationships between Matthew, Mark, and Luke* (New York: Macmillan, 1964) and *Jesus and the Gospel* (Philadelphia: Fortress, 1982). C. S. Mann provides a careful examination of the evidence for the two source hypothesis and then proceeds to treat Mark as a digest of Matthew. *Mark: A New Translation with Introduction and Commentary* (AB 27; Garden City, N.Y.: Doubleday, 1986), 47–71.

[24] See C. M. Tuckett, "Q (Gospel Source)," *ABD* 5:567–72.

biblical studies because it drew attention to the theological perspectives of the editors of the document.[25] Many of the contributions of these critics were sometimes so obscure and esoteric that preachers could make little use of them. Still, redaction criticism enriched biblical theology in general and has become appreciably significant for the church's reading of Scripture.

As we said earlier, *tradition criticism* refers to the whole process of tracing the history of a passage. It combines the work of textual, form, source, and redaction criticism to produce a single proposal for how a passage came to be what is our biblical texts.[26]

CHALLENGES TO HISTORICAL CRITICISM

From its origins in the sixteenth century, historical criticism slowly but decisively came to dominate biblical scholarship until the second half of the twentieth century. By the 1920s a number of major upheavals, along with several powerful scholarly voices, began to undermine its basic assumptions discussed earlier. In the West the Great Depression, World Wars I and II, and, in the United States particularly, the recognition of racism and the Vietnam debacle all combined to weaken, if not crush, the widely accepted Western modernist optimism about human rationality together with its liberal theology. These events dealt a fatal blow to the study of history as a fact-based, objective process of "uncovering" the past and using it as a means for advancing ever upward toward better human goals and ideals. A "new and counter history" began to emerge, which this book explores more fully in the chapters that follow. In the latter half of the twentieth century the study of "secular history" changed radically. Biblical historians, however, were slower to adopt such change, and in some cases seemed desperate to maintain the practices of pre-twentieth century study.

Among the first outspoken opponents of biblical historical criticism in Europe were Karl Barth and his followers in what came to be called neo-orthodox theology. Above all, Barth wanted to "liberate" the Bible from the chains of reason. Added to this were the voices of European existentialism,

---

[25] See Norman Perrin, *What is Redaction Criticism?* (GBS/NT; Philadelphia: Fortress, 1969) who writes, "redaction criticism is vastly increasing our knowledge of the theological history of earliest Christianity" (67).

[26] Robert A. Di Vito suggests, "tradition-historical criticism seeks to reconstruct the history of the transmission of various individual traditions and tradition complexes that are to be found in the Old Testament." "Tradition-Historical Criticism," in *To Each Its Own Meaning: Biblical Criticisms and their Application* (ed. Steven L. McKenzie and Stephen R. Haynes; rev. and exp. ed.; Louisville: Westminster John Knox, 1999), 91.

which in many different ways proclaimed the past dead, the future hopeless, and the present crucial.

The mortal wounding of the whole historical-critical enterprise by European theologians in the first half of the twentieth century did not impact the United States for several more decades. The post–World War II exhilaration carried on for a time the optimism of modernity. In spite of the loss of so many human lives, North Americans did not know the tragedy of the destruction of their homeland and all of their ideals as did the Europeans. As a result, North American liberal theology, to a certain extent, held its own for a time and even flourished. By the end of the 1960s, however, even that changed. The tremors of the modern world were finally felt in North America; the assassination of political and moral leaders, defeat in war, challenges to authority, the failure to resolve poverty in the midst of wealth. These tremors threaten modernism's rationalism, its exaltation of the individual, and its great promise of the future. While modernism's optimistic view of world has not yet finally and decisively collapsed, its demise appears near. We believe that the present now foreshadows a postmodern era.

While the full shape of this new era is still undetermined, it is certain that the idealism and optimism about the human spirit which spawned historical-critical methods of biblical interpretation are relics of the past, as is the view of history as a science. We now face a new world and a new age, in which truth and faith will have to be rethought. The methods of historical criticism have been challenged not just because they were seriously flawed (even though we can see that now) but because the whole culture on which they were based is no longer viable. Indeed, we could conceive of all the interpretative methods in the next chapters as products of postmodernism to some degree or another. To what they will eventually lead us is as yet unknown.

Still, historical criticism remains vital and productive. To understand anything, even things biblical, we have to study them and come to terms with them historically. And yet part of the challenge to historical criticism, as we will see in future chapters, is that it produced newer methods of biblical study. Some of them, such as the social science methods, seek to strengthen traditional historical criticism, while others hope to take the place of the old criticisms. For now it is important that, as preachers, we take stock of our legacy from the "traditional," or modern, view of historical criticism.

THE CONTRIBUTIONS OF THE HISTORICAL METHODS TO PREACHING

In the next chapters we will cite some of the more important problems with the historical-critical methods. Here, however, we address only how preachers, by and large, have responded to this sort of biblical interpretation. Simply put, many preachers have perceived a tendency of some historical critics to concentrate their energies exclusively on the analysis of a biblical passage without ever getting around to ask how, if at all, the passage might be relevant to the Christian community today. Of course, as historians, in the modern (though not necessarily postmodern) sense of that word, scholars may be interested only in the dissection of the passage and not its value for life and faith.

One of the most vivid expressions of this view goes something like this: Historical critics treat Scripture as medical examiners might treat a corpse. First, they assume they are working with a "dead" body of literature, a relic from the past, and then they carefully dissect each and every part of the body. Having done so, the examiners leave the room with the sundry body parts of the passage strewn about the table. The historical critic, it sometimes seems, takes a biblical passage apart, but, having done so, never reassembles or redirects it for the sake of preaching. Preachers and other persons of faith are left to try to put the passage back together again and determine what it means for our lives today.[27] The consequence has sometimes been that preachers have found nothing of relevance for their task of interpreting Scripture in the works and commentaries of the historical critics. In fairness, however, we need to recognize how some scholars within the church utilize historical-critical methods but attempt to do so for the sake of the proclamation of the Christian message. Generations of such scholars have taught and are still teaching in theological seminaries.

Whatever the assessment of traditional historical-critical studies, they have made important contributions that are helpful to those of us who preach. What follows is a brief assessment of a few such contributions.

The Humanity of the Bible

First, even though it is an incomplete assessment for some, the concept of Scripture as a product of human effort composed in a historical context is valuable for preachers. In various ways, we hold that Scripture contains, transmits, or occasions an indispensable message for humanity. However, one of the ways in which the Bible communicates its message today is by means of attracting us to a record of human struggles and searches not unlike our own. If we hold that Scripture is exclusively God's word, we may stand in awe of it but be unable to appropriate it. If, however, we come to understand that

---

[27] We are unable to find the source of this comparison and are actually not sure it ever appeared in print, but it is known to us by means of oral tradition!

the struggles reported and the views advocated by the authors of the Scripture are the result of human endeavors much like our own, we may more readily give those views our attention. In other words, the divine message of Scripture comes to and through humans, who, like us, were imperfect.

Several examples may help to express our view. The fact that the Elijah stories reflect the struggle of a culture going through change and trying to understand God in new ways makes many of us more attentive to and appreciative of the stories. As Elijah had to show that Yahweh was the One who brought the rain (1 Kgs 18), we may be challenged to show that our God is somehow related to the genes and chemicals that order our lives. The contest between Yahweh and Baal, so dramatically told in 1 Kgs 18:20–35, is not unlike the contest people of faith face daily with the gods of materialism, secularism, and affluence.

When we turn to the New Testament, the portrayal of Simon Peter has helped many of us accept ourselves and God's message for us. Although the four Gospels are not identical in their presentation of Peter, they make clear his impulsiveness (Matt 14:22–33), his blindness (Mark 8:31–33), and finally his cowardice (Mark 14:66–72). If such a person as Peter could become Jesus' disciple, the stone on which the church is built and a fearless leader of the early church, then God is calling us to discipleship, as well.

Analogy

The historical-critical view of Scripture as the story of real human struggles is the first contribution it makes to our understanding of preaching the biblical message. Consequently, it becomes possible to connect Scripture with analogous historical situations in our own world. Analogy has long been one of the many ways in which preachers have built a bridge between Scripture and contemporary life, but its usefulness may not be fully appreciated.[28] Historical and situational analogy is one of several ways we sometimes find the human predicament addressed in a biblical passage. We can, for instance, easily identify the lust, the assumption of power, and the arrogance of David in the Bathsheba story (2 Sam 11:2–12:31) as comparable to the temptations lust, power, and pride pose for us today.

---

[28] Stephen Farris has masterfully broadened the category analogy to make it more useful for preaching. *Preaching that Matters: The Bible and Our Lives* (Louisville: Westminster John Knox, 1998). See also Webb, *Old Texts, New Sermons,* 35–58, who gives us a sermon growing out of analogy. In an older study, Ernest Best describes all of the ways in which he believes preachers may link a biblical text to our world today. *From Text to Sermon: Responsible Use of the New Testament in Preaching* (Atlanta: John Knox, 1978), 54–96.

Jonah provides an example of the use of the proposed historical setting of a text as the basis for a comparison with matters of modern Christian faith and life. In the past the comparison was based on the theory that the book of Jonah was actually written in a time when post-exilic Israel was tempted toward exclusivism in its relationships with its neighbors.[29] More recently, this proposal for the setting of Jonah is frequently questioned in Old Testament scholarship and for good reason.[30] The use of a theoretical, proposed historical setting is precisely one of the weaknesses of the historical-critical method, and using it for analogical connections between those proposed historical situations in biblical texts and the contemporary situation of a congregation can sometimes prove misleading. Every proposed setting for a passage is, at best, tenuous. Nonetheless, an analogy based on such a view of Jonah has promise for a powerful sermon which calls into question a church's own exclusion of certain people. (See the sermon in Chapter Three.)

A less tenuous example of the analogical use of Scripture might be a sermon on 1 John 1:1–2:2 (an assigned lesson for the Second Sunday of Easter, series B, in the Revised Common Lectionary—hereafter RCL). There is relative consensus among scholars that 1 John was written to a congregation (or congregations) that had suffered a schism when a group left the church, and the author is trying to reassure those still in the congregation.[31] Suppose a contemporary congregation is faced with a possible schism and that a disgruntled group has threatened to leave the church. First John seeks in part to convince readers that everyone sins but also that everyone has a source of forgiveness. The preacher might parallel the situations and suggest that neither side in the dispute is without sin nor outside the grace of forgiveness.

Liberation from Literalism

A final contribution the historical-critical methods can make to our preaching has to do with addressing the view of Scripture held by some in our congregations. The number of Christians who embrace biblical literalism seems to have grown tremendously in the last decades. This is not the place

---

[29] See, for instance, Hans Walter Wolf, *Obadiah and Jonah: A Commentary* (Minneapolis: Augsburg, 1986), 76–88.

[30] Phyllis Trible, "The Book of Jonah: Introduction, Commentary, and Reflections," *NIB* 7:488–90.

[31] See the excellent commentary by Raymond E. Brown, S.S., *The Epistles of John: Translated with Introduction, Notes, and Commentary* (AB 30; Garden City, N.Y.: Doubleday, 1982) as well as Robert Kysar, *I, II, and III John* (ACNT; Minneapolis: Augsburg, 1986).

to seek the reasons so many are attracted to literalism, because there are surely a number of different factors that converge to make this view so popular.[32] However, pastors share with other congregational leaders a responsibility to aid lay people in finding alternative ways of reading the Bible. While that responsibility can best be fulfilled through Bible studies, sermons hold promise of reaching more of our members than those who participate in Bible studies. By using the tools of historical criticism, pastors can demonstrate the limitations of literalism and help congregants realize that so much of the Bible becomes distorted and misleading when everything is read in strictly literal terms. The critical dimension of these methods is effective in finding and analyzing conflicts in the biblical witness and showing that a more realistic and sophisticated understanding of the composition of the Bible is required. The bold and honest preacher has opportunity to point out some of these matters in the process of preaching on a text while using historical-critical methods. Of course, some of the other critical methods also afford us that same opportunity, as we will see.

What is important, we believe, is that church leaders take seriously the threat posed to the church by literalism and accept the urgency for them to ask their congregations to examine their views of Scripture. Unless leaders become proactive in this matter, more and more laity will likely become literalists *by default!* They will know of no other way to read the Bible than the one demonstrated by some of the television evangelists. The church faces, and will face, a great many threats in this new century, but the growth of literalism (along with authoritarianism) is far from the least of them.

There are a variety of ways in which a sermon might deal with biblical literalism. For example, preaching on one of the Pastoral Epistles presents an opportunity to suggest that they may not have been written by Paul. If one is preaching an Old Testament narrative that can be found in several different places in slightly different forms, one has an opportunity to point out that the editors of the biblical texts have included two or more similar stories from

---

[32] Certainly the growth of literalism in the Protestant churches is one of the indications of the uncertainty and fear that prevails in North American culture. With social values changing so rapidly and the decline of traditional authorities (such as government), as well as many other changes, many are in search for a reliable authority. The literal interpretation of the Bible is presented in some churches as a clear and absolute authority—God's word(s)! Representatives of other views of biblical authority have not been equally successful in making their positions as clear as literalism does. Part of the problem, we suspect, is that so-called mainline Protestant churches are themselves unclear about their views of biblical authority.

different sources. For example, Gen 17:15–21 and 18:1–15 are both stories of the promise of Isaac's birth. As a further example, if one is preaching on a saying in the synoptics, one might comment on its parallel in another gospel. For instance, when we preach on the beatitude in Matt 5:3 ("Blessed are the poor in spirit"), we might point out that Luke's beatitude in 6:20 is significantly different ("Blessed are the poor"). This, naturally, requires that the preacher reflect carefully upon why such an apparently different passage exists and grapple with how to present the differences in the context of the sermon.

Preachers may come under some fire for voicing historical-critical views of Scripture from the pulpit, but doing so may also open up some opportunities for teaching. The degree of response you get to such views will indicate the degree to which your congregation has come under the spell of literalism. Objections to historical-critical views will provide you the occasion to organize a study devoted to how we interpret the Bible.

AN EXAMPLE

To make our suggestions about the preacher's use of the historical-critical methods as specific and concrete as possible, we offer a sermon as an example. This sermon certainly needs further polishing, but it demonstrates how the historical-critical method can help us preach a text. It was written for the fourth Sunday of Advent, series A, on which the RCL proposes we read Matt 1:18–25 alongside of Isa 7:10–16. An historical-critical reading of the two passages helps us explain how the evangelist interprets a passage from the Hebrew Prophets. Of course, on the verge of Christmas, the preacher is well-advised to be careful not to devastate people's faith and sour their Christmas celebration by dealing critically with these beloved words. However, such an occasion may be a near-perfect opportunity for some teaching.

The following sermon shows several clear influences of the historical-critical method as well as a number of challenges for the preacher. Obviously, the sermon assumes that the role of the Hebraic prophets was not to predict the advent of Christ and Christianity—a point for which we are indebted to the historical study of our Old Testament. Moreover, this sermon entails an understanding of how the early Christians used Hebrew Scripture.

In this case, one important task for the preacher is to place Isaiah's words in what scholars believe was their origin historical context. Please note that the preacher makes certain decisions about issues upon which critics are not agreed. You will notice, too, this preacher does not venture into the swampy terrain of the identity of either the woman or the child of whom Isaiah speaks.[33] However, the presentation of the historical scene challenges preachers because it raises the question of how to make such an episode as Isa 7:10–16 interesting for our listeners. Old Testament history often confuses and discourages some people with its strange names and locations. So, the story needs to be told in an interesting and sometimes even dramatic way. Paraphrasing quotations and using colloquial terms to present the action are two of the ways we can effectively tell stories from Scripture.

The historical understanding of how ancient writings were used (and assigned new meaning) is also in the background of this sermon. (See the Introduction.) In this case, the preacher draws an analogy among the needs for assurance of God's presence in Isaiah, Matthew, and today.

---

[33] Almost any historical-critical commentary will summarize some of the issues in interpreting the passage. For example, R. E. Clements, *Isaiah 1–39* (NCB; Grand Rapids: Eerdmans, 1980), 85–89.

"Changing Meaning"

Fourth Sunday of Advent, A
Isaiah 7:10–16
Matthew 1:18–25

I WAS A FRESHMAN IN COLLEGE NOT LONG AFTER THE REVISED STANDARD VERSION of the Bible was published. For the most part, the King James translation had remained the favorite of most Christians, even though some more contemporary translations were available. But some actually believed the Revised translation was the work of the devil! Of course, they would probably have said that about any translation that changed their beloved King James.

One of the most volatile issues was the translation of Isaiah 7:14 in the Revised Standard Version. It reads like this: "Therefore the Lord himself will give you a sign. Behold, a *young woman* shall conceive and bear a son, and shall call his name Immanuel." Of course, the translation of the Hebrew word as "young woman" instead of "virgin" provoked people's anger. However, it's pretty clear that the Hebrew word properly means any woman old enough to marry, virgin or not. And interestingly when Matthew cites this passage, he (or she) uses the ancient Greek translation of the Hebrew word, a Greek word which does explicitly mean "virgin." Some protestors burned copies of the new translation because of this change in the translation of Isaiah.

There is no doubt, I think, that the translation "young woman" is the better rendering of the Hebrew word. What is difficult, perhaps, is the fact that Matthew took this verse not out of the Hebrew text of Isaiah, but out of the Greek translation, itself an interpretation, and then used it to refer to the birth of Jesus. For the most part, scholars agree that in Isaiah the verse *does not refer to the birth of some Messiah* in the future but to a child in the prophet's own day. Imagine a scene like this:

Judah stands teetering on the verge of a crisis. They are dominated by the hated Assyrians. And they are forced to pay tribute to their oppressors as a way of showing their subservience. But then another nation revolts against the Assyrian oppression, and Egypt joins the revolt. Now those rebel-nations pressure Judah to get on board and join the uprising. Ahaz, Judah's king, has to decide what to do. Should he join the rebellion at risk of having his nation destroyed? Or, should he remain neutral and provoke the rage of Judah's neighbors? He must make this terrible decision.

Then here comes this nuisance in the royal court—the one who calls himself a prophet. Should Ahaz really trust him to know what God wants the king to do? This prophet claims that God wants the king to remain neutral. How's one to know whether he is right or wrong? This Isaiah always seems to think God wants Judah to stay clear of violence and war. He keeps harping on that theme.

In this case, the prophet invites the king to ask God for a sign. If Ahaz does not believe the prophet, then the Lord will make it clear. But the king is reluctant to do that. He's afraid to test God. Or, at least, that's what he says. He has enough trouble without angering God by asking for a sign. No, he'll just ignore this prophet.

Then the prophet declares, "Okay, you won't ask God for sign. But God is going to give you a sign anyway—whether you want it or not. There is a young woman right now who's pregnant but has not yet delivered. When the child is born, they will name him 'Immanuel, God with us.' He will be your assurance that God is not going to let the Assyrians overrun you. As a matter of fact, before that kid is old enough to eat solid foods or discern the difference between good and evil, God is going to show you who's in charge. Before then, the Assyrians will be defeated and their land laid waste! Your enemy will be a thing of the past."

Isaiah refers to the birth of an unknown child as a sign of God's presence amid a national crisis. Some eight hundred years later, Matthew takes Isaiah's words and applies them to Jesus. Mary is equated with the pregnant woman. Jesus becomes the child who will be named Immanuel, "God with us." The prophet Isaiah did not speak of a Messiah who would eventually come. He was not predicting the birth of Jesus. He addressed a crisis in his own day. He tried to influence the policy of the king.

Notice how drastically the writer of Matthew changes the meaning of the Old Testament passage he quotes and applies to Jesus. It almost seems Matthew *distorts* Isaiah, twisting his words to mean something other than what the prophet originally meant. If this sort of thing occurred today, there would be cries of protest and most likely legal action. Was Matthew wrong to quote Isaiah this way? Not necessarily.

The situation is a little like this. A friend of mine gave his wife a portable CD player for a Christmas gift. She loved to listen to music, and this compact little player would allow her to take her music with her. Within a year, however, doctors discovered she had severe glaucoma. After only a few months she was nearly blind. *Now* that CD player took on new meaning. It was her constant companion and a source of music in her darkened world. What was originally a sort of electronic gadget had become a reservoir of joy and encouragement. A gift given at one time later took on new meaning.

Isaiah spoke words for his situation. By Matthew's time those words took on a new meaning. For the early Christians, the advent of Christ made everything new—even their Bible, the Hebrew Scriptures. You see, our ancient ancestors believed that written words could come to mean new things in a new situation. We ought to know how true that is.

Words keep changing meanings, don't they? The word "cool" used to mean slightly cold. Now it means fashionable, up-to-date, and "with it." If I had said to my father, "give me five," he would have pulled his billfold out thinking I was again asking him for money. Now, the expression is a gesture of greeting, affirmation, and joy with others. We want to be careful not to describe a movie as "gay," because that word now means something different.

Words change meaning according to the situation in which they are used. Matthew puts Isaiah's words in a new situation—the Advent of Christ. And they have a new meaning in that situation. Isaiah was not predicting the birth of Jesus. But Matthew realized how appropriate the prophet's words were to his story of Jesus' birth.

There is, however, one aspect of both Isaiah's and Matthew's message that is the same. Isaiah was trying to assure King Ahaz that God would not abandon Judah. So, he declared that the child soon to be born would be named *Immanuel.* He would symbolize God's presence with Judah. Eight hundred years later Matthew announced that Christ not only symbolized but was the very presence of God—God with us.

If we haven't already become ensnared by Christmas celebrations, we probably will be very soon. We are likely to be swallowed up in parties, programs, carols, and special music. And sometimes the meaning of the nativity of our Lord gets lost in all the activity. We lose our focus, much as a camera can lose focus on the subject of the picture, and much as king Ahaz lost his focus when faced with an enormous decision with dire consequences.

Isaiah knew that his king needed to believe—to trust—that God was with the nation. Matthew knew that Christian readers of the Gospel would be threatened to doubt that God was with them. So, too, we may sometimes fear that God is no longer with us. Amid the violence and chaos of our nation and our world, at times we may feel that God has abandoned us—left us to destroy ourselves. And sometimes, for some of us, Christmas is not at all a joyful time. It may be a time of loneliness and depression. We may feel we have messed up our lives. And then there is no joy in Christmas.

In those times, and always, we need the simplest meaning of Christmas—*God is with us!* Be assured that after all else is said about the birth of Jesus, this remains the heart of the Christian message. In Christ God is with us and remains with us—no matter what our situation.

Chapter 2

What Difference Do Social-Scientific Theories Make?

Let us return for a moment to our illustration of that note discovered among the books on a used bookstore shelf. The note, you will remember read like this:

> I can no longer contain myself! The anguish and torment is too much to bear. You know that I care deeply about you and the children, but my patience has worn thin. If what I am about to do seems cruel and heartless, then so be it. But I must be true to myself and to my values. If what I am about to do brings you shame and embarrassment, you will have to deal with that. For my part, this is my only honest way out. God help me if I am wrong.

We suggested that historical critics would attempt in any way they could to discover the original setting for the note. Who was the author? What was happening in the area where she or he lived? What were the issues the author faced, and so on. The attempt was to reconstruct, so far as possible, the historical context for the composition of this note. If we could learn what the author had originally meant to say, we would have discovered the note's meaning.

Suppose now that we try a related search but this time asking about the society and culture in which the author lived. What social values are expressed in the note? What social issues might have been at stake? For instance, what is the social significance of the author's concern for the reader and the shame and embarrassment the author's action might cause. Did the society of the time value honor and shame highly? What actions in that society might bring shame and embarrassment for the reader?

These are some of the questions (admittedly in an oversimplified sense) that the social-scientific critic might ask of our imaginary note. These critics actually share many of the same interests as those that motivate the historical critic. Social-scientific critics, however, are concerned with a different dimension of the historical setting than historical critics. Again to oversimplify, whereas historical critics focus on events and persons, social-scientific critics seek to understand the cultural values and practices at work in the lives of the author and the readers. For this reason, we think that social science methods of interpretation are really part of an effort to widen, strengthen, and refocus historical methods.[1]

Some scholars who embrace and use social science methods in interpretation contend that these methods are advanced far beyond typical historical-critical concerns. Hence, the methods of the social sciences are frequently understood as something of a rebellion against historical-critical methods.[2] Others prefer to think of social science methods as supplementary to the classical historical-critical questions.[3]

> The need for a social investigation as part of biblical interpretation is due in large part to the realization that the biblical authors and their readers lived in a much different social and cultural setting than the twenty-first century reader. Much as the Enlightenment brought radical change to our world, so did the Industrial Revolution in the eighteenth and nineteenth centuries. The biblical documents, however, arose out of an agrarian and pre-industrial world. According to two New Testament social-scientific interpreters, the Industrial Revolution "offers a radically different way to interpret human experience and, consequently, a radically different way to construct our interpretations of reality." Therefore, "the distance between ourselves and the Bible is as much *social* as it is temporal and conceptual."[4]

---

[1] The "original" formative social theorists that influence the rise of the social science interpretative methods include Max Weber, Emile Durkheim, and (more recently) Karl Marx.

[2] See Bruce J. Malina's distinction between the traditional methods of historical criticism as "the received view" and the "social science view." Malina believes the social-scientific methods entail entirely different sorts of new research. "The Received View and What It Cannot Do: III John and Hospitality" in *Social-Scientific Criticism of the New Testament and Its Social World* (ed. John H. Elliott; Semeia 35; Atlanta: Scholars, 1986), 171–89.

[3] For instance, at the conclusion of his chapter on sociological interpretation, Christopher Tuckett says, "there is little here which differs fundamentally from the traditional approaches to the text associated with the historical-critical method." *Reading the New Testament: Methods of Interpretation* (Philadelphia: Fortress, 1987), 148.

[4] Bruce J. Malina and Richard L. Rohrbaugh, *Social Science Commentary on the Gospel of John* (Minneapolis: Fortress, 1998), 1–2.

In the course of the nineteenth century, biblical scholars grew more and more interested in the "social world" of the biblical authors and readers.[5] What follows is only a quick survey of a complicated subject. We will first try to categorize the most important types of social-scientific methods offering examples of each. Following that we will look at what we think are some vital issues in these methods. Finally we will explore their use for the preacher.

MAJOR TYPES OF SOCIAL-SCIENTIFIC METHODS

There are a number of ways in which we might summarize the major types of social-scientific method. Some speak simply of "descriptive sociology" and "sociological explanations."[6] Another distinction which has to do with the difference between description and explanation is what some call "social history" and the other "social-scientific." The first group thinks of their task as using the traditional historical-critical methods in order to supplement the history of the biblical communities with attention to social and cultural matters.[7] The second group is more likely to use cross-cultural analysis, to employ anthropological and social models in order to understand biblical communities.[8] We have chosen a somewhat eclectic means of dividing the disciplines but one that allows us to speak of the most important ones.

---

[5] Robert A. Nisbet writes, "No other single concept is as suggestive of the unique role held by sociology among the social sciences in the nineteenth century, or as reflective of its underlying premises about the nature of man [and women] and society, as the concept of the sacred. I use the word to refer to the totality of myth, ritual, sacrament, dogma, and the more in human behavior. . . . What gives distinctiveness to sociology's incorporation of the religio-sacred is not the analytical and descriptive attention such men as Durkheim and Weber gave to religious phenomena. It is rather the utilization of the religio-sacred as a perspective for the understanding of ostensibly non-religious phenomena such as authority, status, community, and personality." *The Sociological Tradition*, 221.

[6] Tuckett, *Reading the New Testament*, 139.

[7] It is interesting that Steven L. McKenzie and Stephen R. Haynes title the section of their excellent book that deals with social, canonical, and rhetorical criticisms, "Expanding the Tradition." *To Each Its Own Meaning: An Introduction to Biblical Criticisms and Their Application* (ed. Steven L. McKenzie and Stephen R. Haynes; rev. ed.; Louisville: Westminster John Knox, 1999), 123.

[8] For more on this distinction see Dale Martin, "Social-Scientific Criticism" in *To Each Its Own Meaning*, 125–32.

Gathering Data

The simplest and yet perhaps the most important kind of social interest in biblical studies has to do with gathering fundamental information about the societies of the biblical periods. This process is little more than "descriptive sociology." Still, all the social-scientific methods depend in large part on the evidence we have for the kinds of social institutions and values that prevailed when the documents in the Bible were written. This is doubtless the oldest of the social-scientific investigations—one which has concerned readers of the Bible for centuries. It is worth pointing out, however, because of its primary role in all the methods.

Gathering evidence with regard to social, economic, and psychological life in biblical times involves several different sorts of investigation. Obviously, the Bible itself tells us something about these matters. The laws in the Old Testament imply certain social phenomena. The regulation about divorce in Deuteronomy 24:1–4, for example, informs us a bit about one major social institution. The regulation about leaving wheat and grapes in the field after harvest for the sake of "the alien, the orphan, and the widow" (Deut 24:19–22) provides insight into provision for the needy of the day. Paul's infamous words about women worshiping with their heads uncovered offers some hints, if not clarity, concerning the expected behavior of women in public spaces in the Corinthian society (1 Cor 11:2–16).

Evidence of social structures and practices may be gleaned, too, from other literature of the time and region. The writings of Josephus are a rich (if not always reliable) resource for information on the social life of the Jewish people and their Roman rulers in the first century C.E. He reports, for instance, that the Pharisees gained the support of the common people while the Sadducees were sustained by the wealthy.[9] In another example in 1 Cor 7:4, Paul states that a husband and wife do not have authority over their own bodies, but the wife has authority over her husband's body and he has authority over her body. Such a view of the marital relationship is clarified by quotations by other authors, the most prominent of whom is the Stoic, Musonius Rufus (a contemporary of Paul's). Among others, Musonius stresses the commonality of marriage even to the point of physical bodies.[10]

---

[9] Josephus, *The Jewish Antiquties* (trans. H. St. J. Thackeray et al; 10 vols; LCL; Cambridge: Harvard University Press, 1926–65) 13.298. For more on the social life of the time, see John E. Stambaugh and David L. Balch, *The New Testament in Its Social Environment* (LEC; Philadelphia: Westminster, 1986).

[10] Musonius Rufus, *What Is the Chief End of Marriage?* (30–100 C.E.) quoted in *Hellenistic Commentary to the New Testament* (ed. M. Eugene Boring, Klaus Berger, and Carsten Colpe; Nashville: Abingdon, 1995), 303.

Still another source of social data is archaeology. The archaeologist finds and analyzes physical evidence of the biblical world. When excavating the site of an ancient building or village, the archaeogists study bits of pottery, remains of houses, and most anything else they come upon. Such finds can help situate information given in the biblical text. For instance, excavators of the sites of Megiddo and Beth-shan in the north of Palestine found evidence of the wealth and culture of a Canaanite king, wealth the likes of which no later Israelite king knew. In another example, when archaeologists unearthed Saul's capitol at Gibeah north of Jerusalem, they found remains which indicated that this small tower was never anything like an elaborate dwelling or palace for that monarch.[11]

Of course, archaeology entails discovery and description of the evidence, but sooner or later analysis becomes important. In recent years, we have heard a renewed discussion of the literature found at Qumran and what kind of a community was located there. The study of the literature found in the caves surrounding the site has demonstrated the existence of a Jewish sect pre-dating the rise of Christianity. Was the original analysis of the literature and the site simply a reflection of the concept of a monastery read back into the archaeological evidence by a fine archaeologist who was also a monk? Did he attribute his own way of life to the Jews who lived at Qumran two millennia earlier? Whatever is finally decided about the site of Qumran and its function in that society, in many ways the literature found in its vicinity has opened the door to our understanding of early Christianity as a Jewish sect.[12]

A good number of studies based on the gathering of evidence are of a descriptive kind. A famous example are the two volumes of Roland de Vaux on the social and religious institutions of ancient Israel.[13] De Vaux's work is a comprehensive assemblage of data for these institutions, without elaborate analysis or theoretical structure. However, the critics have to ask whether or not these scholars have been (or could be) absolutely objective and "scientific" in their work. One might ask, of instance, how the decisions to include some data and exclude other data are made. In this case, sociological critics are in the same predicament as historians who inevitably choose the events which are "worth" recording and counting as historically significant.

---

[11] G. Ernest Wright, *Biblical Archaeology* (abrid. ed.; Philadelphia: Westminster, 1960), 61, 67–68. Martin Noth's encyclopedic work, *The Old Testament World* (trans. Victor I. Gruhn; Philadelphia: Fortress, 1966), is a model of integration of data.

[12] For the argument that Qumran was not the setting of the Essene community, see Yizhar Hirschfeld, *Qumran in Context* (Peabody, Mass.: Hendrickson, 2004).

[13] Roland de Vaux, *Ancient Israel* (2 vols.; New York: McGraw-Hill, 1961).

Nevertheless, these bits and pieces of social description vastly enrich our reading of Scripture. For example, two passages in Mark speak of how a convert to the Jesus movement would receive fellow converts as new siblings and mothers. When told his mother and brothers and sisters were looking for him, Jesus responds that his listeners are his "mother and brothers" (Mark 3:31–35). Additionally, when Peter points out how much the disciples have given up to follow Jesus, he responds that those who follow him receive "a hundredfold now in this age—houses, brothers and sisters, mother and children and fields, with persecutions" (Mark 10:30). Conspicuously absent in these sayings is any references to fathers. In Matt 23:9 Jesus is said to order, "call no one your father on this earth, for you have one Father—the one in heaven."

Having gathered the information concerning the role of fathers in the Greco-Roman world and in Palestine, Stambaugh and Balch write, "Jesus' omission of 'fathers,' his evaluation of children, and his practice of calling women followers differs significantly from the patriarchal structures and values of Greco-Roman cities."[14] While simple attention to the text might make us wonder about the failure to mention fathers, the sociological evidence about the role of the father in the family heightens the contrast for us. In this matter, Jesus seems to have been at odds with the society of his time.

Sociological Models

Sociological models are used to offer explanations of portions of Scripture, particularly those that pose problems of some sort. The principle in this sort of sociological study of the Bible assumes that models of behavior and values found in other times and places afford us a way of understanding what was going on the biblical world. To say it another way, this kind of study uses what we might call "transcultural models" to analyze the biblical communities. The model explains something important about one (sometimes current, sometimes ancient) culture in hopes of helping us to understand the cultures of the biblical era. In this case, anthropological models are equally important as sociological ones.

Social experience and religious faith. We begin with a fairly simple theory regarding the influence of social experience on the formation of a faith community. There is no reason to doubt that our social experience to some degree shapes our religious faith. We may not want to go so far as to say that our religious faith is nothing more than a product of our lives in a society and culture. The question, however, becomes this: to what degree and in what ways do our beliefs reflect our societal and communal lives?

---

[14] Stambaugh and Balch, *The New Testament,* 106.

In 1972 Wayne A. Meeks published an article that had a profound and widespread impact on the study of the Gospel of John and more generally on the rise of social-scientific methods of interpretation. To summarize an argument that is much more complicated and subtle, we will note the major elements of Meeks' thesis. He shares the view of a good many Johannine scholars that the faith of the community behind the fourth Gospel was unique. At the heart of the theology of Gospel of John is the idea that Christ was a revealer who descended from the Father and would again ascend to the Father. It is less clear what it is Christ revealed, except as Rudolf Bultmann said, than it is that he was the revealer.[15] This is what Meeks regards as the *central myth* on which the fourth Gospel builds. The question is what does the myth do: how does it function for the readers, especially the first readers?

Meeks points out that no one has asked what the social function of the descending and ascending myth might be, and he sets out to correct that oversight. In the simplest terms possible, the myth of the Jesus who belongs to another world but descends to this one in order to reveal that he is the revealer and who then ascends again, becomes the basic structure by which the community understands itself. They are not of this world, just as Jesus was not of the world. They are at odds with culture and hence necessarily counter-cultural. In short they are a sect formed by insiders who speak their own language and refrain from becoming identified with outsiders. Hence, it is this religious faith concerning Jesus' identity that becomes the model on which the community comes to understand itself. The community's role and function in its society is the result of what it believes about Christ.

Meeks is careful to say, however, that all the religious faith of the Johannine community cannot be reduced to social self-understanding.

> I do not mean to say that the symbolic universe suggested by the Johannine literature is *only* the reflex or projection of the group's social situation. . . . It is a case of continual, harmonic reinforcement between social experience and ideology.[16]

The question that remains is why this particular myth? That this community would shape its understanding of the world and its Lord in this particular way invites the notion, at least, that the influence may have gone both ways.

---

[15] E.g., Rudolf Bultmann, *The Theology of the New Testament* (2 vols.; trans. Kendrick Grobel; New York: Charles Scribners, 1955), 2:66.

[16] Wayne A. Meeks, "The Man from Heaven in Johannine Sectarianism," in *The Interpretation of John* (2d ed.; ed. John Ashton; Studies in New Testament Interpretation; Edinburgh: T&T Clark, 1997), 194. First published in *The Journal of Biblical Literature* 91 (1972): 44–72.

The myth shaped their understanding of their lives in the world; but it is equally likely that their lives in the world already influenced the myth.

Meeks' definitive thesis became a model for a number of other investigations into the way in which social experience shaped a community's self-understanding and religious faith. One such proposal was offered by John H. Elliott. Elliott suggests that the social situation of the first readers of 1 Peter influenced the language of the text. He says there is a correlation that "involves the terms *paroikos* (-*oi*) and *oikos* (*tou theou*), 'resident aliens' and 'household (of God),' words that, together with the associated imagery in 1 Peter, point to broader details concerning social condition and socio-religious response." They think of themselves as "visiting strangers" (1 Pet 1:1).[17] The language gives expression to the community's experience of social dislocation, estrangement, and limitations of its political, legal, social, and religious rights. Elliott warns us against taking the language of this document as purely figurative or spiritual, for he understands that it is vividly realistic and describes the community's experience.

There is much more to Elliott's book, but this suffices for us to see another example of the theory that social situations mold a community's faith and self-understanding. It should not be overemphasized or misunderstood, but this reality reminds many of us of how the slaves in the history of the United States identified with the exiles in Babylon and with Israel in the Exodus pilgrimage.

Cognitive dissonance in early Christianity. In a 1975 book John G. Gager offered an analysis of early Christianity from a sociological perspective. One of the problems with which he wrestled is why the Christian movement thrived. He compares the early Christian movements with what we today call millenarian movements and finds the comparison yields a number of similarities. For instance, most modern millenarian movements attract those who feel disenfranchised. The first Christians likewise came from those who felt alienated from the political system and felt themselves to be outsiders in the majority culture. The first Christians experienced what Gager calls "cognitive dissonance"—a problematic split between their beliefs and the surrounding reality they were experiencing. They experienced this clash first as a result of Jesus' death (Messiahs do not die as common criminals) and then as a result of the failure of Jesus to return quickly to earth as he had promised. Gager writes,

> Rationalization in connection with important beliefs, specifically the death of Jesus and the delay of the kingdom represents an effort to reduce doubt and despair and thus is evidence of cognitive dissonance. When, in addition, mis-

---

[17] John H. Elliott, *A Home for the Homeless: A Sociological Exegesis of 1 Peter, Its Situation and Strategy* (Philadelphia: Fortress, 1981), 23.

sionary activity is regularly associated with the same beliefs, it can and must be interpreted as a further attempt to reduce dissonance.[18]

However, the most striking result of the disappointment that the kingdom had yet to arrive was the intensified evangelistic efforts on the part of the Christian community and its successful proselytizing of new members. Gager accepts as the reason for this intense and successful evangelism the fact that when more people come to believe what you believe, it seems to confirm that your beliefs are true. "[T]he church initially carried on its mission in an effort to maintain its eschatology."[19]

We will discuss the notion of cognitive dissonance more critically and at greater length below. There we will look at the theory as it has been applied to the Apostle Paul and his Christian calling. Here we shall examine how this theory is used. First, the theory that the early church experienced cognative dissonance relies upon social theory to explain historical events. How did the disciples go on believing after the crucifixion and as the coming of the kingdom was delayed? Second, while we will argue that cognitive dissonance is not exclusively a sociological thesis, the credibility of Gager's thesis depends on how one conceives of this conflict between reality and belief.

Cross cultural models. One of the most interesting but problematic models used to understand biblical literature is that of Mary Douglas, an anthropologist. Her studies of a culture's symbol system have proven important to a number of biblical scholars. She proposes a topology by which she believes she can discern how a society determines its self-understanding. She sees two dimensions to social structure, what she calls "group and grid." Group has to do with the degree of commitment members of a society have to a particular culture. Grid is a way of measuring the degree of control the group exercises over its members. She maintains that any idea of God is rooted in the idea of a society.[20]

In an ingenuous application of Douglas' schema, Jerome H. Neyrey, S.J. seeks to understand the idea that Jesus is equal to God as it is presented in the Gospel of John. He uses Douglas' categories to locate the Johannine

---

[18] John G. Gager, *Kingdom and Community: The Social World of Early Christianity* (Prentice-Hall Studies in Religion Series; Englewood Cliffs, N.J.: Prentice-Hall, 1975), 45–46.

[19] Gager, *Kingdom and Community,* 46. This whole section is an effort to summarize Gager's thought in Chapter Two, 20–56.

[20] Howard Clark Kee, *Knowing the Truth: A Sociological Approach to the New Testament* (Minneapolis: Fortress, 1989), 14–16. Kee cites Mary Douglas, *Natural Symbols: Explorations in Cosmology* (New York: Random House, 1972), 60 and *Purity and Danger* (Boston: Routledge and Kegan Paul, 1976), 115.

community on the group/grid diagram. What he concludes is that the Christology of the Gospel is closely related to the conflict of the community with the synagogue. The high Christology then becomes an ideology of revolt. The revolt is against the synagogue but also all the formal structures in the society. All value in the community, Neyrey argues, is in individualism and not group membership.[21]

Several points are worthy mentioning. First, Neyrey's study shows that social-scientific studies of this kind build upon theories developed in another discipline, namely, anthropology. Second, his study is a good example of one of the basic premises of social science: models by which we can understand one culture are useful in studying others. Third, while we did not note it in detail, Neyrey used a text produced by and for a community of faith to gain clues of how that community understood itself and its world. All three of these points suggest the vulnerability of social-scientific studies.

The Sociology of Knowledge

Howard Clark Kee offers this insightful statement of the mission of sociology of knowledge:

> The historian . . . cannot rest content with the soical description of such phenomena as economic factors, archeological remains, social patterns, institutional forms, or even literary evidence in and of itself. Rather, the historian must seek to enter into the symbolic universe of the community that produced this evidence, and to identify both what the shared assumptions were as well as what explicit claims and norms were declared by the group.[22]

This process of entering "into the symbolic universe" of a community leads to what has been labeled the sociology of knowledge.[23] This science is interested in the relationship between human thought and the social context in which thought takes place. It is more concerned with commonsense, everyday thought than with ideas in general. In other words, its subject matter is what people " 'know' as 'reality.' . . . *The sociology of knowledge must concern itself with everything that passes for 'knowledge' in society.*" Particularly problematic, however, is the relationship between what we take to be "objective

---

[21] Jerome H. Neyrey, *An Ideology of Revolt: John's Christology in Social Science Perspective* (Philadelphia: Fortress, 1988), 209. Cf. Douglas, *Natural Symbols,* 54–64.

[22] Kee, *Knowing the Truth,* 53.

[23] The expression, "sociology of knowledge" (*Wissenssoziologie*) was first used by Max Scheler. See his book *Die Wessensformen und die Gesellschafte* (Bern, France, 1960).

facts," or reality and our subjective sense of the meaning the facts have for us. Reality, it must be noted, is actually a human and social construction.[24]

This means that the interpreter watches for ways in which the symbolic universe is taken for granted and invoked in defense of an author's view. Take, for instance, the rather strange statement Paul makes in his efforts to calm the Corinthian Christian women who are worshiping with their heads uncovered. "For this reason a woman ought to have a symbol of authority on her head, *because of the angels*" (1 Cor 11:10). What does "because of the angels" mean? How has Paul projected his cultural preferences onto the universe?

A far more important critical process is the identification of "legitimation" in a document. According to Berger and Luckmann, "Legitimation produces new meanings that serve to integrate the meanings that already attached to disparate institutional processes." In other words, legitimation links a phemenon with the whole symbolic universe. Berger and Luckmann go on to say that, "Legitimation not only tells the individual why he [or she] *should* perform one action and not another; its also tells him [or her] why things *are* what they are." What we know to be true is the source of our values. Our symbolic universes "are bodies of theoretical tradition that integrate different provinces of meaning and encompass the institutional order in a symbolic totality."[25]

One example of how the sociology of knowledge has been used in biblical studies is Philip Francis Esler's study of the motivations behind Lukan theology. Why does Luke go to such lengths to try to persuade readers that the Roman system of justice was without flaw and to report the many times Roman officials rescued Christian missionaries from danger? Esler claims that Luke wanted to show that Christian faith and Roman rule were harmonious. He calls the Gospel of Luke and Acts of the Apostles "an exercise in the legitimation of a sectarian movement."[26] In effect, the author of Luke-Acts sought to place Christian life and practice in a symbolic universe the readers knew and to which they adhered. Or, as Esler says:

> Luke re-presents traditions relating how the gospel was initially proclaimed by Jesus and later preached throughout the Roman East in such a way as to erect

---

[24] Peter L. Berger and Thomas Luckmann, *The Social Construction of Reality: A Treatise in the Sociology of Knowledge* (AB; Garden City, N.Y.: Doubleday, 1966), 14–15. For the complete discussion see pp. 1–18.

[25] Berger and Luckman, *The Social Construction*, 92, 93–94, 95.

[26] Philip Francis Esler, *Community and Gospel in Luke-Acts: The Social and Political Motivations of Lucan Theology* (SNTSMS 57; Cambridge: Cambridge University Press, 1987), 16–18, 222.

a symbolic universe, a sacred canopy, beneath which the institutional order of his communty is given meaning and justification.[27]

He concludes that Luke's intent was not to present an apology for Christianity but a legitimation.

Anthropology and Psychology

Social-scientific interpretations of the Bible use a vast multitude of themes and methods from all the social sciences, and we do not have time nor space to discuss them all. Instead, we will make short notes on the role of anthropology and psychology.

We have already alluded to the use of *anthropological models* in social analysis and of cross-cultural applications of methods. Anthropological studies have sometimes been called simply culture studies. However, anthropological concerns are usually located on the borders between ancient (or "primitive") and modern cultures.

Bruce J. Malina demonstrates what he calls "cultural anthropology" in his studies of honor and shame. Honor, he suggests, is "the value of a person in his or her own eyes (that is, one's claim to worth) *plus* that person's value in the eyes of his or her social group. Honor is a claim to worth along with the social acknowledgment of worth."[28] It can be acquired or bestowed. Shame, on the other hand, results from loss of honor. "To be or get shamed, thus, is to be thwarted or obstructed in one's personal aspiration to worth or status, along with one's recognition of loss of status involved in this attempt." Symbolically, honor is one's social status. "The purpose of honor is to serve as a sort of social rating which entitles a person to interact in specific ways with his or her equals, according to the prescribed cultural cues of the society."[29]

Probably no other result of social-scientific studies has been more widely disseminated and more widely used than that of honor and shame. Perhaps because honor and shame are categories we can appreciate, we are better able to understand them. If a preacher does little more than employ these categories, she or he has made valuable use of the social-scientific methods. (See the sermon at the end of this chapter.)

The use of *psychological models* for the study of the biblical world is less common than anthropological ones. In this case, psychological means those feelings, attitudes, and behaviors that arise peculiarly from one's self under-

---

[27] Ibid., 222.
[28] Bruce J. Malina, *The New Testament World: Insights from Cultural Anthropology* (Atlanta: John Knox, 1981), 27.
[29] Ibid., 46.

standing. Gerd Theissen defines the psychological exegesis used in New Testament studies simply as the attempt "to describe and explain, as far as possible, human behavior and experience in ancient Christianity." He goes on to define three different "theories" appropriate for exegetic study: learning, psychodynamic approaches, and cognitive approaches.[30] In another study, he uses psychoanalytical theories to argue that the Jesus movement addressed a deep crisis by "diverted, transferred, projected, transformed and symbolized" aggression arising from that crisis.[31]

A very different kind of psychological interpretation is found in Adela Yarbro Collins' provocative study of Revelation. She argues that the Christians to whom Revelation was addressed were discouraged and felt betrayed by a hope and faith that had not been affirmed, but instead had been severely challenged. They had expected a drastic transformation of the world, perhaps even in a public way. Those hopes had been crushed as they suffered social exclusion and powerlessness while living in Roman-ruled Asia Minor. Revelation addresses this disappointment so as to evoke feelings in its readers. Actually the technique of the language of Revelation is to intensify, not subvert, these hostile feelings and to objectify them. A catharsis is achieved by bringing the readers' true feeling to consciousness where they can be dealt with directly.

Revelation enables readers to deal with their aggression in a number of ways. The first is the transference of their anger to another object, in this case, to Christ. "The second method of containing aggression reflected in Revelation is that of internalizing it and reversing it, so that it falls on the subject of the aggressive feelings." This makes the readers more reliant on themselves. Their sense of powerlessness was diminished by the fact that they were privileged to receive a message of heavenly origin and consequently knew something their oppressors did not. In conclusion, Collins writes,

> Through the use of effective symbols and artful plots, the Apocalypse made feelings which were probably latent, vague, complex, and ambiguous explicit, conscious and simple. . . . Fear, the sense of powerlessness, and aggressive feelings are not minimized, but heightened. They are placed in a cosmic framework, projected onto the screen of the heavenly world. This intensification leads to catharsis, a release of the disquieting element of the emotions in question.[32]

---

[30] Gerd Theissen, *Psychological Aspects of Pauline Theology* (trans. John P. Galvin; Philadelphia: Fortress, 1987), 15–39.

[31] Gerd Theissen, *Sociology of Early Palestinian Christianity* (Philadelphia: Fortress, 1978), 110.

[32] Adela Yarbro Collins, *Crisis and Catharsis: The Power of the Apocalypse* (Philadelphia: Westminster, 1984), 157 and 160–61. For the discussion see pp. 141–61.

ISSUES IN SOCIAL-SCIENTIFIC METHODS

Collins' study sparks reflection on some of the issues in social-scientific methods. One of the major problems these methods face is their use of models for the interpretation of social data. We will illustrate what this means, and the danger in it, with a widely-read study by an eminent Jewish theologian, Alan F. Segal, who set out to analyze the conversion of Paul of Tarsus.[33] In seeking to explain why Paul converted from Judaism to Christianity, Segal appropriated a specific theory from social science. The story of Segal's study is a caution for those who would engage in a complex endeavor like social science.

Segal takes Paul's conversion as legitimate, as an experience that must be handled at face value as the way that Paul himself grasped what happened to him. Moreover, from the outset of his study, Segal's interest is on the nature of "conversion" as it is found in Paul. Conversion, he says, is a "decisive and deliberate change in religious community, even when the convert nominally affirms the same religion."[34] On that basis, then, Segal sets the framework for his study by saying he uses Jewish and Christian material from Paul's time as well as contemporary studies of conversion.

One result of Paul's conversion was that he quickly became a proselytizer for his new religious orientation, Christianity. He became Paul, the evangelist, the one summoning his old comrades in Judaism, as well as Gentiles, to the Messiah. Segal argues that Paul's energetic proselytizing was a direct outgrowth of the nature of his conversion experience, a way to deal with what he explains as Paul's "dissonance" over his radical break with his own religious past.

The model, then, to which Segal turns for help is drawn from a study published as *When Prophecy Fails: A Social and Psychological Study of a Modern Group that Predicted the Destruction of the World.*[35] This study dealt with a small religious group that passionately believed they would see the end of the world. When that did not happen, the group had to learn how to cope with failed prophecy. The researchers describe what they thought they saw happening in the group as "cognitive dissonance." Segal picks up and consistently uses cognitive dissonance as a way of drawing specific conclusions

---

[33] Alan F. Segal, *Paul the Convert: The Apostolate and Apostasy of Saul the Pharisee* (New Haven: Yale University Press, 1990).

[34] Ibid., 7.

[35] Leon Festinger, Henry W. Riecken and Stanley Schacter, *When Prophecy Fails: A Social and Psychological Study of a Modern Group that Predicted the Destruction of the World* (New York: Harper & Row, 1956).

concerning the nature of Paul's conversion. (He recognizes, however, the theory of cognitive dissonance has run into many problems over the thirty-five years that it has been in circulation.) Segal tries to account for why Paul set about to "redefine" his old Judaism in new terms, terms that would enable him to "discount" his own "failure" as a Jew and to create a new world of meaning for himself.

Segal's work suggests a number of important issues in the social-scientific methods of biblical interpretation. First, his use of cognitive dissonance is problematic since that model has undergone such debate and criticism. However, the question is more fundamental than an uncertain model. His work also suggests the danger inherent in the use of sociological models by biblical scholars who cross disciplines to adopt a model from a discipline other than her or his own for use in biblical interpretation. The threat also entails using stereotypical sociological terms to explain biblical data. For example, while the title "charismatic prophet" seems to fit Jesus in a certain regard, should we try to include all the data into one term? Tuckett offers a useful summary:

> Now it is certainly the case that the comparison of early Christian communities with other communities widely separated in space and time from the first-century Roman Empire may well be fruitful. Nevertheless, . . . it may be that the New Testament evidence is pressed, by at least some New Testament sociologists, into *sociological* stereotypes in a way which represents an illegitimate use of these categories from the sociological point of view.[36]

All this does not diminish the value and promise of the social-scientific methods but only cautions us against careless use of the critical value of the disciplines.

THE CONTRIBUTIONS OF THE SOCIAL-SCIENTIFIC METHODS TO PREACHING

Social-scientific biblical critics can appear to be rather obscure in their conclusions and most certainly locked up in their own jargon. The use of sociological and anthropological models is sometimes so complicated that those who are not formally trained in the social disciplines will feel alienated. A good example, we think, is the Mary Douglas model of group and grid. It takes some time and thought to figure it out, much less understand how biblical scholars are using it. It is also important to recognize that those who use

---

[36] Tuckett, *Reading the New Testament*, 146.

social-scientific methods may sometimes have no interest whatsoever in a text's message for our day. It may seem, therefore, that the methods we have surveyed have no relevance for the preacher. The opposite is actually the case.

In this section we will first ask why the results of social-scientific exegesis would interest preachers. Then we will try to suggest ways of applying the methods for homiletical purposes, at best offering only some examples. In conclusion we will offer one sermon as an example of how social-scientific methods yield material useful for preaching.

Real-world Settings

We want to make the same point here that we did in the previous chapter under the heading, "The Humanity of the Bible." The methods we have discussed in this chapter take for granted that the communities behind the biblical documents and those that are the subject of the books are human. We assume, that is, they lived in this real world that you and we know. Therefore those communities (including the earliest Christian churches) shared some of the same dynamics that are evident in our societies. We can, for instance, identify with the Israelites when they had to make the transition from a nomadic to an agrarian life. Our culture has gone, first, through the industrial revolution and now is in the midst of the electronic revolution.

An example might help. After the Israelites settled in Canaan, they wondered if Yahweh had anything to do with fertility and farming. They knew Yahweh as a warrior, guide, and provider but not as a source of fertility. The Canaanites had their god and goddess of fertility, Baal and Astarte. In Canaanite religion, changes in the relationships between these deities was the determining factor for the fertility of the land. The name of the Canaanite deity, Baal, would become the Hebrew word for owner or master, perhaps because the Baals were understood by the native Canaanites to be the owners of the land.[37] There is evidence in the Bible that many of the Israelites adopted the worship of Baal alongside their worship of Yahweh. This may well have been because, in the midst of their trying to learn how to farm, they needed to appease the god who controlled the fertility of the land (Judg 2:11–13). In the midst of what seemed an endless drought, the Israelites had to ask the question, Who brings the rain? During the time of the monarchy the prophet Elijah challenged the prophets of Baal to a contest—a superbowl of sorts fought between the gods. As the contestants are gathering on Mount Carmel, Elijah mocked the people: "How long will you go limping with two different opinions?" (1 Kgs 18:21). In effect he says the people cannot go on with their

---

[37] Noth, *The Old Testament World*, 280–81.

worshiping two gods—Baal and Yahweh—but must choose between them. After taunting the four hundred prophets of Baal because their god did not answer them with rain, Elijah appeals to Yahweh, and it starts pouring.[38]

A transition in cultures often calls into question the religious faith and the worldview of the people. Will the God of the past suffice in this new complicated world in which we now live? What does the Christian God have to do with cloning, artificial insemination, mind-altering drugs, stem-cell transplants, and so on? A radical change in our culture makes us ask about the sufficiency of our faith. As we limp about with divided opinions, we understand the transitional pains of the Israelite people.

The social sciences study the biblical world and offer up their findings to us, showing us how the text reflects the larger social and cultural issues of the day. Through their observations we preachers can find analogies (see Chapter One) with our own day. Consider all the issues Paul raised in the first of his epistles addressed to the Corinthian church. There were struggles about wisdom (1 Cor 1–2), sexual immorality with "a man lying with his father's wife" (5:4), lawsuits among believers (6:1–11), marriage and divorce (7:1–39), eating food offered to idols (8:1–13) and so on. We may wonder what kind of a church is this? But the truth is that these young Christians were trying to find their way from the "normal" life in this Greco-Roman city to a "new" Christian life.[39]

The social-scientific methods enable us to see more clearly the real world situations in which the biblical documents are set. Preachers then can use that insight to speak in relevant ways to our congregations.

Community Emphasis

Another contribution the social-scientific methods make to the homiletical interpretation of Scripture entails their concentration on communities. The social sciences are distinguished by their focus on the way humans live in groups, form societies, and interact with one another. Therefore, nearly all of our examples of the methods under consideration have had to do with biblical communities.

How is this community emphasis a contribution to homiletical interpretation? There is much in our western tradition that is precious and important, but we are learning that our tendency is to think of human existence

---

[38] Walter Harrelson, *From Fertility Cult to Worship* (Anchor Books; Garden City, N.Y.: Doubleday, 1970).

[39] See Gordon D. Fee, *The First Epistle to the Corinthians* (NICNT; Grand Rapids: Eerdmans, 1987), 196–97.

first in terms of the individual and only secondarily of our human existence in community. Pastors have learned how hard it is in this day and this culture to nurture community among congregants. There is a natural tendency for us to dwell on individuality rather than community.

That being the case and immersed as we are in our culture, our preaching needs to emphasize community more than it naturally might. One thing the social-scientific methods of interpretation do for us is to focus our perspective more on relationship among people than on individual experience. We are aided by the social-scientific methods because they deal with texts in terms of their relationship with community.

We will provide an example of this community perspective with a social science interpretation of Matt 6:14–15. We are inclined to think of forgiveness in terms of what Malina and Rohrbaugh call "psychological healing." Instead, they ask us to think about these words of Jesus in the context of a honor and shame society.

> [S]in is a breach of interpersonal relations. In the Gospels the closest analogy to forgiveness of sins is the forgiveness of debts (Matt. 6:12; see Luke 11:4). . . . [Debt] made persons poor . . . that is, unable to maintain their social position. Forgiveness would thus have had the character of restoration, a return to both self-sufficiency and one's place in community. . . . *Forgiveness by others meant restoration to community.*[40]

Our inclination to stress the privacy of sin may make it difficult to grasp this idea of sin and forgiveness in an honor and shame society. However, when we think of the way sin so often breaks relationships, alienates us from others, and causes a sense of shame, as well as alienating us from God, then we may see the contemporary parallel to what these social-scientific interpreters are saying.

A Holistic View

Another contribution the social science-oriented methods make is what we might call a holistic view. Theological interpretations tend to emphasize the rational and logical relationship among statements of faith. Ethical interpretations might spend too much time on the commands for behavior. Our more usual approach may be something like a "faith interpretation," meaning that we are looking for something in the text which will strengthen the faith of our listeners.

---

[40] Bruce J. Malina and Richard L. Rohrbaugh, *Social Science Commentary on the Synoptic Gospels* (Minneapolis: Fortress, 1992), 63–64. Italics ours.

Social-scientific methods, however, tend to be as comprehensive as possible in considering the meaning of the text. That is the case because these methods are necessarily interested in whatever shapes the behavior, religion, and worldview of people. This is one of the reasons that a good many different kinds of human sciences come together in what we have been calling social-scientific. For example, one area that has not been mentioned thus far is the attention to economic matters in the biblical world. In chapter four we will consider one form of liberation interpretation that emphasizes the economic concerns of Jesus and his ministry, the poverty of the people, and the heavy taxation laid upon them.

Social-scientific methods have been interested in the relationships among the rich and poor in both Testaments. How was the oppression and occupation of Israel a factor in economic conditions? It is interesting that one of Paul's frequent themes in his later letters is an offering for the poor in Jerusalem (Rom 12:13; 15:25–26; 1 Cor 16:1; 2 Cor 8:4; 9:1). The reason for the collection for the "saints" in Jerusalem is often said to be Paul's concern for uniting the Gentile church with Jewish Christians and for the fulfillment of the directive that the Gentile churches should "remember the poor" (Gal 2:10). Traditional historical-critical commentators tend to make more of Paul's strategy for keeping the church unified. A more keenly economic reading, however, would not exclude the simple fact that the inhabitants of Jerusalem tended for years to be poor and in need of help. Social-scientific critics would likewise stress the importance of the needs of the Jerusalem community.[41]

Contemporary preaching ought to maintain the kind of holistic interpretation we are stressing here. The unity of human life and community is a significant goal for the church's ministry.

Interrogating the Text

We turn now to the question of how preachers can study a text from the perspective of the social-scientific methods without necessarily becoming skilled experts in the discipline. There is, of course, no simple answer to such a question. As we have said above, clearly it entails the task of becoming more sensitive to the social, cultural, and community dimensions of human existence and especially of those in the biblical communities. A sensitivity to these matters will go a long way toward renewing our preaching and ministries.

---

[41] Bengt Holmberg, *Paul and Power: The Structure of Authority in the Primitive Church as Reflected in the Pauline Letters* (Philadelphia: Fortress, 1978), 35–43.

Howard Clark Kee (one of the leading New Testament social-scientific critics) emphasizes that the interpreter of a text needs to take into account the social factors that influenced the document. The preacher needs then to attend to at least these four matters: (1) "the sociocultural environment in which the writing was produced." In other words, how might the context of the author and the intended readers have shaped both their understanding and concerns? (2) "The interpreter of a document must be alert to the effects of [the] process of change within the community by whom and for whom it was produced" and how it might be expressed in a text. (3) "The mode of communication adopted by the writer." Because form plays a social function, preachers need to ask if there is a social reason for the author choosing a particular stylistic form or linguistic tone. Kee goes on to say (4) that what interpreters are looking for is the "life-world" of the author and the first readers.[42]

In an effort to test Kee's suggestions, and with his observations to guide us, we undertake the sketch of an examination of 1 John 1:1–2:2 (the RCL reading for the second Sunday of Easter, year B). Without any pretense of being able to respond thoroughly to Kee's four topics, we shall briefly address them.

The Sociocultural environment. We have no way of knowing in detail what the environment of 1 John might have been, but we can assume that it was in Asia Minor near the turn of the first century C.E. Christians were likely to have been in a minority in the region and surrounded by a multitude of other Greco-Roman religions. The writing suggests that the community or communities to whom the document is addressed has suffered a schism caused by differences between the main church and a group of separatists. The differences between the two groups have to do with both theological thought (Christology) and morality. The tone of the writing hints at the emotional uneasiness this schism has caused. The author tries to condemn the separatists, while reassuring the main body of believers. The environment was rich in religious options and the letter implies that the separatists have chosen to interpret Christianity in terms of other religious perspectives, which we have come to think of as gnostic or pre-gnostic.

The document tries to assure the readers that they have the revelation of the truth and the author witnesses to that revelation. The dualistic language of light and darkness hints at a radical right and wrong perspective which allows for no compromise. As well as access to truth, the author argues that the community has forgiveness for their sins. Finally, Christ is mentioned in sacrificial language.

---

[42] Kee, *Knowing the Truth*, 104–5.

Religious change. First John 1:1–2:2 indicates that the author believes the separatist have changed their position and are challenging the main body of Christians. Caught in the back draft of that change, the readers are fearful, anxious, and uncertain. The change threatens the basic worldview of the readers which included the solidarity of the church. The author's response to this change is defensive. The separatists are wrong and evil, so the readers must hold on to their belief. The strong language used of the separatist suggests defensiveness which arises from uncertainty.

Mode of communication. What is insinuated by the form of this document? Its stylistic form is not certain, for it does not appear to be a letter. Instead, it seems to be a document that might be circulated among the churches or groups of believers. Given the situation we discern from the writing, we may comfortably think of this document as a defense of a religious stance and therefore of vital importance. One stylistic feature is the author's use of the first person, plural pronouns, "we" and "our." The impact of this language is to stress the unity and clarity of communal self-identity between the author(s) and the readers.

Life-world. To summarize, the elements mentioned above hint at a life-world that includes a clear distinction between truth and falsehood. It is based on the experience of the community as the author implies in our reading. However, the security of that world has been threatened, so that it is no longer as stable as it once was.

This exercise has made several things clear for the preacher. First, there is a great deal we do not know, and much that we will never know. We think it is important that preachers realize the limited amount of clarity we have. Therefore, the suggestions made above, while based on the evidence of the document, are nothing more than reconstructions.

Second, we can imagine the sort of atmosphere created by the schism that the church in 1 John seems to have just experienced. The sense of uncertainty, fear, and anxiety is a natural experience in such a situation.

Third, the variety of Christian views supposed in the document is characteristic of a region comprised of a potpourri of religious options. The presence of other religious views was not abnormal in such a syncretistic environment.

Fourth, the challenge to one's religious worldview is a serious matter, since that worldview is fundamental to many. We are then dealing not just with a troublesome variation, but with a radical readjustment.

What, then, might we preach given the results of this interrogation of a text? Certainly a sermon that articulates the trauma of religious change in our society and helps us understand why such change is so frightening would be appropriate. We might wonder why certain issues and changes in our society so upset some people, including ourselves. The fear of homosexuality and the recognition of same gender marriages disrupt the religious worldview of some. It is as if the heavens are shaking. If the social scientists are right in their belief that we fashion for ourselves (or inherit) religious views which are integral to a certain worldview, it is not a single practice that really offends us but the whole idea that our secure religious worldview might come crumbling down. It may be fear of the destruction of their religious worldview that the readers of 1 John were experiencing as a result of their church splitting. Our effort in Christian love is to try to understand how vitally important these matters are and understand the reactions—even the reactions we ourselves feel.

ANOTHER EXAMPLE

Our investigation of the 1 John passage with Kee's suggested topics has perhaps helped us understand how social-scientific exegesis for preaching might be done. Next we need to see how a sermon arises from such exegesis and how that sermon might unfold.

The following sermon is based on one specific insight into the passage under consideration for preaching, Matt 21:28–32. In preparing for the sermon the preacher consulted the book on the parables by Bernard Brandon Scott, who is committed to social-scientific interpretations. Scott writes about this parable that it,

> . . . exploits a fundamental problem with the peasant family system: a conflict between the demands of the family and those of honor. When the parable hearer is asked to choose between the two sons [21:31], a dilemma arises. Both sons have insulted the father, one by saying no, the other by saying yes but doing nothing. . . . Would the father choose to be publicly honored and privately shamed, or publicly shamed and privately honored?[43]

The issue of honor and shame, as we said, is one of the social-cultural features of the biblical material that is clear and easy to understand. We have all felt the difference between honor and shame, and so we can grasp the issues in the biblical context.

Often this seemingly simple parable is taken to be a comment on the importance of obedience and of service. However, Scott deepens the impact of the parable considerably by asking us to look at the honor-shame issue. By

---

[43] Bernard Brandon Scott, *Hear Then the Parable: A Commentary on the Parables of Jesus* (Minneapolis: Fortress, 1989), 84.

claiming that in Jesus' culture both of the sons have shamed their father, each in his own way, he drastically changes the point of the parable and makes us realize that sometimes there is no way out of a dilemma.

This sermon was written on the Matthean text in preparation for preaching on the Nineteenth Sunday After Pentecost (Proper 21, the twenty-sixth Sunday in Ordinary Time). It was prepared for a congregation that the preacher did not know, and therefore of necessity it lacks some of the congregational specifics that are essential to a really good sermon.

"No Way to Go"

Proper 21, A
Matthew 21:28–32

HAVE YOU EVER FOUND YOURSELF TRAPPED BY A FORK IN THE ROAD? YOU MUST decide which way to go. But the sign on one road reads, "Bridge Out Ahead." And the sign on the other road reads, "Road Closed Ahead!" You have no way to go! No matter which you choose, you will find yourself in big trouble down the road. So, what do you do?

The chief priests and elders must have had a bit of that feeling. They were questioning Jesus' authority to teach as he did. They ask him, "By what authority are you doing these things, and who gave you this authority?" Jesus responds with his own question about the authority of John the Baptist. His opponents are stumped. They could not respond without getting themselves in trouble with the people. So, they answer, "We do not know."

Jesus then proposes this situation: The farmer has two sons. He asked one to go into the field to work. The son responds that he would not go. Later he thought better of it, and changed his mind. He went into the field to work.

The father then asked his other son to go and work in the field. And the son answered, "Sure, Dad. I'll do it." But then he did not go.

Now Jesus asks the religious officials who had been challenging him. "Which of the two did the will of the father?" And they respond, "the first."

Actually Matthew's report of the telling of this parable seems to be a bit brief, and we get the feeling that something has been left out. In the culture of Jesus' day, your social position was very important. It was a matter of honor. Now honor is your own sense of your worth, plus the worth you have in the eyes of others. To be shamed is to lose honor. That is, to be demoted from your social status. You felt shame when others looked at you and concluded that you were not as worthy as they once thought. So, it was very important how others thought of you.

I was raised in a small town. It was one of those infamous communities where everyone knew everyone else's business. And what other people thought of you was so very important. I remember clearly how my blessed mother would write on her calendar the day a couple in the village was married. Now I love and appreciate my mother very much. But she kept her little record so that when the first baby arrived, she could count the months since their wedding. Woe be the couple who did not have a good nine months between the wedding and the first baby! For if they didn't, mother and her friends did all they could to get the word around. They hoped to shame the couple by passing the word around about a baby conceived before marriage.

We all know how important honor and shame are to us. In Jesus' day, however, it was even more important. The honor of social position was about all some people had—no money, no fancy houses, or clothes—only the honor of being well regarded by the community.

Now the part of the parable that Matthew apparently chose not to include had to do with honor and shame. These two bratty sons *both* shamed their father. The first son shamed his father by publicly refusing to obey him. However worthy it was of him later to go into the field and work, the harm had already been done. He said no to his father's request and dragged his father's sense of worth down.

The second son did no better. He said, yes, he would obey his father. But then he doesn't! Again the parable suggests that this was a public matter. Everyone knew the second son had agreed to go and work in the field. And everyone knew he didn't do it!

What does this parable have to do with us and our Christian lives? Yes, to be sure, it encourages us to be willing and responsive to God's call. Yes, it suggests that actual service is far more important than our promises—whether we keep them or not.

But something else of importance is tucked away in this parable. Some of us say yes to God but never get around to doing much that's concrete in service of God. Others of us resist saying yes to God but pretty soon find ourselves trying to serve others *and* God.

All of us, however, have shamed God—brought shame on our creator. *All of us!* The yes-sayers and the no-sayers.

The point is that none of us is without blame!

So, here we are at a crossroads. Shall we say yes? Or, shall we say no? Either way we go, we still have no reason to feel proud. None of us has said yes and then done what we know honors our God. So, which way shall we turn?

It feels as if we have *no way to go.* Both roads lead us nowhere. So, what are we to do?

There was a young man who set out on a journey but got lost along the way. He eventually came to a crossroad like the one we have been discussing. Either way he decided to go, he wouldn't get far. Soon he would be stuck. He stood there contemplating his dilemma.

Then here came an elderly woman, wearing an apron and carrying a sack of vegetables. The young man stopped the woman hoping to get some directions. "Which way should I go?" he asked her.

"Oh, it doesn't really matter, because old sister Brown will be along on her tractor soon. She'll take you over the river and beyond the road repairs."

"But I don't know her," the young man complained. "And I have no money to pay her for her services."

Through her laugh, the woman said, "Oh, no problem! You see, young man, sister Brown doesn't do this for money. And she doesn't do it just for her friends. She just wants to help people like us to find our way through this dead-end."[44]

"No Way to Go?" At a dead end? No problem! God's love and grace takes all of us beyond the dead-ends of life. No charge! No special privileges necessary. The divine love is the way to go.

---

[44] This story was conceived by Kysar. Any resemblance to others is unintentional and accidental.

Chapter 3

What Difference Do Literary Criticisms Make?

Recall the imaginary document to which we referred at the beginning of Chapter One. We supposed we had discovered a note, tucked away among the books in a musty used book store. Scribbled in pencil on the back of an envelope, the note reads:

> I can no longer contain myself! The anguish and torment is too much to bear. You know that I care deeply about you and the children, but my patience has worn thin. If what I am about to do seems cruel and heartless, then so be it. But I must be true to myself and to my values. If what I am about to do brings you shame and embarrassment, you will have to deal with that. For my part, this is my only honest way out. God help me if I am wrong.

Efforts to reconstruct the historical situation out of which this note was written would lead us to much speculation and many different theories. Suppose this. Imagine that. Some of those proposed situations might provide interesting ways of reading the note, and some of them might explain (or account for) the note in part or entirely. Ultimately such interpretations prove to be futile, since there is no way we can know the author's intention in the words she or he used. But there are other very different ways of approaching the note.

One such way would be to attend strictly to the words and sentences of the note itself without trying to reconstruct the circumstances under which it was written. We would abandon the notion that we should try to discover the author's intention and instead deal strictly with what the note means in and of itself. How do we respond to the note's cry for understanding? What do the words elicit from you? As we read the expressions of deep emotion, what feelings arise in us? What are we to infer from the relationships among some of the words, such as "values" and "shame?" What are the oppositions we find in the words of the notes—oppositions between the author and some circumstance in life, between the author and the addressee? When we have done such a study of the note, perhaps we have done all that can be done and indeed all that needs to be done. We may then at least understand what the text of the note says, even if we are still bereft of the knowledge of the circumstances under which it was written and the author's intended meaning.

THE MAJOR COMPONENTS OF LITERARY CRITICISM

Our imaginary discovery of the note and our attempts to understand it suggest what seems to many to be the failure of historical-critical methods of biblical interpretation which has the impetus to find other ways of reading a text. The first and perhaps most successful challenge to the dominance of historical-critical methods has come from the rise of new literary-critical methods. The adjective "new" in this title is important for several reasons. First, historical-critical studies have long spoken of "literary criticism." However, by it the critics meant literary matters rooted in the history of the biblical text, such as authorship, sources, and forms.[1] The newer movements are quite different from literary studies done in the context of historical criticism.

The second and more important challenge is the recognition that by referring to the *new literary criticism* in biblical studies, we acknowledge the influence of a movement in general literary criticism (that is, a movement among scholars outside of biblical studies) called "the New Criticism." That movement at its most basic was concerned with how a text affects its reader. As it has been adopted and used by biblical critics, this literary emphasis came to argue that texts do not create meaning, readers do.

The New Criticism was popular in general literary circles between the 1930s and 1950s, but it was the 1970s before it began to influence biblical studies in a significant way. In the 1970s *structuralism* reached biblical interpretation from other disciplines where it was in vogue in the 1950s and 1960s. Within literary studies and other disciplines such as anthropology, structuralism was a means of studying any human production in terms of

---

[1] In college in the mid-1950s, Kysar's text book for an Old Testament class was *The Literature of the Old Testament* by Julius A. Bewer (rev. ed.; New York Columbia University Press, 1933). The first two chapters were respectively, "Early Poems" and "Early Narratives." The literary interest was part of an effort to isolate the earliest bits of literature that lay "behind" and became part of the Old Testament.

"the rules of internal organization."[2] Out of the analyses of language and the way it works arose the conviction that all human understanding entails relationships. We never know one thing in and for itself alone, but only by its relationship to other things. For instance, we never know another person apart from the context in which we met her and deal with her.

In biblical studies structuralism was taken up as a means of analyzing texts in ways which unearthed their "deep structures," that is, their implicit values and convictions. For a time, some biblical scholars pursued this sort of "deep structuralism" in reading texts (and some continue to do so), but within a few decades the movement faded in its importance. Combined with the influence of the New Literary criticism, however, structuralism spawned a number of other biblical enterprises, including deconstruction and semiotics (a study of the structures of language) as well as other critical efforts to move beyond historical-critical studies. Of particular importance for us is the outgrowth of *narrative criticism* from structuralism. (See the more detailed treatment of structuralism below.)

A third movement related to the literary study of biblical texts is *rhetorical criticism.* It arose from an extra-biblical interest in "new rhetoric," the revival of classical analyses of argumentation and persuasion. In one sense, it fits nicely into the literary paradigm, but in another sense it does not. Initially rhetorical criticism was launched by the New Criticism but soon took on a life of its own as scholars tried to restore the values of classic Greco-Roman rhetoric which had been repressed since the Middle Ages. Rhetorical criticism of the Bible began with the Old Testament in the late 1960s[3] and was then adopted by some New Testament interpreters. It is related to structuralism (at least what we will later call "surface structuralism") in that rhetorical criticism deals with the structure of individual units of biblical material. At the same time, it is a relative of literary criticism insofar as it focuses on the way in which passages function to move the listener or hearer. It differs from some other forms of literary criticism, but is similar to structuralism, in that its focus is not on the reader but on the structure of texts. In the discussion below, we will suppose that one form of rhetorical criticism is

---

[2] Early in the development of the movement, William A. Beardslee proposed this definition of literary criticism: "the approach of literary criticism is to accept the form of the work, and the reader's participation in the form, as an intrinsic part of entry into the imaginative world of the work." *Literary Criticism of the New Testament* (GBS/NT; Philadelphia: Fortress, 1970), 13.

[3] See James Muilenberg's crucial article "Form Criticism and Beyond," *JBL* 88 (1969): 1–18. His work began what became a Muilenberg school devoted to the rhetorical criticism of the Old Testament.

primarily literary, while the other is not. It is the literary expression of rhetorical criticism that interests us in this chapter.

The history of these various types of literary criticism is complicated and does not concern us here. However, we must be careful not to equate these three profound developments in late twentieth-century biblical studies—rhetorical criticism, new literary criticism, and structuralism—for they are very different from one another. What they obviously share in common is a concern for a text as it is found by the reader. The historical-critical methods (including the social sciences criticisms discussed in the last chapter) insist that to understand a text one must know something about its origin and development into the form found in our Bibles. As different as they may be, the literary movements about which we are concerned in this chapter both deny or—in the case of rhetorical criticism—seriously qualify the claim that historical investigation is required to understand a text.

LITERARY AND HISTORICAL CRITICISMS

There are a number of other ways to distinguish the larger movement of literary criticism from historical-critical methods. One important distinction between them is their different understandings of *the time of interpretation*. Historical studies assume that an interpreter must refer to a past time, that of the text's origin, in order to read it the present. The interpreter deals with both past and present in the act of reading and understanding a text. Hence, historical criticism has been labeled *diachronic* ("through time") because of its attention to both times. On the other hand, the new literary criticisms (including some expressions of structuralism) may be thought of as *synchronic* ("with time") because of their attention exclusively to the present moment of reading. While these terms are used in a variety of ways, in this case they may help us understand the contrast between historical and literary criticisms.

Moreover, the new literary criticisms emphasize *the unity of the text* and its structure. No critical separation of sources and glosses is necessary. Since the text presents itself as a unity, readers must deal with it as a single unit. Even in reading and interpreting a small portion of a larger work, the interpreter must have the whole of the literary work in mind.[4]

Another break with historical criticism found in the new literary movements concerns *the creation of meaning*. Historical criticism generally insists

---

[4] David Jobling, "Structuralism and Deconstruction," *Dictionary of Biblical Interpretation* 2:510.

that the meaning of any text arises from the meaning it had originally when first written. That meaning is "encoded" in the present text, and historical criticism seeks to discover the "intention" of the author in writing the text. Literary criticism in its first phases of development claimed that the text contains its own meaning now apart from whatever meaning the author had intended. Once the author has written a text, it is freed to mean whatever it is interpreted to mean. Like a piece of art that says more than the artist may have ever intended it to say, a written text may mean more than what its author meant to say.[5] In fact the meanings of any single text are boundless. The literary movements about which we are concerned in this chapter brought to the surface the question of meaning and its origin (see Chapter Six) but by no means finally answered those questions. Thus a focus on the present text and the experience of reading it are what finally matters, not any theory of the text's origin and development. Much of the debate within both literary and structural criticism in more recent years has confronted this question of how meaning occurs.

The question of the text's unity and the source of the meaning of a text have gradually led to a diminished *commitment to formalism.* By formalism we mean only the idea that there is something akin to "true meaning" located somewhere in the universe. Does the text guide the careful reader to a meaning that is beyond the text? Is there an objective body of truth not dependent on human comprehension? Furthermore, does the commitment to the unity of the whole literary work imply that meaning is located in the whole as the parts are related to each other? All of these questions have arisen in what we may think of as the postmodern era in North America.

One unresolved issue for the literary criticisms, however, is what we might term the *inescapable historical connection* of any biblical text. To be as descriptive as possible, we need to acknowledge that literary scholars today are divided over the question of whether one can ever read an ancient text without some acknowledgment of its historical origin. Some will answer yes and others no. Some stand on the cusp between historical and literary criticisms and gladly employ both. Others are absolute in their rejection of anything born of the historicism of the modern age and enthusiastically embrace purely literary methods without reserve. At the time of this writing, biblical criticism is in a transitional period in its history and the outcome is not yet clear—nor is it likely to become clear for at least a decade.

One may at least ask whether readers can honestly ignore the history of a biblical text given the fact that, in many cases, the texts before them are

---

[5] Robert Morgan and John Barton, *Biblical Criticism* (The Oxford Bible Series; Oxford: Oxford University Press, 1988), 217.

translations. Suppose the readers are able to read the original languages, Hebrew, Aramaic, and Greek. Our understanding of these languages is the result
of historical investigations of how the languages were used in the period
when the documents were written. For instance, to understand how to
translate the Greek word *agapē,* scholars must study its use in extra-biblical
as well as biblical examples. Readers may also need to admit that the standard Hebrew and Greek texts are constructions from the fragmentary manuscripts available to us. So, either way—in translation or in the original
languages—biblical texts have a history, that is, are the result of some historical investigations.[6]

These issues will continue to be discussed for some time, but for now it
is clear that a major component of current biblical studies focuses on the text
as it stands before us and on readers of that text without resorting to inquiries
into the historical origin and development of those texts. As we hope to show
at the end of this chapter, literary movements hold considerable promise for
preachers and their ways of doing biblical interpretation.

This chapter treats the enormous and varied field of literary and rhetorical methods under three topics. Since it has connections with historical criticism in some of its forms, we deal first (and briefly) with rhetorical criticism.
Second, we seek some understanding of "reader-oriented criticism."[7] The
third topic is narrative criticism. Finally, as we have in the previous chapters,
we ask what "pay off" each of these literary movements has for homiletic interpretation and then present a sermon based on the literary reading of a text.

RHETORICAL CRITICISM

Rhetorical criticism has emerged as a method that sometimes fits
within historical criticism and sometimes within literary criticism. In both
cases, rhetoric refers to the structure of language within defined limits and
most specifically to the means of argumentation. "Rhetoric is that quality in

---

[6] We think Edgar V. McKnight is right when he writes, "reader-response approaches are capable of accommodating and utilizing approaches followed in more
conventional biblical and literary studies. Historical and sociological exegeses, for
example, are not precluded in reader-response criticism. They are *reconceptualized
and relativized but not made illegitimate as such.*" "Reader-Response Criticism," in *To
Each Its Own Meaning: An Introduction to Biblical Criticisms and Their Application*
(ed. Steven L. Mckenzie and Stephen R. Haynes; rev. ed.; Louisville: Westminster
John Knox, 1999), 240. Italics ours.
[7] Edgar V. McKnight used this title in his book, *Postmodern Use of the Bible:
The Emergence of Reader-Oriented Criticism* (Nashville: Abingdon, 1988).

discourse by which a speaker or writer seeks to accomplish his [or her] purposes."[8] The historical and literary wings of rhetorical criticism are not exclusive of one another but are clearly distinctive. However, sometimes "rhetoric" entails only how language is used in a particular document. In these cases, a linguistic investigation of Mark might be entitled, "The Rhetoric of Mark."

The historical-rhetorical critics seek to find the relationship between biblical instances of rhetoric and those found in the Greco-Roman literature of the biblical period. Moreover, these critics also often inquire into the social setting of any biblical instance of a rhetorical pattern and how that pattern worked in a particular cultural situation. This form of rhetorical criticism has come to be called "socio-rhetorical." While rhetoric is concerned with the structure of texts, Vernon Robbins explains, "the hyphenated prefix 'socio-' refers to the rich resources of modern anthropology and sociology that socio-rhetorical criticism brings to the interpretation of a text."[9] This form of rhetorical criticism is entangled in all the issues treated in the previous chapter on social science criticisms.

However, there has also been a renewed interest in rhetoric within the context of a purely literary investigation. Sometimes called *the new rhetoric* or *modern rhetorical analysis* (as opposed to ancient or Greco-Roman), critics focus on passages with a persuasive intent and ask how such passages attempt to argue their respective points. Within literary criticism, rhetorical analysis has provided a way to approach non-narrative passages (for instance, the New Testament book of Hebrews) in order to discern how urgency and purpose work in argumentative passages. Attention is given to values embedded in an argument, but—perhaps most important—literary rhetorical critics treat such passages not as decoration in a speech, but as integral to the style of a text.[10]

Methods

In its efforts to understand how the rhetoric of a passage functions to persuade readers of the argument the text makes, the new rhetorical criticism is not far from the interests of reader-oriented criticisms. As we will see, reader-response critics attend to the effect of the reading experience rather than to the text itself. However, there is clearly a component of the new literary-rhetorical movement that is indebted to structuralism and works

---

[8] George A. Kennedy, *New Testament Interpretation Through Rhetorical Criticism* (Chapel Hill: University of North Carolina Press, 1984), 3.

[9] Vernon K. Robbins, *Exploring the Texture of Texts: A Guide to Socio-Rhetorical Interpretation* (Valley Forge, Pa.: Trinity Press International, 1996), 1.

[10] D. F. Watson, "Rhetorical Criticism, New Testament," *Dictionary of Biblical Interpretation* 2:399–402.

with non-narrative texts in a way comparable to how narrative criticism deals with stories. In both cases, critics are interested in how the text is put together, how it moves, and what strategies appear in the passage. Still, this method is not to be identified with either of the other two literary methods we are discussing. It has its own methodology and concerns.

George A. Kennedy was instrumental in advancing rhetorical criticism in New Testament studies. However, his understanding of the process was not purely literary, since he believed that the rhetorical critic could make use of the findings of the historical form criticism of the time. In his work we see how the historical interests in the transmissions of biblical forms became a bridge to rhetorical criticism. Nonetheless Kennedy's outline of a process by which rhetorical analysis works is still helpful.

1. The determination of a *rhetorical unit.*

2. Definition of the *rhetorical situation of the unit.* Kennedy means by "situation" the conditions under which "an individual is called upon to make some response," and entails "persons, events, objects and relations."

3. Discover the *rhetorical problem.* Why does the author find it necessary to persuade the listeners of something?

4. Identify the *form* (or genre) *of the argument.* The three classical forms are those which (1) seek to make a judgment on the past (judicial), (2) try to influence a future decision (deliberative), and (3) reinforce or condemn someone or something in order to shape some values (epideictic). Under the influence of the form criticism of the 1980s, Kennedy thought the forms or genre should be related to those advocated by form critics.

5. Identify the *arrangement of the materials.* This involves discerning the subdivisions of the passage.[11]

Others have enriched Kennedy's procedure with two other steps:

6. Identify features of *rhetorical style,* such as the use of questions.

7. Analyze the general *rhetorical strategy* of the passage. In this step one might look at the effectiveness of the whole of the unit.[12]

---

[11] Kennedy, *New Testament Interpretation,* 33–38.

[12] George Aichele et al., eds., *The Postmodern Bible: The Bible and Culture Collective* (New Haven: Yale University Press, 1995), 154–56. As well as adding these

Examples

Burton Mack provides us several good examples of rhetorical criticism in historical perspective, one of which is an analysis of Heb 12:5–17. He proposes that the whole passage is "an exhortation to accept discipleship" comprised of a number of discernable parts. Verse 5 is an introduction, after which the author states the main thesis (vv. 5–7a and b), citing Prov 3:11–12. The argument for the thesis consumes the most space (vv. 7c–11) and cites examples, reasons, and a maxim. The conclusion comes in verses 12–17: "Therefore lift your drooping hands and strengthen your weak knees, and make straight paths for your feet, so that what is lame may not be put out of joint, but rather be healed" (a paraphrase of Isa 35:3 and 12:12–13). Arising from that conclusion comes the author's exhortation: "Pursue peace with everyone, and the holiness without which no one will see the Lord."[13]

As Kennedy suggests, rhetorical criticism identifies the form of an argument (see Chapter One). As we have already noted, interest in various genre or forms of literature in the Bible is certainly not unique to rhetorical criticism, or even literary criticism in general.[14] "Form" provided a basis for the development of form criticism in historical-critical studies. The literary critic, of course, is not interested in the historical development of different genres and forms but in the way they work in a text and in the mind of the reader. Rhetorical criticism names different forms of argument, but other literary critics also take seriously the fact that genre and form shape reading. For instance, apocalyptic literature piques the imagination and demands a different kind of attention than, say, historical narratives. In the case of form, a Psalm of lament evokes a different sort of reading than a Psalm of praise. The rhetorical critics find a general form for most of the biblical material but then go on to distinguish among what they call "specific rhetorical functions," such as an exhortation (for example, Luke 12:22–31) and a *chria* (a memorable saying such as the one found in Mark 2:23–28).[15]

As we will argue later, the potential of rhetorical criticism as an aid to interpretation for preaching is obvious. Rhetorical criticism (of either the historical or literary type) can provide preachers with helpful understandings of

---

steps, this group also offers some revisions and refinements to Kennedy's five steps. See Kennedy, *New Testament Interpretation,* 150–54.

[13] Burton I. Mack, *Rhetoric and the New Testament* (GBS/NT; Philadelphia: Fortress, 1990), 77–78. This book is a good general introduction to rhetorical criticism with ample examples of the method.

[14] See James L. Bailey and Lyle D. Vander Broek, *Literary Forms in the New Testament: A Handbook* (Louisville: Westminster John Knox, 1992), 11–15.

[15] Mack, *Rhetoric and the New Testament,* 25–48.

the structure of a passage and its major point. As a method, however, rhetorical criticism of a literary type needs to clarify the relationship between the text and the reader. One of its weaknesses is that sometimes the method focuses on the text without asking what the reader brings to the process. Moreover, if we are interested in argument, how do we define the relationship between individual units and the argument of the whole book? If the part is not meaningful without the whole, then it would seem that rhetorical criticism must include an analysis of the whole of the book in which a passage is found. All of these remarks suggest that rhetorical criticism needs the insights of other methods.[16]

READER-ORIENTED CRITICISM

Few areas of criticism are as complicated, or as difficult to categorize, as the one known as reader-oriented criticism or, sometimes, reader-response criticism. The perspective emerged in secular literary criticism in the middle years of the twentieth century when it began to dawn on scholars that the search for "truth in the text" was being regularly subverted by the inability of capable students to agree on a text's "truth." Different scholars were seeing and reacting to the same texts in strikingly different ways. Consensus over meaning, let alone truth, seemed difficult if not impossible to achieve. So the question of literary study itself began to change. Instead of "What does a text mean?" the question turned toward some variation of "Why does one react to the text, both intellectually and emotionally, as one does?" The spotlight of literary criticism moved from the text itself and its "meaning" to the situation of the one studying it—its "reader."[17]

Others would put this discussion elsewhere in this book, which is not inconceivable. Our view, though, is that it belongs about midway between traditional literary criticism and various postmodern forms that we will look at later. So we choose to discuss it in this context of other literary criticisms. We will try to back up and treat it in as straight-forward a way as we can.

One impulse behind focusing on the *reader* of a text lies in the gradual recognition of the limitations of what humans can know. A text, for instance,

---

[16] This is precisely the task that Vernon Robbins undertakes with some success in *Exploring the Texture of Texts*. He proposes socio-rhetorical criticism can be used profitably in connection with all the other contemporary critical methods and thereby pull them together.

[17] Webb's explanation of the history and meaning of reader-response theory is found in the first chapter of his book, "Ready and Responding to a Text," *Old Texts, New Sermons* (St. Louis, Mo.: Chalice, 2000).

does not convey information about some objective truth in the universe. In this way, the rise of reader-response criticism both contributes to and results from the emergence of a postmodernist perspective. Instead of seeking knowledge about what is beyond the reader and the text, reader orientation stresses what the text does to, or means to, the reader in terms of values, attitudes, and responses. In other words, *the goal of reading a text is not to learn about truth that lies beyond the text but to learn about oneself and the human interaction with a text.* Consequently, two related threats have haunted reader-response criticism. The first is the threat of relativism and the second is the question of how and on what a community can agree when reading a text. What is shared in a reading experience? The movement has raised any number of issues, some of which will be addressed in subsequent chapters.

As a way of getting inside the reader-oriented criticisms, we ask that you read the following familiar paragraph focusing your attention on what the text arouses in you as well as on what you bring to the text intellectually and emotionally that prompts your reaction to it. Avoid thinking about ways to "explain" the text and simply allow yourself to become vulnerable to these words:

> Do not think that I have come to bring peace to the earth; I have not come to bring peace, but a sword. For I have come to set a man against his father, and a daughter against her mother, and a daughter-in-law against her mother-in-law; and one's foes will be members of one's own household. Whoever loves father or mother more than me is not worthy of me; and whoever loves son or daughter more than me is not worthy of me; and whoever does not take up the cross and follow me is not worthy of me. Those who find their life will lose it, and those who lose their life for my sake will find it. (Matt 10:34–39)

What did you experience or feel while reading this passage? You may have felt confusion or perhaps betrayal, because your Jesus should not speak like this. Maybe the declaration that we cannot love our parents more than we love Christ worries us. The words may judge and convict us. If we were freed of the notion that these words are somehow sacred Scripture, we might feel anger and disgust to such a degree that we would discard the passage. What does your response to this text tell you about it or, more to the point, about yourself?

In reader-response criticism, attention is shifted away from the text to the reader. The text is no longer thought to contain meaning which the interpreter must dig out the way one digs in the ground for buried treasure. Instead, the primary focus for the origin of meaning is on the reader. Admittedly, there is still much debate even among reader-response critics as to whether the reader alone creates meaning or whether meaning arises from a dialogue between reader and text. Many biblical reader-response critics still tend to side with those who believe that the text is in some sense independent of the reader and provides a stability of meaning, but only the future will tell how long this will be the case. Actually, reader-response (or reader-oriented) criticism is an umbrella term that covers a great variety of methods, so that it is impossible to say for certain what will become of the movement.

You may immediately sense that there is something terribly individualistic about the sort of experiment to which we have subjected you, and you may be inclined to conclude that reader-response would ultimately lead us to a relativism in which each individual has her or his own reading of every passage. Moreover, that makes every reading "true" (to someone), and no one reading can claim to be the only "true" interpretation.

Who Is the Reader?

The contrast between historical and literary methods has been characterized as the difference between looking through a window and into a mirror.[18] Understanding a text as a window to the past is typical of the historical-critical enterprises which attempt to go "through" or "behind" the text to discover its meaning in its historical context. To understand a text as a mirror, however, is to allow the text to illumine the present and in particular the present reader. Of course, the imagery of window and mirror raises some troubling questions for reader-response criticism. Not least, the mirror analogy seems to suggest that readers *create themselves* in the text. The text is reduced to a means by which readers clarify their own convictions, and it may not present a message that challenges readers. Some critics would say that this conclusion is precisely right, while others will still maintain that the experience is more like encountering another person than looking into a mirror to encounter oneself. In that case, the text then has an integrity and identity of its own, which stands over against its readers.

Doubtless the most pressing question for reader-response criticism is what kind of reader one is as he or she reads a text.[19] Among those who employ this sort of reading technique, there are at least three different images of the reader. On the one hand, some reader-response critics seem to think that contemporary readers should mimic how they believe the original and first

---

[18] This metaphor was apparently first suggested by Murray Krieger, *A Window to Criticism: Shakespeare's Sonnets and Modern Poetics* (Princeton: Princeton University Press, 1964), 3–4. See also Joseph M. Webb, *Old Texts, New Sermons: The Quiet Revolution in Biblical Preaching* (St. Louis: Chalice, 2000).

[19] Stephen Moore systematically discusses each of the options for understanding the reader in reader-response criticism in Chapter Seven of *Literary Criticism and the Gospels: The Theoretical Challenge* (New Haven: Yale University Press, 1989), 107–30.

readers would have interpreted the text. Such a view, however, seems to revert to a historical paradigm for understanding a text, since it would require knowing something about the first readers.

On the other hand, some suppose that the readers are "ideal" interpreters of the text, which means that readers follow precisely the clues a text gives as to how it is to be interpreted. These critics speak of "an interaction between text and reader," and thereby attempt to hold together some sense of formalism or structuralism which claims meaning is at least "mapped" in the text. Ideal readers of the Matthew passage given above, therefore, are faithful to what they find in the passage and allow it to lead them along to a deeper understanding of their own commitments and accept the words as a genuine challenge of Christian discipleship. The concept of the ideal reader assumes that the text creates a path toward its interpretation and that readers can discern and follow that path along which the text leads them. In most cases, this view depends on the notion of the *implied reader* in the text, which we will discuss later under narrative criticism.

Still other literary critics view the reader as the actual and particular reader of the moment. Readers are simply those who approach and attempt to understand the text today—not necessarily attempt to understand it the way the original readers would or to understand it as would some abstract "ideal reader." This view makes reading a text a very personal experience. As we encouraged you to attend to your own responses to the Matthew passage above, so readers are always and properly going to do so. Reading is totally subjective, since in the reading experience one's perception of the text is always one's own construction of the text. This view, however, raises as many questions as it answers. For instance, how do I keep my own social and psychological situation from creating the message of the text? My "social location" (as critics call it) is an essential element in shaping my particular interpretation of a text. Furthermore, how do communities (like the church) engage in such readings? Can the church practice a reader-oriented approach to the Bible without eventually fragmenting itself into as many interpretations as there are church members?

Since a given reader is always embedded in a particular historical and social position, some critics seek to think of the reader as a social being, representing a social setting and creating meaning out of a text suited for that setting. A "social" orientation assumes that the individual reader is always a part of some interpretative community. In this case, reader-oriented interpretation is always a communal undertaking.[20]

---

[20] Joseph M. Webb, "Deconstruction/Reconstruction: New Preaching from Old Texts," *Quarterly Review* 16 (1996): 447, n. 4. This entire article is a discussion

Another way of dissecting reader-response theories entails how readers approach a text. Each of these two broadly-conceived approaches could be coupled with any one of the views of the reader described above. In the first approach, readers allow themselves to become *vulnerable to the text.* They put themselves at the mercy of the text. In this case, the emotional and personal responses to a text are most important, not unlike what we invited you to do in the little exercise above. Being vulnerable to the text stresses the identity of the reader, and what is at stake for readers of a text is their personal identities—how they understand themselves. The other approach to the text fosters the idea of the "resistant reader"—one who is suspicious of a text and its message. The best (but not only) examples of this sort of reader-response are found within the feminist approach to biblical interpretation to which we will turn in the next chapter. The resisting reader refuses to be subjugated to a text's point of view, so that reading becomes an experience of vigorous dialogue with a text.

Among the most important issues these various ways of defining the reader raise is the matter of social location. As we suggested above, some critics stress the social identity of readers, insisting that interpretation is shaped by certain social pressures and customs. This view leads to the necessity of readers knowing themselves well enough to be able to identify the social reasons for their reading a text the way they do. For instance, contemporary readers tend to ease the threat implicit in Jesus' words about the family divisions that may result from discipleship, and they do so quite simply because of the importance our culture attaches to family. A reader's social position and power are another concern for such a reading. We naturally interpret a text from a social position so as to protect our status and empowerment.[21]

---

of the new movements in biblical interpretation and their influence on preaching. Webb also discusses four lectionary texts in the light of these new movements. See also Webb's book, *Old Texts, New Sermons.*

[21] There is currently a vigorous movement committed to the importance of the "social location" of reading. Among the claims the advocates of this movement make is that an honest interpretation of a passage always necessitates that readers first of all describe their social location, in order that others know how the interpretation may be shaped (even unconsciously) by the interpreter's position, background, and social identity. This movement has included a good number of interpreters from other parts of the world, since their "social locations" differ radically from those of the middle class, white, empowered, male, affluent North Americans. See *Reading from this Place: Social Location and Biblical Interpretation in the United States* (2 vols.; ed. Fernando F. Segovia and Mary Ann Tolbert; Minneapolis: Fortress, 1995) and *Reading from this Place: Social Location and Biblical Interpretation in Global Perspective,* vol. 2, by the same editors and publisher.

No better example of this protectiveness is found than in the relative importance of the first beatitude in the Gospels of Matthew and Luke. As you know, Matthew's text reads, "Blessed are the poor in spirit" (5:3), while Luke has simply, "Blessed are the poor" (6:20). Among white, middle and upper class North Americans, Matthew's version is much more widely known, and some even claim to have never heard Luke's version. Social location can filter out that which threatens us. We preachers should carefully and honestly identify our own "social locations" as best we can in order that we might understand how and why we read certain texts as we do.

The importance of the reader in this sort of literary criticism has led some to say that reader-response criticism inevitably results in *autobiography*. No matter how hard we may try, we cannot attain a purely objective reading of a text, and indeed one of the virtues of reader-response criticism is that it takes seriously the personal nature of interpreting a text. Therefore, a careful study of our interpretations of the Bible reveals our own histories and identities.[22]

One final perspective on readers comes from what has been called the more "radical views of reader-response."[23] In this case, reading is understood as an experience of self-transcendence in which readers move beyond themselves into another world from which they find their basic life experiences illumined. Hence, reading becomes a means by which we can overcome the separation between subject and object. Readers enter into the object, the text, and transform it into subject. In doing so they themselves are subjectively transformed. Such a view of readers clearly breaks with the modern Cartesian separation of subject and object.[24]

What Is Language?

Understandably, language and how it is conceived play important roles in any literary criticism. Indeed, the movement toward literary criticism has been intertwined with new concerns for language. Language, however, is understood and analyzed in various ways. As scholars began to scrutinize the traditional view of language as referential (referring to some reality beyond

---

[22] The clearest example of this movement toward autobiography is Jeffrey L. Staley's provocative *Reading with a Passion: Rhetoric, Autobiography and the American West in the Gospel of John* (New York: Continuum, 1985). Other examples include Ingrid Rosa Kitzberger, ed., *Autobiographical Biblical Criticism* (Leiden: Dio, 2003) and Janice Chapel Anderson and Jeffrey L. Staley, eds., *Taking it Personally: Autobiographical Criticism* (Semeia: 72 Atlanta: Scholars, 1995).

[23] See E. V. McKnight, "Reader-Response Criticism," *Dictionary of Biblical Interpretation* 2:372–73.

[24] See Webb, "Deconstruction/Reconstruction," 448, n. 6.

itself), new understandings were advanced. The history of the study of language is very complex and lies outside the scope of this book. In simplest terms, language has in recent years been deprived of its signification of truth and has come to be understood as a unstable means of human expression appropriate to particular social groupings. Language interests literary critics in two quite different ways. Structuralists study language for the deep values it exposes, and they appreciate the organic nature of language. The reader-oriented critics, however, value language for how it *functions* in the experience of reading a text.

Lucy Atkinson Rose's discussion of language in preaching is helpful as a kind of summary of the changes in the perception of language during the twentieth century. She traces the understanding of preaching from the traditional view of language to the present "transformative" view of language. The traditional view, as we suggested, assumes that language expressed truth and represented some transcendent truth built into the universe. "The focus" in the transformative perspective, Rose writes, "is on the change in the human situation created by words." Among the central convictions of such a position is that "language shapes human consciousness" and that "words are events." More recently, this view of language, Rose points out, has changed due to a fresh honesty about the "biased and limited nature of language that reflects its historical conditioning." All language is relative to concrete historical situations and always ambiguous.[25] The power of language, on the one hand, and its social limitations and ambiguity, on the other, are both essential to the view that literary criticism brings to reading the Bible.

Although Norman Perrin was not primarily a literary critic and his major contributions actually antedate the period when the new literary criticism became prominent, his important study of the expression "kingdom of God" opened the way for a new and different understanding of religious language. He maintained the expression "kingdom of God"

> is a symbol that functions within a larger mythological conception of God's activity in history. . . . If we view the symbol Kingdom of God in ancient Judaism in this light, then we can see that fundamentally it is a tensive symbol and that its meaning could never be exhausted, nor adequately expressed by any one referent.

Jesus' proclamation of the kingdom was not an effort to communicate an idea but, through language, to evoke from the listener a sense of God's presence in their lives. Perrin goes on to study the parables as poetic metaphors that broke

---

[25] Lucy Atkinson Rose, *Sharing the Word: Preaching in the Roundtable Church* (Louisville: Westminster John Knox, 1997), 67, 79–80.

into the listeners' world with new possibilities.[26] His study was a precursor to a new appreciation of biblical language as poetic and metaphorical.

Probably nothing about language is more consequential in literary criticism than its openness or its *instability,* what has come to be called its *tensive* quality. Openness refers to the fact that the meaning of language is never once and for all discovered but that the interpretation of an incident of language goes on forever. Tensive is used here as the opposite of *steno* which is language that supposedly has a one-to-one equation with some referent. (For example, the word "chair" refers unequivocally to the object it names.) Instability refers to the fact that meaning is never fixed but always fluid, and that different readers experience the same language in different ways. This instability of language is one of the hallmarks of deconstructive criticism, as you will see in chapter five. In reader-response criticism this view of language is accompanied by a sense that each reading of a text is, in effect, a "performance" of that text, if only in the experience of the reader, and that each performance is unique. As Perrin came to think of kingdom of God, many literary critics have come to think of all language as metaphorical in the sense that it works to stimulate readers with different possibilities rather than some single meaning.[27] For the literary critic, therefore, language is never simply equated with this or that referent nor is its power to take on new meaning ever exhausted.[28]

---

[26] Norman Perrin, *Jesus and the Language of the Kingdom: Symbol and Metaphor in New Testament Interpretation* (Philadelphia: Fortress, 1976), 31. See also Amos N. Wilder, *The Language of the Gospel: Early Christian Rhetoric* (New York: Harper & Row, 1964). Perrin's book provides an excellent survey of parable interpretation up to the publication of the book.

[27] See Joseph M. Webb's discussion of symbolism in *Preaching and the Challenge of Pluralism* (St. Louis: Chalice, 1998) and Chapters One and Two and the discussion of language and relanguaging in Robert G. Hughes and Robert Kysar, *Preaching Doctrine for the Twenty-First Century* (Fortress Resources for Preaching; Minneapolis: Fortress, 1997), 13–16, 29–32. For two examples of reader-response interpretations of metaphor, see these articles by Robert Kysar: "Johannine Metaphor—Meaning and Function: A Case Study," in *The Fourth Gospel From a Literary Perspective* (ed. R. Alan Culpepper and Fernando F. Segovia; Semeia 53; Atlanta: Scholars, 1991), 81–111, and "The Making of Metaphor: Another Reading of John 3:1–15" in *"What Is John?" Readers and Readings of the Fourth Gospel* (ed. Fernando F. Segovia; SBLSymS; Atlanta: Scholars Press, 1996), 21–41.

[28] Speech Act theory argues that a speaker *does something* with language and causes certain effects in the hearer. However, some speech act theorists claim the text and not the reader is responsible for the act. For example, Anthony C. Thiselton, "Reader-Response Hermeneutics, Action Models and the Parables of Jesus," in *The Responsibility of Hermeneutics* (ed. Anthony C. Thiselton, Roger Lundin, and Clarence Walhout; Grand Rapids: Eerdmans, 1985), especially 103–10.

The implicit power and ambiguity of language forms one of the important assumptions of reader-response criticism, since it is the language of the text that effects the reader. At least as reader-response criticism has evolved in the last several decades, the instability of language has come to play a more and more important role. As we will see in Chapter Five, deconstruction criticisms take this view of language even further.

An Example

We can offer only a summary of a reader-response interpretation of a passage,[29] and for that purpose we have selected the parable of the workers in the vineyard found in Matthew 20:1–16. One reading experience of this parable revolves around readers' reaction to the major characters of the parable and what is attributed to them. One might well experience both empathy and antipathy toward the story's characters and find oneself shifting identifications in the course of the story—first admiring, then disliking the major character. As we begin the story, we may be won over by the generous landowner who went out to hire workers four separate times, each time promising to pay his temporary employees a just wage (although that is not explicit in the case of the last group of workers, vv. 1–7). Here is a just and generous employer!

But then we are shocked by the employer's harshness in responding to the complaint of the first group of workers. The landowner is arbitrary (v. 14) and selfish (v. 15a) and then dismisses the complaining workers with an accusation that their demands are envious and wrong (actually that they have an "evil eye," v. 15b). The narrative leads us to think like the workers who were first hired, namely, that, if the last group of workers is paid a full day's wage, then those who arrive first on the job should be paid more than a single day's wage. Consequently, the employer's harsh reply in verses 14–15a shocks the reader. The generous and kind man suddenly seems to change character. Readers may be left confused by this mysterious character whose actions are inexplicable, and we may side with the employees who had been in the first group to be hired.

A reader-response study of this parable may leave readers puzzled and bewildered, and feeling some ambivalence toward the employer. Our sense of justice is suddenly shaken. The employer's charge that the first group of employees has "an evil eye" forces us to ask whether our own sense of justice is conceived with evil eyes. Perhaps just such confusion and sense of injustice

---

[29] For a fuller example, see McKnight, "Reader-Response Criticism," 240–47.

are what we are supposed to feel having read this provocative parable.[30] The keys to this strategy are the identification (or empathy) and repulsion solicited by the story, both of which we will discuss later.

NARRATIVE CRITICISM

For reasons far too complex to list here, as biblical structuralism waned, there arose in its place what was christened *narrative criticism*.[31] Narrative criticism's indebtedness to structuralism is complicated, since the New Literary Criticism clearly influenced the inception of narrative criticism along with structuralism. Since it is at least one of the ancestors of narrative criticism, we will sketch the biblical structural criticism that is still practiced and advocated by some. Having briefly summarized structuralism, we will turn to the task of describing narrative criticism.

Structuralism

Structuralism had its beginning in the linguistics of Ferdinand de Saussure in the 1950s. Working at the level of individual sentences, he insisted that any portion of a sentence had no meaning, except as it is related to other linguistic elements, and his work stimulated the consideration of how a story was a complex interweaving of parts. Claude Levi–Strauss claimed that cultural systems were related in much the same way as de Saussure proposed language was. A myth within a culture could be analyzed as a complex sentence and, when compared to other myths, could expose the "deep structures" of a society, that is, its values and worldviews. With this understanding of language, structuralism spread into anthropology.

Efforts to investigate the structures of narratives inspired biblical critics to use the methods of structuralism in their studies. Along with others, Daniel Patte in the United States took as the goal of structuralism the identification of the values and convictions that generate a text. Patte explicitly presented structural analysis as an alternative to historical-critical methods. Unlike those who implemented historical methods, the structural critic is interested not in what

---

[30] Robert Kysar, "Matthew 20:1–16: A Narrative Reading" in *Academy of Homiletics: Papers of the Annual Meeting, 1997*, 123–27. For Kysar's sermon on this passage, using his reading experience of the parable, see Joseph M. Webb and Robert Kysar, *Greek for Preachers* (St. Louis: Chalice, 2002), 193–96.

[31] Apparently David Rhoads was the first to use this title in a consistent way for what he saw happening in the study of Mark. See his article, "Narrative Criticism and the Gospel of Mark," *JAAR* 50 (1982): 411–34.

the author intended to say in a passage but in the structures implicit in that passage. As a matter of fact, the "deep structure" of a narrative reveals convictions and beliefs sometimes hidden in an author's unconsciousness. Some of the variety of meanings in narratives are discovered when critics compare the structure of a biblical text with other texts—including those in the Bible, in extra-biblical literature, and literature of a later time.

Patte identified three types or levels of deep structures, of which the first two are constraints imposed on the author by either culture or the author's own situation. Below (or behind) those are the convictions rooted in a person by virtue of human nature, and the discovery of these is the primarily goal of structural exegesis. The structural exegete first identifies a system of signs in a text and then tries to distinguish between the deep structures and the other two which function as constraints.

Patte's proposals for analyzing narratives are probably related to the origin of narrative criticism. There are, he claimed, several specific matters to which the narrative exegete must attend. The first of these is the sequence that provides a narrative its basic framework and the smaller narrative elements comprising a sequence. These are in turn made up of narrative statements, which are descriptions of one person's action in relationship to that of other persons or things. "Canonical narrative functions" is Patte's term for a series of pairs of opposites, such as domination versus submission and attribution versus deprivation.[32] Finally, narrative statements are made up of six *actants* (what the actors do) which are related in three different ways: communication, volition, and power. The model looks like this:

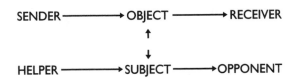

The binary nature of these elements enables an exegete to see the basic values expressed in a passage, whatever the author may have intended to say.[33]

The complexity of structuralist theory doubtless contributed to its failure to make a lasting place for itself in biblical studies. More helpful, perhaps, are the actual interpretations Patte and others have published. For instance, in his commentary on Matthew, Patte explains his exegetical strategy. He

---

[32] Daniel Patte and Aline Patte, *Structural Exegesis: From Theory to Practice* (Philadelphia: Fortress, 1978), 18–21.

[33] This summary is drawn from Daniel Patte, *What is Structural Exegesis?* (GBS/NT; Philadelphia: Fortress, 1976).

seeks the convictions of the evangelist, and these are evident in cases where Matthew says both what he means and then what he does not mean. "Discovering Matthew's conviction is, therefore, a matter of *identifying in each passage the points Matthew makes by setting up explicit oppositions*—the narrative oppositions in his story." The oppositions the exegete looks for are of two kinds—semantic oppositions (opposing terms) and narrative oppositions (opposing actions). From these, as we shall see, one can discern Matthew's convictions.[34]

In his exegesis of Matt 15:1–9, Patte initially says the passage is comprised of "no fewer than four closely interrelated narrative oppositions, a signal that something important is at stake for Matthew."[35] The first opposition (15:2–3) is between Jesus and the Pharisees and scribes who question Jesus regarding his interpretation of the "tradition of the elders." Their deeper question is, on what basis might one judge another guilty of a transgression? The story informs us that God's Word (Scripture) and not "the tradition of the Elders" is the proper basis for such a judgment. However, another opposition in the same verses contrasts the disciples' violation of tradition and the Pharisees' transgression against God's commandment.

A third opposition found in 15:4–5 is the contrast between what God says and what the Pharisees say. The final opposition (15:4–9) entails God's command, on the one hand (honor one's father), and, on the other hand, the teaching of the Pharisees that allowed one to violate that command in favor of something that is dedicated to God (*korban*). In other words having dedicated his wealth to God, a son no longer had to share it with his parents. Patte concludes, "[in] sum, the Pharisees and scribes are 'hypocrites' because they confuse their own teaching and their own will (established in their 'heart,' see 15:8–9) with God's commandment and his will. And thus when they want to honor and worship God, they do so in vain."[36]

A number of problems continue to plague structuralism, the first of which is the unnecessarily bewildering tangle of theories and technical language. Moreover, sometimes one wonders if the elaborate analysis of a passage is worth the little that it yields—often only what is already evident to any careful reader. (The analysis of Matt 15:1–9 summarized above is a good

---

[34] Daniel Patte, *The Gospel According to Matthew: A Structural Commentary on Matthew's Faith* (Philadelphia: Fortress Press, 1987), frontal page and 5–8. The quotation is from the frontal page.

[35] Daniel Patte, *The Gospel According to Matthew*, 216–18. See also his *Paul's Faith and the Power of the Gospel: A Structural Introduction to the Pauline Letters* (Philadelphia: Fortress, 1983) and *Preaching Paul* (Fortress Resources for Preaching; Philadelphia: Fortress, 1984).

[36] Ibid., 216–18.

example.) But more important is the fact that, as a method for biblical exegesis, structuralism assumes there are discernible patterns of truth concealed in the text. In his declaration that the actual intention of the author is not recoverable, Patte broke with historical criticism, but he nonetheless speaks freely of learning "Matthew's convictions." If those convictions are sometimes unconscious ones, then the exegete claims to learn something about the original that is more elusive even than the author's intent.

Another point at which structuralism is vulnerable is its notion that convictions are uncovered through binary opposition. This "binary opposition" seems to be understood as truth in some objective and even universal sense. So, the text and not the reader is the focus of structural criticism, and it implies formalism. This is to say, "structuralists have often claimed a global, objective validity for their models." As a method then it "tried to pattern itself on the model of an objective natural science; theoretically, any reader using its technique will discover the same structure."[37]

The structuralism of Patte and others is often called "high" or "deep" structuralism to distinguish it from analyses of the *surface* of a text, namely, narrative criticism. However, the fact that we now speak of *poststructuralism* to refer to nearly every other method that is different from deep structuralism testifies to the importance of structuralism in the history of criticism. Hence, reader-oriented, narrative, and even rhetorical criticisms are in some way efforts to go beyond structuralism. Most characteristic of poststructuralism, however, is deconstruction criticism, which we will address in a later chapter.[38]

Assumptions of Narrative Criticism

Narrative criticism is closely related to reader-response criticism in part due to their shared history within North American biblical study. Narrative criticism clearly owes its life to its predecessors. Its attention to the structure of the narrative and the way it moves comes out of structuralism, although with radical differences. Furthermore, its concentration on the Gospels in their final form grew out of redaction criticism. Redaction criticism, of course, took for granted the history of the text, namely, that behind the text are sources, both written and oral. The evangelists undertook the task of editing these sources as they incorporated them into their work. The redactional-critical study, in either its Old or New Testament form, viewed the docu-

---

[37] Aichele, *The Postmodern Bible,* 98.

[38] The *Dictionary of Biblical Interpretation* treats structuralism and deconstruction together. David Jobling, "Structuralism and Deconstruction," 2:509–14.

ments under consideration as a unified whole. Closely related to redaction criticism is *composition criticism* (as we pointed out in Chapter One), which is less interested in the sources behind the text than in the wholeness of the present text. However, like redaction criticism, composition criticism sought to understand the theology of a work. Narrative criticism is a close cousin of composition criticism but, unlike its cousin, narrative criticism is interested not so much in theology as in story.[39]

There are a number of matters that are basic to narrative criticism, and these may offer us an entry into its method. To isolate these assumptions is not to say that there is no difference among narrative critics on these issues, for there certainly is. However, the majority of these critics would, we believe, agree with these assumptions, though with some qualifications.

1. Narrative critics assume that the biblical documents are unified wholes, so that in order to interpret any one part of the document one must view it in the light of the entire book. What comes before and what follows a text are essential components for interpretation. Narrative critics are opposed to the fragmentation of source criticism operative in historical-critical methods.

2. Narrative criticism (along with other expressions of the new literary criticism) assumes that form and content are inseparably wedded. Careful readers cannot isolate one from the other.

3. Narrative critics take for granted that story is a basic ingredient to the biblical literature and to human life. Faith comes to expression most vividly through the stories of the believers. In this way this critical method is a part of the larger narrative movement in theology.[40]

4. Regardless of what historical reference a biblical story may have, narrative critics believe it works poetically to stimulate readers' imaginations. Therefore stories shape the way readers understand themselves in part because self-understanding is most often narrative.

---

[39] See Moore, *Literary Criticism and the Gospels,* 6.

[40] See the momentous work of Hans Frei, *The Eclipse of Biblical Narrative: A Study in Eighteenth and Nineteenth Century Hermeneutics* (New Haven: Yale University Press, 1974); George W. Stroup, *The Promise of Narrative Theology* (Atlanta: John Knox, 1981); Gabriel Fackre, "Narrative Theology: An Overview," *Int* 37 (1983): 343–51; and Mark Ellingsen, *The Integrity of Biblical Narrative: Story in Theology and Proclamation* (Philadelphia: Fortress, 1990).

5. The interpretative key to any text, say narrative critics, lies within the text and not beyond it. Along with rhetorical and structural criticism, and opposed to reader-response criticism, narrative critics assume that meaning (at least to some degree) is embedded in the text and not in a text's historical origin or in the mind of the reader.

6. Narrative criticism assumes a communication model as the basis for the interpretation of a biblical text. That is, the sender (the author) transmits a message (the text) to a receiver (the reader). This is opposed to a historical model which supposes a development of a text from its origin through various forms of transmission (such as oral tradition and written sources). The assumption of a communication model is, of course, shared by other forms of literary criticism.[41]

Concerns of Narrative Criticism

With these assumptions in mind, we now turn to a discussion of some of the issues most important for a narrative critic when analyzing a biblical story: readers and authors, plot, characters, gaps and inconsistencies, and narrative world.[42]

Readers and authors. Practitioners of narrative criticism have developed ways of understanding how a text normally works to bring about the results it does. In particular, the communication entailed in the reading experience described above is fleshed out more fully. The following diagram represents a model narrative critics often use.[43]

Real Reader ←{ Implied Reader ← Narratee ← Narrator ←Implied Author }← Real Author

The text *implies* a certain kind of author and reader, both of which are to be distinguished from a story's narrator. Note that these are *constructions*

---

[41] Mark Allen Powell, *What Is Narrative Criticism?* (GBS/NT: Philadelphia: Fortress, 1990), 8–10.

[42] David M. Gunn provides a useful definition of narrative criticism in his article on this method in *To Each Its Own Meaning,* 201. In narrative criticism "meaning is to be found by close reading that identifies formal and conventional structures of the narrative, determines plot, develops characterization, distinguishes point of view, exposes language play, and relates all to some overarching, encapsulating theme."

[43] This schema was first devised by Seymour Chatman, *Story and Discourse: Narrative Structure in Fiction and Film* (Ithaca: Cornell University Press, 1978), 151. Since then it has been widely cited and employed.

from what the text says. Alan Culpepper defines the "implied author" this way: "The implied author is the sum of the choices made by the real author in writing the narrative, but the implied author is neither the real author (who wrote) nor the narrator (who tells)."[44] Likewise, a text always assumes certain things about the reader and from the clues in a text that hints at those assumptions we create an image of the kind of reader the text takes for granted. For instance, the Matthew text we cited above implies a reader who may be inclined to think Jesus came to bring peace.

A "real reader" gradually gains an impression of the author and reader implied in the text and reads accordingly. For instance, we gain the impression that the implied readers of Job feel themselves caught, as Job himself is, between their own sense of innocence and indignation, on the one hand, and the counsel of their "friends," on the other hand, who keep insisting that Job must be guilty. Furthermore, the absence of God for the entirety of Job 3–37 suggests the implied author leads the readers to a sense of the loss of God.

It is important for the critic to detect the way the implied reader is to go about understanding the text and follow those clues in the text. The implied reader supplies the real reader with a "point of view" which is required for a successful story. This point of view enables the reader to make correct judgments about events and characters in the narrative. Therefore, narrative critics maintain that the proper reading (and meaning) of a text is implicit in the text itself.

The narrator is a voice in the narrative itself that guides the readers to some understanding of the story. The narrator's voice provides a point of view for the story, which the reader may assume is the perspective from which the narrative makes sense. Readers are usually required to trust the narrator and how that voice interprets events and characters. However, narrators are not always reliable and may mislead the implied reader. Furthermore, they are not always all-knowing in their perspective and are therefore limited in what they can say about the narrative. Jeffrey Staley argues that in John 7:1–10 the narrator transmits false information and bad judgments so that the implied reader becomes the victim of an untrustworthy narrator.[45]

---

[44] R. Alan Culpepper, *Anatomy of the Fourth Gospel: A Study in Literary Design* (Foundations and Facets: New Testament; Philadelphia: Fortress, 1983), 16.

[45] Jeffrey Lloyd Staley, *The Print's First Kiss: A Rhetorical Investigation of the Implied Reader in the Fourth Gospel* (SBLDS 82; Atlanta: Scholars, 1988). Staley goes on to say that suffering at the hands of a faulty narrator may produce tensions in readers "which might help us better understand the rhetorical strategy and theological purpose of the gospel" (95–96).

The narrator seems to be speaking to some imaginary "narratee" who is other than the actual reader. The effect of this, according to narrative critics, is that readers feel they are listening in as someone tells another person the story.[46]

Plot. With this rather complicated understanding of readers, authors, and narrators, narrative criticism goes about reading a story with special attention to several of its features, the first of which is plot. Plot is nothing more than the sequence of events which is described by the narrator and within which the story's action takes place. It is plot that supplies the "what" and the "why" of a narrative.[47] Temporal order and some relationship between cause and effect usually determine the sequence. Mark's frequent use of the word "immediately" (*euthus*) connects the previous and the next episodes with a reference to time (for example, 1:29). Having experienced rejection at Nazareth so that Jesus "could do no mighty work there," Mark tells us he went among the other villages (6:6). In this case, the previous episode causes the next one.

More important for the narrative critic, however, is the theme that emerges from the sequence of events. In some cases, the larger sequence sustains a conflict, such as the one found in the Gospel of Mark—a conflict between God and the forces of evil.[48] In other cases, such as in the Abraham and Sarah story (Gen 12–25), the theme may be faithfulness to God. Theme is constructed by the particular events that are narrated or simply referred to, the order of the events, and most importantly by their impact on characters. Abraham and Sarah's faithfulness is tested by God's delay in bestowing the divine blessing on them (12:1–3), so the events (and in this case the absence of events) leads the story on.

Plots generally exhibit unity and completeness; although that does not mean that the plot always moves to resolution. The most common plot structure entails movement from equilibrium, to disruption, and finally to resolution. The plot of the parable usually called "the prodigal son" is a ready example. The equilibrium is the complete family living together; the disruption is the son's request of his inheritance and his departure; and the resolution occurs with his return and his acceptance by his father. In another example, David disrupts the status quo with his desire for Bathsheba and his

---

[46] For an Old Testament example of narrative criticism, see Gunn's article in *To Each Its Own Meaning*, 212–24.

[47] Elizabeth Struthers Malbon, *In the Company of Jesus: Characters in Mark's Gospel* (Louisville: Westminster John Knox, 2000), 15.

[48] See Jack Dean Kingsbury, *Conflict in Mark: Jesus, Authorities, Disciples* (Minneapolis: Fortress, 1989), 27–29.

murder of her husband, and the resolution comes only with the death of their son and David's repentance (2 Sam 11:1–12:23). The resolution of Job's dilemma comes with the prose conclusion to the story in which his wealth is restored and more (42:10–17).

However, plots may leave readers without resolution. The absence of resurrection appearances in the earliest manuscript of Mark may suggest a plot that remains open, that is, one that does not reach final resolution. Sometimes a story ends with a promise or reference to something that is beyond the limits of the story. The Gospel of Luke concludes with Jesus promising the disciples they will be "clothed with power from on high" and then his ascension (24:49–53). That promise is fulfilled in the beginning of the story in the Acts of the Apostles (the day of Pentecost, 2:1–47). However, Acts concludes with Paul under house arrest in Rome (28:11–31). In one sense, this ending fulfills the promise of the story that the disciples would witness to Jesus "to the ends of the earth" (1:8), but Paul's fate is left unresolved.[49]

An unresolved plot constitutes a narrative strategy sometimes designed to provoke response and invite readers to write their own conclusion to the story. Again, the parable of the prodigal son is a good example. It ends with the father's plea to the elder brother to come and join the party to celebrate his younger brother's return, but the narrator never tells us if he did! So, we are left to answer the question: Will the elder brother accept his father's invitation or not? Will we accept it?

The classic types of plot are the tragedy and the comedy. In tragedy, the final resolution is an undesirable one and, in comedy, desirable (at least for the main character of the story). The biblical literature contains marvelous examples of both. Saul's story is tragic. First, God rejects him (1 Sam 15:10–33) and then he must take his own life to avoid capture (31). The four Gospels, however, are comedies, or, more precisely, examples of what appear to be unfolding tragedies that only turn into comic endings with Jesus' resurrection.[50]

Characters. The actors in a narrative are of central interest to the literary critic as they are perceived by the implied reader. Narrative criticism is attentive to the role characters play in a story and it seeks to describe those who come to life through the course of a plot. In other words, narrative

---

[49] See Robert L. Brawley, *Centering on God: Method and Message in Luke-Acts* (Literary Currents in Biblical Interpretation; Louisville: Westminster John Knox, 1990). Brawley writes, "Acts ends with a sense both of closure and openness. . . . Thus, Luke-Acts projects toward the future so that by extension its story can include modern readers" (32–33).

[50] See Joseph M. Webb, *Comedy and Preaching* (St. Louis: Chalice, 1999).

critics are concerned with *characters in their narrative setting.* Reader-response critics, on the other hand, may focus on how characters affect readers, how readers respond to character portrayals, and how characters are like, or different from, the expectations the narrative seems to create. In either case, characters are of interest to all forms of literary criticism, but especially so for narrative critics.

Characters are of two basic types. Some are *round* in the sense that they are described fully enough that they emerge as whole persons. The main characters of a plot are usually round, however, others are *flat.*[51] They seem to play one limited role in a narrative or epistle and nothing more. In Mark, for instance, while Peter emerges as a rather full (however puzzling) character, Jesus' mother and brothers are mentioned only to set the stage for his pronouncement, "Whoever does the will of God is my brother and sister and mother" (Mark 3:35).

Flat characters, however, are not necessarily minor characters. The story in 2 Samuel 11 and 12 treats the reader to a rather full picture of David, while Nathan has no function except to bring David to repentance. The significance of Nathan's role is major, but the narrative presents only the bare essentials of his character. The Jewish leaders in the Gospels are flat characters, because we learn nothing about them except in their relations to Jesus. They are, however, clearly major characters.[52] In Paul's letters most of the characters are not described in any detail. An exception is perhaps Philemon (and maybe Onesimus), about whom we are told a good deal.

God is a major character in a good many of the biblical stories, especially in the Old Testament. In fact, God becomes a round character in a good many instances, changing the divine mind, being angry, sorrowing, deciding, and acting. Consider the deeply emotional God implied in Hosea 11:1–9. Notice, too, the different portrayals of God in the two creation stories in Genesis. In the first (1:1–2:4a) God is so powerful that the divine word brings things from nothingness into being. In the second story (2:4–25), God creates by getting down in the dust and fashioning the human, and then using a part of the male to create the female. God then asks of these humans, "Where are you?" in 3:9. In the biblical narrative God becomes a character sometimes fully sketched and sometimes mysteriously veiled.[53]

---

[51] E. M. Forster first made this distinction in his book *Aspects of the Novel* (New York: Harcourt, Brace, 1927), 103–18.

[52] Malbon, *In the Company of Jesus,* 10–12.

[53] See Jack Miles, *God: A Biography* (Vintage Books; New York: Random House, 1995).

Three specific things about characters in narrative criticism are worth pointing out. The first is that they are actually *the implied reader's constructs*, and they are assigned some specific role in the story. Readers learn about a character by what the character does or says; by what others say about or do to another character; or by what the narrator tells us about the character.[54] The narrator may explicitly tell the implied reader about a character, as is the case in John 13:27, where the narrator tells us that "Satan entered into him [Judas]." Or the story may show us the character by what he or she does. In the story of Saul's tragic decline, the narrative describes, first, how he offers an unlawful sacrifice in Samuel's absence (1 Sam 13:8–15) and then how he seeks the guidance of a medium (2 Sam 28:3–25). The implied reader learns of Saul's weaknesses through what the narrator tells us he does.

A second matter about characters is the phenomenon of *the unnamed character*. When a person goes unidentified, the critic may usually assume that her or his role in a story or letter is not important enough to be personally identified. For instance, the widow of Zarephath seems to have no function but to provide Elijah two occasions for wondrous deeds (1 Kgs 17), but we wonder why she goes unnamed. An unnamed character seems to play a particular role in a story and is no more important than that role.[55] On the other hand, both reader-response and narrative critics have wondered if perhaps the nameless character creates an opening for readers to enter the story and become that unnamed person. In other words, whether intended or not, unnamed characters may invite reader identification.[56] Such is the case, some think, with the mysterious unnamed person whom the narrator calls simply "the disciple Jesus loved" in the Gospel of John (for example, 13:23). This instance of anonymity entices readers into identifying with this model of discipleship.

A third aspect of characterization is *identification*. Do readers identify with this character or are they repulsed by him or her? Is a character admirable and to be emulated, or is she or he a negative example? Identification may be one of the ways a narrative draws readers into the story and carries them along with it. Furthermore, trying to ascertain how the implied author wishes us to think of a character may keep us involved in a story. Narrative critics suggest that such an identification with a main character helps tie the

---

[54] Malbon, *In the Company of Jesus*, 11.

[55] Some critics have quite properly become concerned by the number of unnamed female characters throughout the Bible and have argued that this is a demonstration of the patriarchal character of Scripture. See Chapter Four.

[56] David R. Beck, *The Discipleship Paradigm: Readers and Anonymous Characters in the Fourth Gospel* (Biblical Interpretation Series 27; Leiden: Brill, 1997).

whole story together. Our example of a reader-response interpretation of the parable of the workers in the vineyard (Matt 20:1–16) demonstrates the importance of identification.

Gaps and Inconsistencies. Some narrative critics contend that what goes unsaid can be as important as what is said. This is particularly true when it comes to "gaps" in a story or an argument. What do such lapses mean? A historical critic might argue that these gaps are indications of the ineptness of the writer or, even more likely, that they constitutes a "seam" between the author's own words and the inclusion of source material. Narrative critics, however, pursue what gaps in a plot say in the context of the narrative now rather than in the past.

Equally important is an inconsistency in the text. The conclusion of Amos (9:11–15) seems contradictory to the rest of the book, which is filled with promises of judgment and suffering as a result of Israel's sin. Suddenly in the last chapter, the text reverses the mood, and Israel is promised restoration and abundance. Source critics are quick to suggest that a later editor added a hopeful theme to Amos. Narrative critics might, however, see the reversal as the completion of the story of God's sovereignty. Certainly the reader-response critic would deal with the story's conclusion in terms of the reader's own judgment and hopefulness—restoration comes only after conviction.

Another example of a narrative gap (and inconsistency) occurs in Elijah's abrupt swing in emotions between his exhilaration in victory at Mount Carmel and his flight to Mount Horeb when he learned Jezebel had put a contract out on his life. Is the brave Elijah, who faced four hundred and fifty prophets of Baal without flinching, now so afraid of the queen? Has he turned coward? Or, is there something left out of the story at this point—something that would complete the portrayal of the prophet? (See the sermon at the end of this chapter.) The narrative critic asks: how important is what has been omitted? The critic may puzzle over the gap for a time but then fill it in with the fruit of imagination. A gap is seen as an opportunity to enter the story and become a participant in it by making one's own contribution.

A classic example of a gap and an inconsistency occurs in the account of Jesus' trial in John. We are told that Jesus is brought to "the high priest," Annas, and questioned. Then the text declares, "Annas sent him bound to Caiaphas, the high priest" (18:19–24). The scene immediately shifts to report Peter's second and third denials of Jesus (18:25–27). In another abrupt change of scene, Jesus is taken from Caiaphas to Pilate's headquarters (18:28). What happened during Jesus' appearance before Caiaphas? Why does the narrator bother to tell us that Annas sent Jesus to Caiaphas but then not report anything of what occurred in that conversation? Add to this gap the inconsistency that in the course of six verses the narrator calls both Annas and Caiaphas "high priest," and you have a considerable quandary that invites our participation and tickles our curiosity. Rather than trying to solve the problem as the historical critic would, with historical suppositions of one kind or another, narrative criticism invites us to savor the puzzle.

Narrative World. Narrative critics are especially intrigued by the environment created by the narrator of a story. To some degree every story fashions a "world" in which the story takes place and which influences the actors in a story. Some critics would even define narrative criticism by its insistence that a story presents a unified world. Stephen Moore summarizes this feature of narrative criticism by saying a narrative "generates a world of persons, places and events . . . that has its own internal consistency and validity independent of its resemblance or non-resemblance to the real world."[57] The key to the understanding of a story's world is its completeness in and of itself without reference to any other "world."

The narrative world may be very much like that of the real reader's world or it may be very different. For instance, the two "Toy Story" movies ask viewers to enter a strange realm in which inanimate toys come to life, speak, have feelings, and possess all the other features we associate with humans. The biblical worlds are not all that different. The story of Balaam in Numbers 25 first asks the implied reader to believe that a prophet's curse actually brings disaster. Then the story solicits the implied reader's belief that a donkey might perceive an angel of the Lord when the prophet does not and furthermore that donkeys can indeed speak. In another example, Proverbs 1 describes "Woman Wisdom" as the personification of wisdom, crying out in the streets (1:20).

A narrative critic traces the emergence of the story's world, the detail in which it is painted, and what role it plays in the plot. Could the plot be located in another narrative world? If not, how is it integrated with this particular narrative environment? A critical reader of Luke notices the significant role of angels in chapters 1–2, these heavenly figures do not appear again until two angels meet the women at the empty tomb in chapter 24 (vv. 4 and 23). (In contrast to Mark 1:13 and Matthew 4:11, Luke does not mention angels serving Jesus in the wilderness at the time of his temptations.) Or, after the devil tempts Jesus in Luke 4:1–13, he then "departed from [Jesus] until an opportune time" (4:13), when he enters into Judas to inspire his betrayal (22:3).[58] What do these narrative features of the world of Jesus' ministry suggest?

---

[57] Moore, *Literary Criticism and the Gospels,* 8.

[58] The redaction critic, Hans Conzelmann, pointed out that in Luke Jesus's ministry was "a period free from Satan . . . an epoch of a special kind in the centre of the whole course of redemptive history." *The Theology of St. Luke* (trans. Geoffrey

The Gospel of Mark supplies another good example of a narrative world. The surroundings of this story conjure up the scene of a cosmic struggle between God and Satan in which there is no great divide between humans and God, even though the two realms of heaven and earth remain intact. Likewise, the Marcan story supposes two temporal periods—the present age and the one to come. Readers are enticed into this world to be participants in the Jesus story.[59]

The implied reader in a story gives the real reader clues as to how they are to participate in the story's world. The story's effectiveness often depends on how willing readers are to allow themselves to enter or participate in that world and then how consistently that worldview is maintained throughout the whole narrative. If the narrative world is unclear or ambiguous and incomplete, it is less effective.

Impact of Narrative Criticism

How productive narrative criticism is and how widely used it will be are questions we cannot answer. At present it is a strong and lively movement, equal in strength to, if not stronger than, reader-response criticism, and there is little reason to think that it will diminish in significance, at least in the near future. What may be at least one determinative factor in the future of narrative criticism is its reliance on the idea that the text has within itself a structure and implicitly therefore a truth. That is, what challenges narrative criticism is its commitment to a certain kind of formalism—the concept of some truth in the text that transcends the text itself. While narrative criticism grew out of structuralism, it may not be thoroughly post-structuralist because it perpetuates the idea of meaning within text. Reader-response criticism moves us closer to the view that meaning is strictly a reader's creation (although, as we have said, that issue is yet to be settled among reader-response critics). Narrative criticism, however, remains joined inseparably to the idea of some truth that transcends both reader and text, but which is discovered in the text. Once again Stephen Moore captures the issue confronting not only narrative criticism but all biblical criticisms:

> The propensity in each biblical scholar to speak and write as though we might one day stumble on those hidden chambers of content within our biblical texts, as we gradually hone our methods—coming ever closer to finding the concealed lever and seeing the secret doors swing open—bespeaks the "lingering strain of

Busell; New York: Harper & Row, 1961), 28. See the discussion of redaction criticism in Chapter One.

[59] See Kingsbury, *Conflict in Mark*, 1–3.

naive Platonism" that befuddles our critical thinking. Hypostatize Content, invariant and discoverable, is the enabling fiction of our exegetical practice.[60]

THE CONTRIBUTIONS OF LITERARY CRITICISMS TO PREACHING

Our concern is not to judge the durability of any critical method but to describe it and then to ask how we preachers might best utilize it in our ministries. Since the literary criticisms we have surveyed in this chapter are so varied, we cannot offer many sweeping generalities about what difference they make to our preaching. Instead, for the most part, we will have to speak briefly and separately of the value of rhetorical, narrative, and reader-response criticisms.

Before doing so, however, there are several features of literary criticisms in general which are important for preachers. The first is the obvious fact that *these critical methods concentrate on the text as we have it before us.* One need not access ancient history to understand and find meaning in a text. We have a hunch that most preachers most often concentrate their study of a text on its "surface" appearance, rather than pursuing historical enterprises to place the text in its original context. One of the reasons we favor the present text to studying its history may be that it is the present form of the text that concerns our congregations. Daily, devotional reading of the Bible by lay people seldom entails exhaustive historical investigations of the text's background. Speaking with the congregation on a text most often leads us to focus on what the present text says now.

In other words, literary criticisms are probably more akin to our daily practice of reading Scripture than are historical criticisms. As such, literary criticisms are more immediately relevant to our homiletical task. Moreover, *concentration on the present form of the text does not require specialized expertise as do the historical methods.* One does not have to be an expert in ancient Near Eastern history to preach on a text in 2 Kings. While the literary methods have developed their own complicated jargon and theoretical foundations, the novice can work with the surface of a biblical text in creative and productive ways. The weakening of historical criticisms challenges the notion that only the experts can read and interpret Scripture, thereby returning the Bible to the people.

---

[60] Moore, *Literary Criticism and the Gospels,* 66. The quotation comes from Barbara Herrnstein, "Narrative Versions, Narrative Theories," *Critical Inquiry* 7 (1980): 213.

Rhetorical Criticism

Our concern here, once again, is with what we might call the new (or surface) rhetorical criticism and not with those older historical efforts to link the rhetoric of a text to historical antecedents. We have already suggested that rhetorical criticism is helpful to preachers in its effort to discern what the text is trying to do, because that effort is one of our major tasks as well. When we see what the text does, it helps inform us as to the purpose of our sermon. Moreover, our preaching often entails the effort to persuade the congregation to cling to the Gospel message. Rhetorical criticism may enable us to see how a biblical text does the same thing.

Suppose we intend to preach on the parts of 1 Cor 15 on successive Sundays. If you follow the RCL, the lessons are 15:1–11 for the fifth Sunday after the Epiphany, Year C, and on the next three Sundays the lectionary assigns portions of verses 12–58. The whole chapter, however, is a single argument, so to know what each of the individual readings attempts to do requires that we have the whole chapter in mind. With the whole chapter in view, we see that Paul is trying to convince the Corinthians that there will be a resurrection. Verses 12–19 suggest Paul is answering some among the readers who have challenged the Corinthians' belief in the resurrection. He begins by reminding the readers of the essential Gospel message which he passed on to them, having himself received it from others. He summarizes that message in verses 3–7 before claiming that he himself witnessed the risen Christ (vv. 8–11). Paul grounds his argument in the content of the Gospel message and authenticates his understanding of that message as "one untimely born." Notice that Paul is first of all documenting his credentials for making the argument that follows.

In verses 13–19, Paul uses a series of linked statements:

If there is no resurrection of the dead, *then* Christ has not been raised; . . .

If Christ has not been raised, *then* our proclamation has been in vain and your faith has been in vain. . . .

If the dead are not raised, *then* Christ has not been raised.

If Christ has not been raised, your faith is futile and you are still in your sins.

Then he declares that Christ has been raised from the dead (v. 20). His argument that Christians will be raised begins with verses 21–28 in which he appeals to a Christ-Adam contrast in order to show that Christ brought life. This is followed by two examples of what Christian practices result from Christ's gift of life—baptizing on behalf of the dead (v. 29) and risking danger everyday (vv. 30–32a). This is opposed to the notion that there is no life

(vv. 32b–34). Next, Paul uses two analogies for the resurrection—a seed that dies before it comes to life (vv. 35–37) and the variety of kinds of bodies (vv. 38–44). Another proof of Paul's argument comes from Genesis (vv. 45–50). Verse 50 is a summary of Paul's argument, after which he begins his conclusion in verse 51. That conclusion is a narrative description of the resurrection of the dead (vv. 51–55), along with a citation of Isa 27:13 (vv. 54–55), a thanksgiving (vv. 56–57), and an exhortation to hold fast to faith and the practice of Christian discipleship (v. 58).[61]

Preaching on any part of the chapter requires that we see it in relationship to Paul's larger argument. Essentially, the purpose of our sermon is to present the resurrection of the dead as a viable conviction today. We cannot, of course, depend exclusively on some of Paul's reasons for believing in the resurrection—in fact, we may regard some of them ineffectual. For instance, we find difficult the statement that the resurrection is the reason we baptize on behalf of the dead (v. 29). Paul's powerful statement in verse 19 may be the most important argument for today: "If for this life only we have hoped in Christ, we are of all people most to be pitied."

The principle that makes rhetorical criticism relevant for us today is simply that *the sermon should attempt to accomplish what the text seeks to accomplish.* Thus any critical method which helps us understand what a passage seems to achieve, or seeks to achieve, is especially helpful to preachers.

Preachers, moreover, are naturally interested in *how a text uses language* because we ourselves seek to use language in effective ways. We could treat language under any of the various literary criticisms, but we do it here because rhetorical criticism is sometimes broadly defined simply as the study of the language of a (biblical) text. Consider a couple of examples of the rhetoric of a biblical passage and what that means for preaching the passage. Psalm 22:12–18 is a lament concerning the psalmist's condition. The language is poignantly descriptive—even shocking. The speaker characterizes her or himself in evocative ways: encircled by bulls who act like lions and later dogs; "poured out like water"; "bones out of joint"; possessing a heart like melting wax; having a dried-out mouth with a tongue stuck to the roof of the mouth; limited by shriveled feet; so emaciated that all the speaker's bones are visible; humiliated by those who "stare and gloat over me." It taxes the reader to experience this successive piling of one image on another. Imagine using this sort of description to portray the way we sometimes feel when the whole of life seems to be crumbling about us. Think of the bulls, lions, and dogs as circumstances which threaten us, our own helplessness as having a melting heart or being poured out like water. The use of language in the Psalm gives

---

[61] Mack, *Rhetoric and the New Testament,* 56–59.

preachers models for depicting the worst of life's experiences. Note, however, that the psalmist abruptly turns a corner and concludes his lament with hope in God's rescue.

Another example of the vividness of biblical language which may be duplicated in a sermon is found in the Matthean beatitudes in 5:3–11. The repetition of the phrase "blessed are" does not strike the reader as redundant so much as it keeps hammering the point. We notice the unlikely people Jesus calls blessed: "the poor in spirit," mourners, "the meek," those who "hunger and thirst for righteousness," "the merciful," "the pure in heart," "the peacemakers," and the "persecuted." This language demonstrates how ridiculous these sayings are—how absolutely contrary they are to what we think is "blessed!" We thank God for the blessings of economic security, for prosperity, for success, for a family, and for all the other plenty we value. But the beatitudes reverse those values and do so with language that relentlessly surprises us. The language is almost a trap for us. When we hear "blessed are . . . ," we start to finish the sentence only to be brought up short by Jesus' claims of what it is to be blessed.

Rhetorical criticism, then, stands at the service of preachers both in the way it helps us identify the purpose of a passage and by drawing our attention to a passage's use of language.

Reader-response

Probably the easiest literary critical method to adopt and use is reader-response. We say this not because it is easy to become a skilled reader-response critic but because we all know what it means to attend to ourselves and our reactions as we read a biblical passage. What may be difficult in this process, however, is our tendency to concentrate on the passage and some truth that lies beyond it and to which it refers, rather than focusing on ourselves as we read. It may even strike us as self-centered to attend to our own feelings and reactions instead of fixing our attention on the words of the passage. Still, the primary nature of reader-response requires no special knowledge, no special techniques, and no special training, even if it does require some practice. To be sure, reader-response critics have their own technical vocabulary and an arsenal of theories, but we maintain that preachers can practice and profit from what we might call a fledgling reader-response.

Reader-response criticism helps preachers enter into a personal dialogue with a passage which can then be carried over into sermons. What is required, however, is a certain self-honesty and openness to both the text and one's reactions to the text. The results are often new experiences of passages which we may have thought we knew very well.

For example, a careful and involved reading of the "bread of life" discourse in John 6:25–71 provides an experience of the elusiveness of faith. At times the passage pulls readers toward the idea that they must decide to believe or not to believe—that humans are responsible for their faith in response to God's act in Christ (for example, v. 24). However, then the passage confronts readers with the notion that faith is entirely a gift from God—that God alone implants faith—and that it is not dependent on human decision (v. 44). As a matter of fact, Jesus' words in this passage fatally question "decisional faith." The final result of this sort of passionate and personal reading of the discourse is a complex and tensive understanding of faith: Humans cannot take credit for believing, but neither can they evade their responsibility to accept the gift God gives in Christ.[62]

Reader-response criticism offers preachers a way to prepare themselves for what might be called "witness" to a particular passage. Thankfully, the understanding of witness is returning to homiletics, and we think the content of such witness should most often entail an experience of reading the Scripture lesson for the day. This understanding of preaching assumes that we invite our listeners into a dialogue with the biblical text. We are not trying to explain the text, but we want our congregants to *experience the text,* as we ourselves have experienced it, although their experience need not be the same as ours. What better way to seek this goal than by sharing one's own experience of reading the text?

Now, there are some risks entailed in this sort of biblical interpretation and preaching. Among them is that the preacher-interpreter has to be willing to admit that the text puzzles, confuses, and even makes outrageous demands. In other words, the risk is being honest, and, when you are honest about your reading of a text, you may suggest that you do not immediately and in every case believe exactly as the text might seem to say you should. Those who take the text as the words of God, directly and faithfully transcribed by the biblical writer, may find it hard to listen to their pastor share her or his doubts about a passage.

One way to preach out of reader-response criticism is to ask your congregation to come with you on "a journey through the text," allowing it to challenge and question us as we read and experience it anew. Naturally, some listeners will allow themselves to become emotionally and intellectually

---

[62] Robert Kysar, "The Dismantling of Decisional Faith: A Reading of John 6:25–71" in *Critical Readings of John 6* (ed. R. Alan Culpepper; Biblical Interpretation Series; Leiden: E. J. Brill, 1997), 161–82. For a sermon on this passage which arose from his experience of reading this passage, see his *Preaching John* (Fortress Resources for Preaching; Minneapolis: Fortress, 2002), 67–70.

involved in reading a text, while others will stand cautiously aloof. With time, however, as listeners come to understand this sort of a sermon, more and more will join our journeys through texts.

A reader-response summary of the famous parable or apocalyptic vision of the sheep and goats in Matt 25:31–46 is a fitting final example. Without tracing the whole reading experience, note how readers of this passage encounter first one shock and then another. The first shock comes when the Son of Man initially commends the righteous, "for I was hungry and you gave me food, I was thirsty and you gave me something to drink, I was a stranger and you welcomed me, I was in prison and you visited me" (vv. 35–36). That may be nothing compared with the sudden surprise of the response of the righteous:

> Then the righteous will answer him, "Lord, when was it that we saw you hungry and gave you food, or thirsty and gave you something to drink? And when was it that we saw you a stranger and welcomed you, or naked and gave you clothing? And when was it that we saw you sick or in prison and visited you?" (vv. 37–39)

They are surprised that they had encountered Christ—most certainly in those conditions! They had no idea they had served Christ! Finally, imagine the shock one experiences when Christ responds: "And the king will answer them, 'Truly I tell you, just as you did it to one of the least of these who are members of my family, you did it to me'" (v. 40).

If we could read this passage as if we had never read it before, it jolts us with the facts, first, that we meet Christ in the needy and, secondly, that when we serve the needy we have no idea we are serving Christ. In a sermon based on this kind of reading experience of a well-known passage, the preacher might share a series of lightening bolts of the unexpected. Furthermore, preachers might try leading their listeners through the passage, asking them to imagine they were hearing it for the very first time.

Narrative Criticism

Narrative criticism is as rich for homiletical use as are the rhetorical and reader-response methods, and some preachers think even richer. In fact, the list of those issues with which the narrative critic is concerned (plot, character, gaps, and narrative world, as well as others) provides an even more varied resource for homiletical interpretation.[63] Preachers can take any one of these

---

[63] See David J. Ourisman, *From Gospel to Sermon: Preaching Synoptic Texts* (St. Louis: Chalice, 2000). Ourisman describes the process of preaching on "the stories of Jesus" and then devotes one chapter to each of the synoptics.

and examine a passage with that one element of narrative criticism in mind. Almost any biblical narrative yields up some interesting insights when you ask specifically about any one of these elements, whether plot, character, gaps, or the narrative world.[64]

Before we go on to explore some possibilities for narrative criticism, we need to ask a troubling question: How does narrative criticism work on a passage that is *not a narrative?* The Bible is filled with stories, but there are an equal number of passages which are not narratives. How is narrative criticism useful when preaching from one of the epistles of the New Testament, from the book of Proverbs, or from one of the collections of law found in the Hebrew Scripture? Some narrative critics openly confess that their method is intended strictly for narrative passages.

The answer is, however, ambiguous, because, on the one hand, narrative criticism is not as useful on a non-narrative passage as it is on a narrative passage, but on the other hand, may provide a way which is more useful. Sometimes there are clues to a narrative in a non-narrative passage, and one can look for and reconstruct a plot from those clues. For instance, let us apply narrative criticism to what would seem the most difficult type of non-narrative passage: a law. It is sometimes possible to construct a history—a story—from what a law proscribes. Deuteronomy 24:19–22 commands that farmers leave a portion of their harvest (grain, olives, grapes) in the field in order that "the alien, the orphan, and the widow" may have something to eat. Along with the farmer, these three comprise the characters of an implicit story. The plot we construct assumes that there was a time when the needy went hungry. The story is simply the tale of those people searching for nourishment, who much to their delight are surprised to find a harvested field in which there remain a good many grapes— enough of them to make a meal. They eat and continue on their journey— a plot with a happy ending. Moreover, as a sanction for these laws, Deut 24:22 invites the readers to *remember their own stories:* "Remember that you were a slave in the land of Egypt; therefore I am commanding you to do this." The clues, of course, call on our imagination to fill in the details of the story. Obviously, this is not narrative criticism as it is formally known, but it is a means by which we can understand a passage to have narrative features.[65]

---

[64]See the appendix, entitled "Using Narrative Criticism in Exegesis," of Powell's *What Is Narrative Criticism,* 103–5. Powell provides a detailed description of how we approach a narrative passage and interpret it for preaching.

[65]Another example of this way of using narrative criticism on non-narrative passages is found in Hughes and Kysar, *Preaching Doctrine,* 65.

Plot. Plot is perhaps the easiest of the interests of narrative criticism to use in preparation for preaching. Like humans have from the earliest time, contemporary congregations love a good story. Moreover, their culture immerses them in story, thanks primarily to television. In most cases your congregations will be more than willing to follow as you retell and examine the plot of a biblical story. It may be true that the people in many of our congregations are not used to thinking critically about a story's plot. To start, the most demanding feature of preaching on a biblical plot is the challenge of retelling the story in an engaging way. The congregation, after all, initially hears the story as it is read to them in the Scripture lesson. Obviously preachers need to repeat the story during the sermon in different words.

The preacher asks where the story leads. This does not mean drawing a "moral" from a story, so much as reflecting on the plot and its meaning for our lives. We are well advised to invite the congregation to reflect on a story for themselves, rather than telling them what it means. Then, having told the story again, we raise questions about it.[66] What does it mean to in our lives today? Does the story replicate something that we have experienced? Is it realistic? Sometimes biblical stories (especially those in the Hebrew Scriptures) may seem very unrealistic to a twenty-first century Christian. Second Kings 2:23–25 provides a good example. Narrative criticism, of course, insists that we place a story such as this one in its broader context. This is not an easy task to preach a tale about bears attacking boys.

Gap. Gaps within a plot are wonderful occasions to ask your listeners to imagine what should go in the gaps and how inconsistencies in a story might be reconciled. In a sermon on Nicodemus in the Gospel of John (3:1–9; 7:50; 19:39), we might invite our listeners to imagine whether or not the Jewish leader became a disciple. The preacher, too, can "write" several different conclusions to a story and then suggest the listeners write their own. Incomplete or open-ended conclusions are an opportunity to prepare an imaginary "what-if" sermon, making sure that your listeners understand that you are going beyond the biblical story itself. What if Paul were eventually released from his imprisonment in Rome (where he is at the end of Acts)? What might he have done? This kind of what-if sermon leads us to characters.

Character. Characters provide good sermon material, as most of us already know. As they are with stories, contemporary North Americans are intrigued by characters, both as a result of exposure to television and because of our preoccupation with celebrities. Narrative criticism provides us with a discipline by which we discover characters more fully. There is, however, a po-

---

[66] Ibid., *Preaching Doctrine*, 69–73.

tential danger in our efforts to psychologize biblical characters, that is, to ask the questions a contemporary biography would ask. In fact, the biblical writers knew nothing of psychology, so it may be pointless to look for such material on a character in biblical stories. Now this should not keep us from using imagination to flesh out a character; but it should caution us against trying to psychoanalyze biblical characters.

Narrative world. The narrative world, as we have already said, offers considerable potential for homiletic interpretation. To tap that potential, preachers have to do several things. First, one must read the passage in the context of its own narrative world. This entails entering the text's world in order to read and understand the message. This requires that we trust the story's narrator to take us into her or his frame of reference. We suspend our own critical capacities for a time and grant that the world of the text is a real world. We surrender our objectivity and enter the text subjectively. Some of us are prone to maintain objectivity with regard to a text because it is a way of trying to be the text's master. To enter the narrative world completely requires that we allow the text to be our master. This step away from objectivity is an effort to span the distance between the text and ourselves, that is, to transcend the text's foreignness. This is much like reading a novel about a world foreign to ours.

Second, having experienced the text's world for ourselves, we begin to compare its world with our own, at least as we perceive both. How is the text's world like our own? How is it different? As an example, while reading Jonah, we immerse ourselves in that book's world, but then we have to admit that people cannot live in the gut of a big fish; that storms do not cease once a guilty person is thrown into the water; and that a repentant city is not likely to clothe their livestock in sackcloth. Still, we find places at which the text's world intersects with ours. Jonah's bigotry toward the people of Nineveh is much like the attitude some have toward persons of other races, sexual preferences, or religious faiths. Some may recognize Jonah's experience when they consider how God's call may nag us no matter how hard we try to run from it.

Comparing our world and the text's world also entails allowing the latter to critique the former. What is it about the other world that challenges ours? A God whose love includes the enemy may challenge the popularity of demonizing our nation's opponents. In another case, the narrative world of Acts involves the ever-present and active Holy Spirit. This world and its interaction with the Holy Spirit calls into question the secularization of our world where we wonder how, if at all, God may be present and active in it. What can we learn about the weaknesses of how we perceive our world in the light of the world of biblical narrative?

Preachers facilitate the collision of the text's world with the world of the congregation. We might say that *we preach from the biblical world to the listeners' world for the sake of a new world.* Of course, this is not easy! Yet we try to retell the biblical narrative in ways that invite listeners into the story's world, so that they may experience it as we did in our preparation to preach the text.

AN EXAMPLE

As an example of how narrative criticism can work for the preacher, we look more carefully at Jonah. The RCL assigns passages from Jonah on only two occasions: Epiphany 3, Year B (where 3:1–5, 10 is to be read) and Proper 20, Year A (where the assigned reading is 3:10–4:11). The following sermon was written for the latter occasion. However, to preach either of these passages requires that we must convey the whole Jonah story to the congregation. There will likely be a good number of congregants who know nothing about Jonah except the "big fish" story. The Jonah story is a good example of how you cannot single out a group of verses, or even a whole chapter, without understanding the whole plot—a point narrative critics emphasize.

Our homiletical study of this book stresses both the plot and also the character of Jonah. The story's plot builds around God's call and Jonah's reluctance, and Jonah's reluctance is the problem that disrupts the equilibrium in the narrative. The search for resolution in one sense is successful—Jonah finally preaches in Nineveh and the city repents. Nevertheless, the disequilibrium of Jonah's reluctance remains to the end of the story. We leave Jonah sitting on that hill outside the city whining and we never learn if he accepts God's mercy for the Assyrians.

The sermon takes its title, "I Knew It!" from Jonah 4:2 and is intended to anticipate the question of what it really means to "know" God's mercy.

"I Knew It!"

Epiphany 3, Year B
Jonah 3:1–5, 10

Proper 20, Year A
Jonah 3:10–4:11

JONAH IS A FASCINATING, BUT ALSO A CONFUSING, CHARACTER, ISN'T HE? HE REALLY troubles me. We know he is a prophet. The introduction makes that clear: "The word of the Lord came to Jonah, 'Arise, and go to Nineveh, that great city.'"

We know he is called to be a prophet. And so, in a sense, his reluctance doesn't surprise us all that much. Prophets are often reluctant to accept God's call. They often make their excuses for not accepting their mission. Remember?

Moses was reluctant, and made all kinds of excuses. He said he wasn't skilled in speech. He failed public speaking 101 in school. So, God had to appoint Aaron as his spokesperson. Isaiah was reluctant. He thought he was too sinful. So, God had to cleanse his lips for service. Jeremiah's excuse was that he was too young. But God wouldn't buy that. God had formed him in the womb for his special calling.

And you and I may have had our own excuses—reasons we could not accept the call of discipleship. You know them! You remember your own reluctance from time to time.

But Jonah! Talk about reluctance! The word of the Lord comes to him, and he takes a cruise—sails off to the south of Spain—the opposite way from Nineveh! Now, of course, you must understand, Nineveh was the last place in the world Jonah wanted to go. The Assyrians were the despised enemies of Israel at the time. And Nineveh was their capitol city. This is the last place Jonah wanted to go. He might well have imagined the reception he would get there!

Well, you know the story. Jonah takes a ship for Tarshish—a city thought to be on the very outer edge of the world! But they sail right into a hurricane. The ship is about to sink. And Jonah thinks he knows why. So, he volunteers to go overboard. The crew is hesitant. It appears these Gentile sailors are sensitive about taking the life of an innocent man. The crew finally and hesitantly accepts Jonah's offer. And they throw Jonah into the drink. The storm ceases immediately.

Now that famous "great fish" enters the story. (The Bible doesn't call the fish a whale; that name is for us the biggest sea animal we know.) Jonah is swallowed by the fish. And in the belly of that creature, he prays his heart out for three long days and nights. Finally, our reluctant prophet is spit out on shore. Then the word of the Lord comes to him a second time.

"NOW, will you go to Nineveh, Jonah?"

We may still not surprised by the story. God is persistent. We don't easily escape God's call, do we? God keeps chasing us, until we finally yield to the call to mission.

So, Jonah goes off to Nineveh, albeit still reluctantly. And there he preaches the shortest sermon in recorded history. Walking through this great city, Jonah mutters the words: "Forty days more, and Nineveh shall be overthrown!" Eight words! Only eight words! (Actually, only four in the Hebrew.) But the whole city repents! They declare a fast! Every one of them—the great and the small—put on sackcloth. The king even repents, and orders that all the people of Nineveh, and even the animals, should wear sackcloth. Imagine what it would be like today: a city with all its creatures, human and otherwise, cats and dogs, dressed in garments of repentance!

What marvelous results from a sermon! And such a short one at that! What a powerful sermon that must have been! Don't we all wish that our pastors could preach sermons that get those kinds of results (and that are that short?). Why, as it is, we clergy are absolutely ecstatic if one single person repents as a result of one of our sermons!

But Jonah? Now we are really surprised, puzzled, and even confused. Jonah is displeased! Angry! Even depressed! He goes out of town and mopes! He wishes that he were dead, and asks God to take his life. "I knew it! I just knew it! You are a gracious God and merciful, abounding in steadfast love! I knew it! I just knew you would save the city!" Jonah is depressed and angry, because God used him to redeem Nineveh. Now the story begins to become clear to us: *Jonah didn't want this city or its people redeemed—not the Assyrians.*

So, God has to give Jonah a short object lesson. God plants a little tree there on the outskirts of the city to shade Jonah. And Jonah likes that. But then God destroys the plant, and Jonah is angry again. He pities the little tree. Why should he be surprised that God has pitied Nineveh? But we are never sure that Jonah gets it, even after God's little object lesson.

How puzzling this Jonah is! We can understand his reluctance. We can identify with his experience of God's persistent call. But what can we make of this anger of his? Why should he be angry? He knew that God was gracious and loving. He has his theology straight. He understands the love of God. But he is depressed and angry that God should love and save *this* city. What can we make of this Jonah character? Why does he not want the Assyrians to know what he knows?

Well, I wonder. Jonah had learned the concepts well. He knows God is merciful and loving. But he seems unable to want God to be merciful and loving *to everyone.* I wonder about Jonah when I consider the possibility that I may not want some to be redeemed. I wonder when I remember certain persons. Do I really want them to know God's mercy? Do I sometimes secretly wish that God would not be merciful? At least, not to some people?

I am not sure I wanted that man to know God's mercy—at least in my congregation that day. The service had begun in this small congregation of only about twenty-five middle-class, proper, and staid worshipers. Then he appeared. Ragged clothes the odor of which told us they hadn't seen soap and water for months. He had an unkept beard, that only partially concealed a filthy face. His eyes were glassy, shifting back and forth. He stumbled his way to a pew—of course in the front row, and right in front of the pulpit! The silence of the congregation was deafening. The unease with his presence nearly paralyzing.

Nervous though we were, we continued the service. Not even I paid much attention to my own sermon that day. I am ashamed to admit it, but I was relieved to see him leave during the last hymn. I would not have to greet him at the door. Not a soul spoke to that man. No one welcomed him to the service. No one really wanted him there, for, you see, he was not "one of us." I knew then, as I know now, that God is loving and merciful. But did I want this stranger to know my God? Did I want him in my congregation?

What about you? You know God is merciful, but are there some you secretly wish might not experience God's mercy? Are there some toward whom you feel as Jonah felt toward the Assyrians? Are there individuals, or groups of individuals, about whom you feel revulsion, reluctant to welcome them into your circle of friends? Maybe it's "those people," those immoral people, those unworthy of God's love, those who don't deserve the Gospel? Or, maybe it's just those who are different from us, like that man who appeared in my congregation years ago.

Do we want some *not* to know God's grace and love? We know God is gracious and loving, don't we? But do we sometimes put boundaries on that grace and love? Do we sometimes put fences around it? Do we say, "God's love and grace can only reach so far"? Do we say, "There has to be limits to God's forgiveness"?

That may be it! Now the story is clear! Maybe Jonah was a fence builder! Fencing certain people off from the gracious God he knew—in particular the hated Assyrians. Putting up these boundaries beyond which God is not allowed to go. And perhaps some of you are like me. You may recognize that you too have sometimes built those fences, erected boundaries. Perhaps you can sense some fences here in this congregation.

Who is fenced out?

But God is a great fence jumper!

A friend of mine learned about fence jumpers. John is a high-powered, brilliant, and successful Philadelphia lawyer. He's also passionate about his hobby of gardening. When we visited his home some years ago, he was locked in mental conflict with gophers who had invaded his garden. It was a battle of wit. Who could outsmart the other? The gopher or the lawyer? But all of John's best ideas to fence the gophers out had failed. No matter what idea he came up with, the gophers found a way through to his garden. They went over or under or through every barrier John could conceive. The gophers were outwitting the Philadelphia lawyer!

God seems to outwit our best efforts to fence certain people out of the garden of grace. God finds a way under, around, or through our boundaries. God finds a way through the boundaries that keep us from the divine grace. God jumps some fences to reach us! In Christ God leaps a fence, crosses a boundary, to love you and me, to embrace us with that boundless love and that limitless grace. In God's eyes we were dirty with sin, dressed in smelly clothes, unkept, and stumbling in our walk, but that doesn't stop the fencing-jumping God! That doesn't stop God from reaching us and leading us into the garden!

That's why we can say with Jonah, "I knew it!" I knew you were a gracious and merciful God. So, if we know it, God now asks us to take a look at our fences. Take a look: Are we ready for *everyone* to know what we know? Take a look: Tear down our fences and dismantle our boundaries. Tear them down for whomever it may be that we have fenced off; whatever type or class of persons we have tried to put beyond the reach of the love we know in Christ.

This God of ours is a gracious God and merciful, slow to anger, and abounding in steadfast love. We know it; and through us may all others come to know it!

Chapter 4

What Difference Do Liberation Criticisms Make?

Then the LORD said, "I have observed the misery of my people who are in Egypt; I have heard their cry on account of their taskmasters. Indeed, I know their sufferings, and I have come down to deliver them from the Egyptians, and to bring them up out of that land to a good and broad land, a land flowing with milk and honey, to the country of the Canaanites, the Hittites, the Amorites, the Perizzites, the Hivites, and the Jebusites. The cry of the Israelites has now come to me; I have also seen how the Egyptians oppress them. So come, I will send you to Pharaoh to bring my people, the Israelites, out of Egypt." (Exod 3:7–10, NRSV)

When [Jesus] came to Nazareth, where he had been brought up, he went to the synagogue on the Sabbath day, as was his custom. He stood up to read, and the scroll of the prophet Isaiah was given to him. He unrolled the scroll and found the place where it was written: "The Spirit of the Lord is upon me, because he has anointed me to bring good news to the poor. He has sent me to proclaim release to the captives and recovery of sight to the blind, to let the oppressed go free, to proclaim the year of the Lord's favor." And he rolled up the scroll, gave it back to the attendant, and sat down. The eyes of all in the synagogue were fixed on him. Then he began to say to them, "Today this Scripture has been fulfilled in your hearing" (Luke 4:17–21, NRSV).

The theme of liberation is common in Scripture, so it is not surprising that methods of interpretation cluster around that theme. Indeed in the late twentieth century, liberation interpretation of Scripture flourished and expanded. Scripture itself enabled groups of people to acknowledge their oppression and empowered them to seek liberation. However, it is also the case that recent social developments sometimes forced recognition of oppression of others within the church, and only then did some seek and find freedom through the message of Scripture. As we shall see, liberation interpretation produced numerous foci in the quest for freedom, but they all share one common basic assumption: *the biblical God seeks to free humans from all that binds us and keeps us from being what we were created to be.*[1] The liberation interpretation of Scripture seeks to uncover God's liberating purpose expressed there.[2]

All liberation interpretations arise from and seek to overcome some sort of oppression. Chief among the liberation interpretations in North America has been liberation from racial and economic oppression. The *feminist interpretation* of Scripture begins with a commitment to the liberation of women in the patriarchal society of the USA, and the *womanist movement* broadens the task to include economic and racial matters. In Latin America the movement has focused on Scripture's potency to empower people to seek freedom from political, economic, and colonial oppression. Alongside of and sometimes joined with one of these movements has been what we will call *socio-historical liberation*, a movement which flourishes among a group of ethnically and nationally diverse scholars. Finally, a still different interest has arisen on the fringe of the liberation movement, namely, *ideological criticism*. Each of these is complex in and of itself, pulling together numerous approaches to reading Scripture, and together they form a matrix of what we treat under the general rubric of liberation interpretations. In the process of describing these, we hope to show how each is related to the broader theme of liberation.

SOME GENERAL PRINCIPLES OF LIBERATION INTERPRETATION

With so many different expressions of what we are calling liberation interpretation, the isolation of some general principles that prevail in many, if not all, of these critical methods is a difficult task. However, we will offer a number of principles which will at least help readers to understand the broader movements in this critical method.

The Canon and Canons

The canon is an issue in nearly every form of liberation interpretation, because the traditional assumption is that the *whole* of Scripture is somehow

---

[1] See for example the little book by Elsa Tamez, *Bible of the Oppressed* (trans. Matthew J. O'Connell; Maryknoll: Orbis, 1982).

[2] For an introduction to the variety of biblical interpretations for liberation see the articles in Katie Geneva Cannon and Elizabeth Schüssler Fiorenza, eds., *Interpretation for Liberation* (*Semeia* 47; Atlanta: Scholars, 1989).

authoritative for Christian life and faith.[3] The difficulty of this view of canon for some liberation interpreters is that not all the texts of the Bible foster human freedom and, as a matter of fact, some of it seems to encourage slavery. Hence, for example, the *Haustafeln* (rules for relationships within a household) in the New Testament are problematic for liberation interpreters because of the manner in which it subjects women and slaves to the authority of the husband or father of the house (see Col 3:18–4:1; Eph 5:21–6:9; and 1 Pet 2:18–3:7). It troubles many that Paul encourages Onesimus to return to Philemon and once again subject himself to slavery.

Interpreters invariably read Scripture with some sort of criteria for distinguishing passages that are authoritative from those that are not. Among liberation interpreters, this is usually a conscious and explicit practice, but sometimes readers may not be entirely clear about the reasons for such distinctions. Of course, this problem and its resolution are not unique to liberation interpreters and it goes back to the process begun in the creation of the canon in the first centuries following the death of Jesus until at least the exegetical work of Martin Luther in the sixteeth century.[4]

Canon as canon. The first of the three most common views of the canon that we find among liberation interpreters, as well as among others, is what we might call *canon as canon.* This view supposes that the whole of Scripture is authoritative for the Christian, but its authority depends on proper interpretation. So, for instance, if the interpreter begins with the right perspective—that of the rights of the poor or of women—the whole of Scripture yields up its message of God's liberation. No revision of the canon is necessary, only a proper approach to it.

Canon within the canon. The second view supposes *a canon within the canon.* As problematic as this view may sometimes be, it provides readers with a criterion on which to measure the authority of any biblical view. In most Christian liberation interpretations that criterion is, of course, Christ—his message and his ministry. When the household duties are measured against Christ, the interpreter immediately discovers those rules which contradict the revelation of God in Christ. According to some who use this criterion, when Philemon is asked to treat Onesimus as a brother in Christ, the institution of slavery is undone.

---

[3] Phyllis A. Bird speaks of the "twofold canon: its dual character as a word from the past, which is always to some degree alien and unrepeatable, and as a word for the present informing and forming faith" in "The Authority of the Bible," *NIB* 1:48.

[4] See Robert Kysar, *Opening the Bible: What It is, Where It Came From, What It Means for You* (Minneapolis: Augsbug Fortress, 1999), 32–49.

Canon outside the canon. The third view identifies *a canon outside the canon* and uses it as the measuring rod for what is, and what is not, God's message for today in Scripture. In this case, readers bring to the biblical texts values which provide the condition for judging a passage. Fernando F. Segovia points out that for some Hispanic American women the canon outside the canon is their lives and liberation. "In other words, the Bible can be both liberation and oppressive for Hispanic women, *and only Hispanic women can make a decision in this regard in the light of their experiential norm.*"[5] Elisabeth Schüssler Fiorenza is even more specific in identifying the canon outside the canon for feminist interpretation: that which is canon furthers "the liberation of women from oppressive sexist structures, institutions, and internalized values."[6]

It is fair to say we see one or more of these three views of canon operating in each of the liberation interpretations we will discuss. Moreover, in the view of some, it is liberationists who have been the most forthcoming and honest about their dependence on some canon within or outside the canon. We have a hunch that a good many interpreters, including pastors as well as biblical scholars, practice some sort of a canon within or from without the canon, but may not always be intentional about it. (The discussion in Chapter Six bears upon this matter.)

Truth and Practice

Among the assumptions that are operative in nearly every liberationist interpretation are two which merit attention at an early stage in the discussion. The first of these is a particular view of *the relationship between truth and practice.* The "classical" view of this relationship assumes that there is a body of truth, "a world of truth, a universe complete in itself which is copied or reproduced in 'correct' propositions." In this case, all statements and actions are tested for their truthfulness against this external body of truth which has ontological status. Its reality is beyond history and independent of historical situation. Liberation theologians, however, have advocated a different view. "They are saying, in fact, that there is no truth outside or beyond the concrete historical events in which men [*and women*] are involved as agents. There is, therefore, no knowledge except in action itself, in the process of transforming the

---

[5] Fernando F. Segovia, "Reading the Bible as Hispanic Americans," *NIB* 1:170. Italics ours. The discussion of the three views of canon are drawn from Segovia's article (167–73).

[6] Elisabeth Schüssler Fiorenza, *Bread Not Stone: The Challenge of Feminist Biblical Interpretation* (Boston: Beacon, 1984), 60.

world through participation in history."[7] This means that truth resides exclusively in specific historical situations and actions and has no separate and ontological status. Hence, truth and practice are not separate.

Context and Interpretation

A second assumption arises out of this fundamental understanding of epistemology but has to do more narrowly with the interpretation of a text. It is the assumption that the *interpreter's context is as much a part of the interpretative process as the text.* If truth resides in concrete historical situations, then interpretation requires that those situations play as important a part in interpretation as does the text itself. C. René Padilla suggests that the contextual approach to interpretation differs from both what may be called the "intuitive" and "scientific" approaches. In the first of these the interpreter seeks an immediate and personal application of the text's meaning. In the second, all the tools of interpretation we have mentioned (literary, historical, sociological, etc.) are used to uncover the text's meaning. A contextual approach, however, recognizes both the historical origin of the text and its relevance to an individual reader. However, the readers' own world shapes what the text is understood to say. This means that interpretation requires as much attention to the readers' present situation as to the text's historical situation. For liberation interpreters this means that their context within a situation of oppression is vital for a proper reading of a text. (See Chapter Six where we will offer what we think is a homiletical-contextual, interpretative method.)

Needless to say, liberation interpreters do not pretend to approach the Bible without presuppositions and particular perspective. While many of them continue to use historical-critical methods to some degree, none would claim to undertake a purely objective, disinterested inquiry into a text's meaning. Quite the contrary, the liberationist's commitment to overcoming oppression is the reason for interpretation. Thus in their own way the methods we will discuss in this chapter all propose radical departures from the historical-critical method described in Chapter One.

Other General Principles

These are some of the other views embraced in various ways among the specific forms of liberation interpretation:

---

[7] José Miguez Bonino, "Hermeneutics, Truth, and Praxis," in *A Guide to Contemporary Hermeneutics: Major Trends in Biblical Interpretation* (ed. Donald K. McKim; Grand Rapids: Eerdmans, 1986), 345–46. First published in Bonino's *Doing Theology in a Revolutionary Situation* (Philadelphia: Fortress, 1975), 86–105.

The biblical message has to do with material and political and not exclusively "spiritual" matters. One interpreter explains that "the term 'materialist' is intended to assert that an investigation of the economic, social, political, and ideological situation of the writers and addressees of biblical texts is indispensable for an understanding of these texts."[8] Such a reading of the Bible has three distinctive goals in mind. First, it hopes to show that the poor are the "real subject" of Scripture. Second, it seeks to rescue the Bible from those who blurred its focus on poverty and oppression. Finally, the materialistic reading,

> aims at reading the Bible in such a way that in its light our political praxis will receive a new clarification, and at the same time this practice and its clarification will help us find in the writings of the Old and New Testaments hitherto undiscovered paradigms of a subversive praxis.[9]

Social class shapes the reading of Scripture. Social class is part of the emphasis on the readers' context in liberation interpretation. Class influences what we find in the Bible and class is the Bible's major subject. Liberation interpretations often seek to overcome any privatization and individualization of the Bible.[10]

Social struggle of some kind is present throughout the Bible and must be the focus of attention. Each community represented in the Bible had its peculiar struggle. One example is Israel's conflict with the Philistines, and another is the early Christian's strife with the Hellenistic culture of the first century C.E. These struggles guide and empower contemporary readers who are immersed in social conflict. In connection with this general principle, Marxism has proven to be helpful to some liberation theologians and biblical interpreters.[11]

With this brief introduction to the general principles of liberation criticism, this chapter will discuss more specific expressions of this movement such as racial and ethnic liberation (including political and economic free-

---

[8] Willy Schottroff and Wolfgang Stegemann, eds., *God of the Lowly: Socio-Historical Interpretations of the Bible* (Maryknoll: Orbis, 1984), 83. See Michel Clévenot, *Materialist Approaches to the Bible* (Maryknoll: Orbis, 1985).

[9] Kuno Füssel, "Materialist Readings of the Bible: Report on an Alternative Approach to Biblical Texts," in *God of the Lowly*, 18–19.

[10] As Wolfgang Stegemann declares in "Our Affluence Demands a Socio-historical Exegesis." *The Gospel and the Poor* (Philadelphia: Fortress, 1984), 57.

[11] Some examples are the works of José Miranda, in particular *Marx and the Bible: A Critique of the Philosophy of Liberation* (Maryknoll: Orbis, 1974) and *Communism in the Bible* (Maryknoll: Orbis, 1982). In the latter Miranda claims Christianity is communism.

dom), feminist and womanist interpretations, and finally ideological criticism. The order only roughly represents the history of these criticisms. Following the discussion of these three broad categories, we ask what liberation criticisms offer the preacher and conclude with a sermon that arises from this sort of interpretation of a biblical passage.

RACIAL AND ETHNIC LIBERATION

Two related forms of liberation criticism arose nearly simultaneously in the course of the 1960s—the biblical criticism which is a part of black theology in the US and the Latin American liberation theologies. In North America, James Cone launched what was to become a liberating theology for African Americans,[12] and in South America, Roman Catholic priests formed Bible study groups which asked how Scripture empowers people oppressed by political tyranny and economic deprivation. Each of these two movements was focused on its own particular situation, and therein lies one of the important features of liberation interpretations. As we have suggested, the readers' immediate, concrete, and material situation provides the beginning point for interpretation. Readers are expected to bring their real life conditions to the task of understanding biblical passages, giving priority to their needs, especially their material needs and not solely their so-called "spiritual" needs. So, in the case of black theology and Latin American liberation theology, as well as in feminist and womanist interpretations, the plight of a specific group of humans is the beginning of the process of interpretation.

In Martin Luther King Jr.'s use of Scripture we find examples of this practical grounding for interpretation. Faced with the dehumanizing forces of racial prejudice and discrimination, King interpreted Scripture in ways that directly addressed the needs of African Americans. In his famous speech, "I have a dream," King describes in eloquent and poetic language what he hoped would one day be real in America. He uses that refrain "I have a dream" repeatedly in reference to contemporary situations, and then says, "I have a dream that one day, . . . little black boys and black girls will be able to join hands with the little white boys and white girls as sisters and brothers. I have a dream today!" In the next paragraph, however, he suddenly puts Scripture in the context of that social hope: "I have a dream that one day every

---

[12] James H. Cone, *Black Theology and Black Power* (New York: Seabury, 1969) and *God of the Oppressed* (San Francisco: Harper, 1984). Cone's work sent shock waves through the church and North American society.

valley shall be exalted, every hill and mountain shall be made low, the rough places will be made plain and the crooked places will be made straight and the glory of the Lord shall be revealed and all flesh shall see it together."[13] King reads Isaiah 40:4–5 through the lenses of hope for an end to oppression and for a world of justice. The plight of African Americans allows him to interpret the Isaiah passage in a new way that empowers people to overthrow oppressive powers.

This foundation in the human condition is equally obvious in Latin American liberation theology. The hermeneutic espoused by many of the interpreters in this movement depends on "base Christian communities." In these small groups, participants share their real life struggles, their problems, read Scripture together, and then devised strategies for returning to the fight for freedom. Christian practice precedes biblical interpretation, and biblical interpretation shapes practice.

As we have seen, another basic element in liberation criticisms arises from its grounding in a people's real concrete situation: *spiritual truth and reality are related to, tied up with, and expressed through physical and material reality.*[14] In many cases this view seems a radical move, since the Bible is often read exclusively for its "spiritual meaning," and that meaning is isolated from political, economic, and social realities. Unfortunately, this purely spiritual (and often individualistic) biblical interpretation still persists and tries to ward off the very thought that the biblical message has anything to do with our society. However, bridging the gap between spiritual and material, liberation interpretations quickly entail political and social action. Evil is not a disembodied reality that transcends the real material world but one that lives and grows within earthly institutions and practices. This view is clearly advanced by Walter Wink's study which began with the New Testament references to "principalities and powers."[15]

---

[13] Quoted from David J. Garrow, *Bearing the Cross: Martin Luther King, Jr. and the Southern Christian Leadership Conference* (New York: William Morrow, 1986), 284.

[14] See, for example, Fernando Belo, *A Materialist Reading of the Gospel of Mark* (trans. Matthew J. O'Connell; Maryknoll: Orbis, 1981).

[15] Walter Wink, *Naming the Powers: The Language of Power in the New Testament* (vol. 1 of *The Powers;* Philadelphia: Fortress, 1984); *Unmasking the Powers: The Invisible Forces That Determine Human Existence* (vol. 2 of *The Powers;* Philadelphia: Fortress, 1986); *Engaging the Powers: Discernment and Resistance in a World of Domination* (vol. 3 of *The Powers;* Minneapolis: Fortress 1992); and *When the Powers Fall: Reconciliation in the Healing of Nations* (vol. 4 of *The Powers;* Minneapolis: Fortress, 1999).

African American Liberation Interpretation

Closing the gap between the spiritual and material worlds was crucial to the birth of liberation interpretation among African Americans. Ironically, the slave masters often tried to teach slaves Christianity and the Bible as one way, among others, of keeping them subservient. However, the very different interpretation of the Bible by slaves, as they themselves knew it, is often found in the "Negro spirituals" which sustained them in their troubles.[16]

Vincent L. Wimbush distinguishes a number of different periods of Bible reading among African Americans. The first was a period of suspicion and rejection of the white people's Bible, but in the second period African Americans began reading Scripture in the light of their own experience. Their reading tended to be free and even playful with the biblical language. The third period is comprised of the formation of free Black churches in the nineteenth century where the Bible was read as a source of self-identity and strength against social oppression. In the twentieth century a fundamentalism and literalism spread through Black churches and created a tension between the more experiential reading and a "proper" one, that is, proper from the perspective of a literalist.[17] Sometimes, although not always, the literalistic reading of the Bible tended to defuse its message of any direct racial and social importance.

However, during the 1960s and 1970s the rise of a distinctive African American liberation interpretation of Scripture was intimately interwoven with the Black freedom movement in the United States. The efforts of African Americans to overcome segregation and take their place in American society as equals really found its beginnings as a movement in Black churches. Congregations and their pastors were often leaders in demonstrations, boycotts, and legal assaults on white racism, and the meetings at which these activities were planned often took place in the Black churches.[18] The formation and application of "Black Power" was clearly a stimulus for the rise of liberation preaching, as the title of James Cone's first book indicates: *Black Theology and Black Power.* The fact is, of course, that the Black clergy had a tradition (that many still practice) of leading congregations in political and social affairs. Strikingly, the Black church is nearly always "political," while in

---

[16] James Earl Massey, "Reading the Bible as African Americans," *NIB* 1:154–55.

[17] Vincent L. Wimbush, "The Bible and African Americans: An Outline of an Interpretation History," in *Stony the Road We Trod: African American Biblical Interpretation* (ed. Cain Hope Felder; Minneapolis: Fortress, 1991), 81–97.

[18] See Garrow, *Bearing the Cross,* which traces the formation of the Southern Christian Leadership Conference in great detail and corroborates the role of Black congregations in the process.

the majority of White congregations great efforts are made to keep religion and politics "separate."

The African American liberation interpretation combines a number of assumptions which are essential to its application. (Some of these assumptions are typical of other liberation interpretations, as well.) The first assumption is the conviction that *the biblical God favors the poor and oppressed.* The poor are privileged insofar as God is consistently seeking their liberation. Jesus' identification with the poor and oppressed is a model for understanding God, as is the more fundamental belief that Christ himself was poor and oppressed. The privileging of the poor is not a view strictly limited to African American interpretation, of course, and is a conclusion to which many biblical scholars have come.[19]

The second major assumption in African American liberation interpretation is *the decisive role of the exodus from Egypt.* Blacks locate the experience and story of their own people in the enslavement of the Hebrews in Egypt and God's emancipation of them. James Cone's provocative use of the image of the Exodus as a lens through which to find "Black Power" has become a typical liberation reading. In this way, liberation interpretation within the Black church tends to make greater use of the Hebrew Scriptures than is typical of many of the mainline White Protestant churches.

Still a third element in the mix of African American interpretation has been a *re-reading of key biblical passages.* The collection of essays in *Stony the Road We Trod* gives us a clue as to the importance of certain passages. First, there is a call for the reevaluation of passages mentioning slaves.[20] What are the actual settings for these passages and should they be regarded as authoritative? Second, it is important that African Americans find their ancestors in the story of the Hebrew people—a presence long overlooked.[21] Persons of African descent were surely among those slaves in Egypt. This recognition of the presence and important role of Africans in the biblical stories has been called "Afrocentric Biblical interpretation." Cain Hope Felder writes, "Afrocentricity is the

---

[19] See, for instance, Schottroff and Stegemann, *God of the Lowly;* Conrad Boerma, *The Rich, the Poor, and the Bible* (trans. John Bowden; Philadelphia: Westminster, 1978); and Walter E. Pilgrim, *Good News to the Poor: Wealth and Poverty in Luke-Acts* (Minneapolis: Augsburg, 1981).

[20] See, for instance, these articles in *Stony the Road We Trod:* John W. Waters, "Who Was Hagar?" 187–205; Claire J. Martin, "The *Haustafeln* (Household Codes) in African American Biblical Interpretation: 'Free Slaves' and 'Subordinate Women,'" 206–31; and Lloyd A. Lewis, "An African American Appraisal of the Philemon-Paul-Onesimus Triangle," 232–46.

[21] Charles Copher, "The Black Presence in the Old Testament," in *Stony the Road We Trod*, 146–65.

concept that Africa and persons of African descent must be understood as making significant contributions to world civilization as proactive subjects within history, rather than being regarded as mere passive objects in the course of history." Felder goes on to argue that the discussion cannot be limited to "Black Theology" but must acknowledge the role Africa and its people play in biblical history.[22] As we shall see, the femininist movement involves a similar call for the recognition of the role of women in biblical history.

To some degree, African American liberation interpretation of the Bible has taken shape within the larger context of liberation movements. Therefore, much of what we will have to say later is also related to Black theological interpretations.

Latin American Liberation Interpretation

The early colonialists often forbade the native peoples of South America to read the Bible for themselves, but their regular use of the Bible to enlighten and encourage the indigenous people can be traced back to the 1920s (although its precursors can be found as early as the sixteenth century). From its beginning Latin American liberation theology was dependent on the Bible, although the actual involvement in revolutionary efforts was often more important than biblical studies.

The most common characteristic the African American interpretation shares with its Latin American counterpart is its engagement in the practice of securing freedom. The basic model for a number of liberation methods of reading Scripture entails three clear steps. The first step in the process is engagement in a discussion of an actual situation in which participants openly express their concerns. The second step is choosing and describing a biblical text so that the actual situation under consideration is seen in the light of the biblical passage. The third step is planning some concrete strategy for dealing with the situation.[23] Note the importance in this process of *"popular" interpretation*, the people's reading, and the significance of *action*. For many liberation theologians, action precedes theology, and theology grows out of practice.[24]

---

[22] Cain Hope Felder, "Afrocentric Biblical Interpretation," *Dictionary of Biblical Interpretation*, 1:13.

[23] Thomas Schmeller, "Liberation Theologies," *Dictionary of Biblical Interpretation*, 2:70.

[24] An interesting reader-response commentary on Mark argues that the second Gospel should be read as a "model for action." John Paul Heil, *The Gospel of Mark as a Model for Action: A Reader-Response Commentary* (New York: Paulist, 1992).

Robert McAfee Brown was one of the most important interpreters of Latin American theology for North American Christians. He summarizes what he experienced in the Bible studies held in the base communities that he studied as a cyclical movement from reflection to action. Base communities [*communidades de base*] were small groups of lay people who studied the Bible in the light of local parishioners' basic needs and acted to address those needs. According to Brown, the process goes something like this:

1. *Action* in the world leads to jarring experiences.

2. Our overall understandings are shattered, and we *reflect* on the need for new ones.

3. We turn to Scriptures with *new questions,* arising from our shattered understandings.

4. This leads to a new level of *action.*

5. The *scope* of the action widens. (And we return to #1.)

Brown concludes, "only in the midst of commitment, of *doing* the truth, will we ever discover [the Bible's] truth for us."[25]

Out of this popular exegesis emerged what some call the basic principle of Latin American liberation interpretation, which they speak of as "co-naturality." Co-naturality means only that readers find a shared experience with the people of the Bible. This connection with the biblical story encourages the notion that the Bible contains not only the mandate for social and political action but also hints at strategies and methods. In some cases, this connection has been understood as a direct identification—the readers and the people of the Bible are the same. Others, however, are cautious about such a one-to-one equation and seek limited identification through the investigation of comparisons of the biblical situations with those of contemporary readers on economic, political, social, and ideological matters. Readers ask how their lives and the lives of biblical persons are alike or different in each of these four areas.[26]

---

[25] Actually Brown uses this cycle (which he calls a "modified hermeneutical cycle") to describe the experience of the disciples on the road to Emmaus when the risen Christ appeared to them. *Unexpected News: Reading the Bible with Third World Eyes* (Philadelphia: Westminster, 1984), 30–31. See Boerma, *The Rich, the Poor and the Bible.*

[26] For examples of liberation interpretation, see Christopher Rowland and Mark Corner, *Liberating Exegesis: The Challenge of Liberation Theology to Biblical Studies* (Louisville: Westminster John Knox, 1989), 7–34.

The African American interpretation of the Bible in terms of Black Power sometimes led to extreme actions as a means of securing freedom from racism. In a similar manner, the conditions of many of the Latin American base communities are so oppressive that the strategies they draw from Scripture lead them to radical political action. Forms of Marxism have provided possibilities for seeking a new life free of both political and economic oppression, because in many Latin American countries hunger and injustice are so severe that only drastic action can yield any positive change.[27] Most controversial is the fact that Bible study has sometimes resulted in the endorsement, encouragement, and even use of violent revolution against colonial oppressors. There is no single rationale for the use of violence in the ministry of Jesus, but it is not uncommon for liberationists to believe that the Bible as a whole, and Jesus' ministry in particular, does not prohibit such radical actions.[28] However extreme the political, economic, and social orientation of Latin American liberation interpretation may seem, God's freeing power is important in terms of human sin and alienation as well as in material matters. Many biblical leaders in South America contend that God's liberation is holistic, inclusive of every dimension of human life.[29]

A distinctive version of liberation interpretation has grown up among Hispanic Americans. In some respects it takes its basic clues from Latin American liberation, but, since the situation of Hispanic Americans is unique, it has its own emphases. This population is rapidly increasing in North America, and that fact alone makes it important that we say a few words about the interpretative methods that are emerging among them.

The peculiar task of Hispanic Americans arises from their intercultural lives. Since they are the "other" in the North American culture, Fernando Segovia stresses that their way of reading the Bible is shaped by otherness. The text itself, Segovia argues, is an "other" to Hispanic Americans because they themselves are bi-cultural. Within that context a number of different approaches to biblical interpretation are espoused. One of the most popular of those stems from the identification the Hispanic American feels with the biblical exiles. They are themselves in exile from their homeland, and, their Bible study, therefore, must include four main characteristics:

---

[27] See the works cited in footnote 11 above.

[28] José Miguez Bonino provides an interesting defense of Latin American liberation thought and practice in his article, "Hermeneutics, Truth, and Praxis," 344–57.

[29] For most of this description of Latin American liberation interpretation, the authors acknowledge their indebtedness to Thomas Schmeller's helpful article, "Liberation Theologies," *Dictionary of Biblical Interpretation* 2:66–74.

(1) It must focus throughout on the question of power and powerlessness in the Bible. (2) It must see the Bible as addressing the community of faith. (3) It must be particularly attuned to what the poor and the simple find in the Bible. (4) It must let itself be interpreted by the Bible in terms of its own historical pilgrimage.[30]

SOCIO-HISTORICAL LIBERATION

Running historically parallel to African American and Latin American understandings of biblical interpretation is another form of liberation exegesis which has both influenced these two and been influenced by them. However, over time socio-historical liberation has developed its own unique perspective. The reason for the adjective "socio-historical" is that these liberation interpretations are founded on the results of investigations into the social nature of the biblical witnesses.[31] In other words, out of the study of the historical situations of the biblical communities, there has evolved a liberation reading of Scripture. These basic investigations on which the liberation theme is based are similar to those discussed in Chapter Two of this book and are susceptible to some of the same weaknesses we have pointed out there. Still, the results of these particular investigations have had an unusual impact on biblical interpretation in North America, in part because it proposes a hermeneutic which is relevant to those who are not included in the other liberation movements we discuss in this chapter. The scholars are both European and North American and are, for the most part, practitioners of a revised historical-critical methodology (see Chapter One).

More specifically, this method of liberation interpretation is a result of efforts to gather data about the social, political, and economic situations out of which biblical material was written. As we have noted, biblical interpretation on the basis of the social sciences has used such historical data as well as

---

[30] Fernando F. Segovia, "Reading the Bible as Hispanic Americans," *NIB* 1:167–73. The quotation is from p. 171. On pp. 171–73, Segovia describes the "biculturalism" and unique "otherness" he experiences as a Hispanic American. This first volume of *NIB* contains similar such articles written from the perspectives of Asian and Native Americans. James Earl Massey introduces the series on particular reading perspectives with another article, "Reading the Bible from Particular Social Locations: An Introduction": 150–53.

[31] A very good example is Luise Schottroff and Wolfgang Stegemann, *Jesus and the Hope of the Poor* (Maryknoll: Orbis, 1986). The authors use some of the best of the historical-critical method to demonstrate the social conditions of Jesus and the earliest Christians.

theories espoused by contemporary social scientists (see Chapter Two). However, the rise of social science interpretations has resulted in a vast amount of "raw data" to which liberation biblical scholars had not been privy until the late twentieth century. One of the clearest examples of such data has to do with the economic conditions of the Jews and of the earliest Christians during the first century C.E. Of course, both the gathering and interpretation of the data occasionally raises some methodological difficulties and must be critically assessed in individual cases. However, the research has rather decisively shown the widespread poverty of Palestinian Jews in the first century, on the one hand, and, on the other hand, the variety of social stations among the early Christians in the Hellenistic world.[32] The availability of such insights into the social, economic, and political worlds of the biblical documents has become one of the most important tools in the socio-historical liberation methods.

The beginnings of this movement can be traced to a special issue of the journal *Radical Religion* devoted to "Class Origins and Class Readings of the Bible" published in 1976.[33] Since that publication, the movement has grown alongside social science methods in interpreting the Bible. Norman K. Gottwald was one of the two editors of the *Radical Religion* publication and has remained a key participant in the special attention to liberation arising from sociological studies of the Bible.

The simplest way to summarize the method of this particular form of liberation interpretation is to say that it privileges investigations into the social settings of biblical materials, how those settings shape the meaning of passages, and how contemporary readers understand those passages in their own social settings. Gottwald made his mark on Old Testament studies by proposing a fresh theory for the origin of Israel. He argued that indigenous Canaanite tribes united in an effort to improve their social and economic situation and form a more egalitarian society, and this tribal alliance eventually became the people of Israel.[34] His students, as well as a good many European scholars, have persistently and steadily advanced this form of liberation interpretation.

---

[32] As examples see Wayne A. Meeks' influential volume, *The First Urban Christians: The Social World of the Apostle Paul* (New Haven: Yale University Press, 1983) and John E. Stambaugh and David L. Balch, *The New Testament in Its Social Environment* (LEC; Philadelphia: Westminster, 1986), 1.

[33] *Radical Religion* 2/2–3 (1976). See *The Bible and Liberation: Political and Social Hermeneutics* (Norman K. Gottwald, ed.; Maryknoll: Orbis, 1984), 1. This volume is a revised edition of the first anthology published by *Radical Religion*.

[34] Norman K. Gottwald, *The Tribes of Israel: A Sociology of the Religion of Liberated Israel, 1250–1050 B.C.E.* (Maryknoll: Orbis, 1979).

A good example of how social analysis leads to the liberation theme is found in some of the work done on the historical Jesus. For instance, as the socio-historical liberation interpreters read it, Mark 2:23–27 (the conflict over the plucking of ears of corn) teaches that hunger takes precedence over Sabbath law and suggests that hunger was a real historical context for Jesus' disciples. In this brief Markan story, the disciples actually have had too little to eat (as did the poor of Palestine), because Jesus and his disciples were themselves among the poor. By confronting the religious leaders of the day, Jesus hoped to awaken them to the fact that the time had come and that those who desired to serve God must unite with the poor of the land. Indeed, "everything that God has promised to Israel by way of salvation belongs to the poor." The usual interpretation of Mark 2:23–27 contends that it has to do with the Sabbath law about harvesting. But some liberation interpreters claim that this is not an adequate reading of the story, because it cannot be properly interpreted apart from an appreciation for the poverty among the common people in Palestine during the time of Jesus and the growth of the Gospels.[35]

Many of the scholars who embrace and practice this socio-historical perspective are not necessarily themselves oppressed. Unlike the Latin American liberation interpretations that depend on the "reading from below" (that is, from among the common people), the socio-historical liberation interpretations come, for the most part, from the scholarly classes. Yet these scholars are committed to creating an atmosphere of liberation among Christians and decisively orienting the ministry of the church toward the poor and needy.

Ched Myers, for example, makes clear that he wants his work to join that of the Latin American liberation theologians in cultivating a "radical discipleship" among Christians. In his case, Myers is interested in the formation of a Christian sub-culture that will oppose many of the political views advocated by leaders in the "first world" (that is, the Western and Northern world). His political reading of Mark is an effort to reclaim the radical political perspective of the second Gospel for Christians and snatch it away from those who interpret the Gospel so as to make it politically palatable among the middle class of the USA. Myer also advances the important role of ideology, to which we will turn later.[36]

---

[35] Luise Schottroff and Wolfgang Stegemann, "The Sabbath Was Made for Man: The Interpretation of Mark 2:23–28," in *God of the Lowly*, 118–28. The quotation is from p. 125.

[36] Ched Myers, *Binding the Strong Man: A Political Reading of Mark's Story of Jesus* (Maryknoll: Orbis, 1988). Myers' thesis is that the Gospel of Mark was written during the Jewish revolt against Roman oppression (66–70 C.E.) and that the evan-

FEMINIST AND WOMANIST LIBERATION

In the process of the woman's movement in the late nineteenth and early twentieth centuries, women began to believe that they needed and had the right to read and interpret the Bible in full consciousness that they were female. In 1895 Elizabeth Cady Stanton and a group of women published *The Woman's Bible,* the first commentary of its kind.[37] Up to that time, the interpretation of the Bible had been the exclusive domain of men, and biblical scholars were invariably male. The sense that women ought to read and interpret Scripture *as women* grew only very gradually out of their new self-consciousness in North America. There most certainly must have been women who brought their own particular selves and station to interpreting the Bible before Stanton and her colleagues, but, if that was the case, it remained a very private matter. The publication of the first *Woman's Bible* unleashed a new force in society and began a movement that continues on to this day.[38]

Feminist and womanist interpretations are really nothing more than the self-conscious reading of the Bible by women as women, but that simple process has had enormous consequences. We can speak of that general movement as a whole, before distinguishing the contributions of women of color. Women now read and interpret the Bible in all of the ways male scholars do. However, some women believe, and have demonstrated, that they have something unique to offer the field of biblical scholarship. Both of your authors can testify to how important the influence of female biblical interpreters has been in our lives, which is but a miniature of the wider impact of feminist scholarship.[39]

---

gelist sought to undermine the symbolic world order advanced by the occupation forces and establish another which was God's reign. For another interpretation of Mark from a similar perspective and influenced by the author's experience in the "third world," see Herman C. Waetjen, *A Reordering of Power: A Socio-Political Reading of Mark's Gospel* (Minneapolis: Fortress, 1989).

[37] Elizabeth Cady Stanton, ed., *The Woman's Bible* (2 vols.; New York: European, 1895–98).

[38] The publication of *The Women's Bible Commentary* both honors the original *Woman's Bible* and extends its influence into the contemporary world. For that reason this one volume commentary is a memorable publication. Carol A. Newsom and Sharon H. Ringe, eds., *The Women's Bible Commentary* (Louisville: Westminster John Knox, 1992). In 1998 the same publisher issued an expanded edition which includes the Apocrypha.

[39] For a historical sketch of the rise of feminist biblical studies see, Vicki C. Phillips, "Feminist Interpretation," *Dictionary of Biblical Interpretation* 1:388–92.

Feminist biblical scholarship has been and remains a single element in the wider movement of feminist theology and as such it seeks to contribute to the whole enterprise of the formation of a Christian faith and life that reflects the experience of women. In biblical scholarship the movement began in what may have seemed an innocent fashion—the study of the women of the Bible. That stage of the process brought attention to the important role of women in the biblical drama, such as Miriam's song of celebration beside the Red Sea (Exod 15:20–21) which has always been dwarfed by the lengthy song of Moses that precedes it (even though a good number of critics believe that Miriam's song is older and more authentic than Moses'). Female scholars ask us to notice the importance of female names in Paul's letter, for example, Nympha who hosted a Christian congregation in her house (Col 4:15). They pique our curiosity about the unnamed women in the ministry of Jesus (e.g., Mark 5:25–34) and bring our attention to women whom Jesus used as models of faith (for example, Mark 12:41–44 and Luke 15:8–10). In this way, feminist interpretation first *liberated the women of the Bible from their obscurity.*

However, the movement soon sought more. As women moved into scholarship and positions of leadership, their contributions widened and deepened. It soon became apparent that there was something special women brought to biblical interpretation and theology in general and that something began to unsettle the "private men's clubs" of Christian biblical scholarship. Women found empowerment in the process of reading the Bible in full consciousness of their womanhood and doing it in communities of other women.[40]

As the movement developed, women became more and more sensitive to their sisters in other countries and of different ethnic heritages. In North America the woman's movement began as an enterprise of and for white, middle-class women, and that was to some extent true of feminine biblical scholarship. However, the woman's movement eventually, especially in Christian circles, took up the cause of all the marginalized of our world, and that continues to be one of the characteristic concerns of feminist scholarship.[41]

---

[40] One of the most influential of the books that brought feminist interpretation to pastors is Phyllis Trible, *God and the Rhetoric of Sexuality* (OBT; Philadelphia: Fortress, 1978).

[41] The effort to be more inclusive in its representation of women is evident in *Searching the Scriptures: A Feminist Introduction* and *Searching the Scriptures: A Feminist Commentary,* both edited by Elizabeth Schüssler Fiorenza (New York: Crossroads, 1993 and 1994). In the introduction of the first volume, the editor points out that Stanton's *Woman's Bible* included only white, middle class women but that *Searching the Scriptures* project "brings together some of the finest scholarship in

The distinctive concerns of women of color in North America and around the world stimulated what came to be called the "womanist" movement. That movement merits consideration on its own merits as a related but distinct endeavor to feminism.

Feminist Liberation Interpretation

In the 1960s and 1970s women were moving into prominence in biblical scholarship and, while there was something like a single methodology among them, the variety of interests and methods grew. What they all share is the conviction that women have the right and duty to read Scripture in the light of their own experience and to resist all efforts to subordinate them to male scholarship. However, like male scholars, they do not all share the same view of the authority of Scripture, and we find among them the three general views of canon we mentioned earlier in the introduction to this chapter. There are, first, those who embrace the Bible as the means of the Word of God and who believe that it affirms women, when it is properly interpreted. Second, there are those who try to distinguish as clearly as possible between the oppressive side of Scripture—the patriarchal dimension, which is the result of the cultural settings out of which much of it was written—and the liberating side, which stresses the biblical message that continues to be true. This group distinguishes between the contingent and the eternal, just as do a good many Christians. The third group is comprised of those who claim that only the liberating message of Scripture is authoritative and the distinction is not so much between contingent and eternal as between oppressive and liberating.[42]

As early as 1979, Sharon H. Ringe tried to articulate the basic assumptions of a "nonsexist interpretation of the Bible." The first assumption is that the biblical texts are "alien" to the contemporary reader, coming as they do out of another historical setting with an entirely different worldview. For this reason historical criticism offers valuable insights into the Bible. However, the second assumption of feminist interpretation is that readers analyze the way a text is put together, what it seeks to do, and how it creates new relationships. In struggling with the text in this manner, one reaches the third assumption, namely that the reader and the text share a common humanity. According to Ringe, two implications follow out of this third assumption:

---

contemporary biblical and historical studies, not only from the United States but from around the world" (ix).

[42] Phillips, "Feminist Interpretation," 392.

First, because human existence is a social existence—and, furthermore, because the texts themselves have their original locus in the community that gathered and preserved them—a group or corporate context seems to yield the most fruitful studies of the Biblical texts. . . . The second implication of the common humanity of reader and texts is that a part of the total process of interpretation involves the reader's entering into the story primarily through its human characters.

The last of Ringe's characteristics of feminist biblical study is a faith perspective that comes with the reader to the text in anticipation of receiving God's message there.[43]

While there appears to be nothing peculiarly feminist about Ringe's assumptions, the emphasis on the shared humanity of the text and reader leads us to some important conclusions about feminist liberation interpretation. Those who practice this type of interpretation attempt to work within communities and in a collaborative way. Furthermore, Ringe's assumptions are related to the heart of feminist interpretation which Rosemary Radford Ruether has called the "correlation of feminist and biblical critical principles" (which is similar to the co-naturality of Latin American liberation interpretations mentioned earlier). The source of the liberating power of Scripture, she writes, is this correlation. The Bible itself expresses the critical principle of "prophetic-messianic tradition" which is the Bible's continual reevaluation of situations and new contexts in the light of the radical message of its tradition. The prophetic tradition continually critiqued structures that produced injustice and inequality. The structures of sexism are not among those the tradition addresses within the scope of the Bible, but the task of feminist liberation is to continue and extend that prophetic tradition into our own day and thereby undermine the patriarchal structures of our society.[44] Hence the liberation one experiences in reading Scripture is not so much the emancipation from oppression as it is the empowerment to act for that emancipation.

The hermeneutic of feminist interpretation is difficult to summarize, precisely because it is so varied. However, Vicki C. Phillips helps us by trying to describe the range of interpretative concerns women bring to biblical study. The critical study of a text requires a *hermeneutic of suspicion* especially with regard to the traditional masculine interpretation of the passage. Only

---

[43] Sharon H. Ringe, "Biblical Authority and Interpretation," in *The Liberating Word: A Guide to Nonsexist Interpretation of the Bible* (Letty M. Russell, ed.; Philadelphia: Westminster, 1976), 35–38. The quotation is from p. 37.

[44] Rosemary Radford Ruether, "Feminist Interpretation: A Method of Correlation," in *Feminist Interpretation of the Bible* (Letty M. Russell, ed.; Philadelphia: Westminster, 1985), 116–20.

after having exposed that tradition does the feminist employ the *hermeneutic of remembrance.* This works out of an awareness of the role of women in the origins of the Jewish and Christian traditions, and thereby constructs a new history freed of male dominion.[45] This style of interpretative work strips the text of its patriarchal elements and offers women power to act. That in turn calls for a *hermeneutic of proclamation,* by which the interpreter relates the newly constructed understanding of the text to her current situation.[46] Finally, a *hermeneutic of imagination* seeks to correct the assumption of the dominant male interpretative tradition that all knowledge is cognitive and does so by expressing the tradition in more imaginative ways (for example, artistic expressions).[47]

While the categories of different feminist liberation hermeneutics described by Vicki Phillips (suspicion, remembrance, proclamation, and imagination) are important in womanist interpretation, more important is what has been called the *hermeneutic of survival.* This is not, however, simply a method of *understanding* the world, it is a method of *changing* the world and it is rooted in practice. The starting point for reading the Bible, and for discerning its authority, is the struggle to survive in this society. "It is a hermeneutics that distinguished between a message of liberation hidden in a text and waiting for retrieval and a liberating reading performed by people engaged in a struggle against injustice."[48] The reader digs in a text to get behind its oppressive message to some liberating word, but that liberating word is "not given by the text but claimed from it by the oppressed."[49] This view is similar to the one we saw in Latin American liberation interpretation in that both stress struggling against oppressive situations.

Elisabeth Schüssler Fiorenza makes a distinction that is helpful in further understanding feminist interpretation. In several of her writings she argues that *the Bible should be taken not as "archetype" but as "prototype."* This

---

[45] For example see the one constructed by Elisabeth Schüssler Fiorenza, *In Memory of Her: A Feminist Theological Reconstruction of Christian Origins* (New York: Crossroad, 1984).

[46] One of the most impressive treatments of proclamation from a feminist perspective is Rebecca S. Chopp, *The Power to Speak: Feminism, Language, God* (New York: Crossroad, 1991). Her interpretation of Luke 4:16–30, while intricate, is a model of feminist interpretation for what Chopp calls "emancipatory transformation" (45–66).

[47] Phillips, "Feminist Interpretation," 393–94.

[48] George Aichele et al., eds., *The Postmodern Bible: The Bible and Culture Collective* (New Haven: Yale University Press, 1995), 253.

[49] Sheila Briggs, "Can an Enslaved God Liberate? Hermeneutical Reflections on Philippians 2:6–11," in *Interpretation of Liberation*, 151.

means the Bible does not contain ideal forms but simply original forms that must yet be developed—"rough drafts," we might call them. In this way of viewing Scripture, we understand that biblical views are open to change and transformation. In the current context, the Christian community shares the responsibility of shaping and improving biblical mandates.[50] Consequently, for instance, the family duties mentioned in the New Testament (the *Haustafeln*) are not to be imitated literally (that is, taken as archetypes), but should be read in terms of what they suggest about the importance of relationships within a family and reshaping those relationships in ways appropriate for today (that is, taking them as prototypes). Fiorenza concludes that the proposal to treat the Bible as prototype and not archetype "locates revelation not in texts but in Christian experience and community."[51] The message of the Bible is not, in itself, revelatory but may become so by what the community does with the message!

Feminist liberation interpretation is not limited to any one of the critical methods practiced today. Some female scholars practice a historical-critical method, having purged it of its androcentric characteristics; others use newer literary and social science criticisms.[52] The result is that feminist liberation interpretation is spread through the whole of biblical criticism.

Womanist Liberation Interpretation

Alice Walker first used the title *womanist,* and by it meant (among other definitions) the woman whose behavior was "outrageous, audacious, courageous, or willful."[53] It was then adopted to refer to African American women who have the courage to struggle for their liberation. Specifically, womanist theologians stress the total context of Black women in today's society, including the racist, classist, homophobic, and ecologic oppression they

---

[50] Fiorenza, *In Memory of Her,* 33–34; *Bread Not Stone,* 61–62.

[51] Fiorenza, *In Memory of Her,* 34.

[52] As an example of a feminine literary study see Tina Pippin, *Death and Desire: The Rhetoric of Gender in the Apocalypse of John* (Literary Currents in Biblical Interpretation; Louisville: Westminster John Knox, 1992). For an example of how a feminist views the social science criticisms see, Carolyn Osiek, R.S.C.J., *What Are They Saying About the Social Setting of the New Testament?* (rev. ed.; New York: Paulist, 1992). For a discussion of the varieties of feminist critique and construction, see Janice Capel Anderson, "Feminist Criticism: The Dancing Daughter," in *Mark and Method: New Approaches in Biblical Studies* (ed. Janice Capel Anderson and Stephen D. Moore; Minneapolis: Fortress, 1992), 103–12.

[53] Alice Walker, *In Search of Our Mothers' Gardens: Womanist Prose* (San Diego: Harcourt Brace Jovanovich, 1983), xi–xii.

experience. Womanists distinguish themselves from feminists by emphasizing that their issue is not simply sexism but all of the oppressive forces at work in their lives. Some womanists tend to view the feminist movement as the property of white, middle-class North American women, and they wish to keep in mind the life conditions of women all around the world.[54]

Some womanists are even more critical of the feminist movement, charging white women with becoming identified with the patriarchal system of oppression. The level of exploitation is more severe in the case of African American women, for the experience of slavery forever affects Black women.[55] The degree of conversation between the two groups of scholars varies, but for the most part there is a recognition of what they share in common, as well as of their distinctive callings.

One of the most powerful and controversial contributions of the womanist movement to biblical theology is the critique of the doctrine of atonement, as it has been nurtured for centuries in the white churches. Integral to the traditional (male) views of the redemptive value of the cross, contends Delores Williams, is the idea that Jesus is forced to serve as a surrogate. For African American women, surrogacy means the role forced on the Black "mammy" and the tradition of Black women as "breeders." Jesus is thought of as the supreme surrogate, insofar as he took our death upon himself. Williams, along with other womanist theologians, reject Jesus' death as the sole source of redemption and instead emphasizes his whole life and ministry. His ministry shows humans how to live peacefully and abundantly. That ministry involves Jesus teachings,

> A healing ministry of touch and being touched, . . . a militant ministry of expelling evil forces, . . . a ministry grounded in the power of faith, . . . a ministry of prayer . . . [and] a ministry of compassion and love. Humankind is, then, redeemed through Jesus' ministerial vision of life and not through his death.[56]

With this refocusing of the doctrine of redemption off the cross and onto Jesus' whole ministry, biblical interpretation shifts in both emphasis and attention. The so-called mission "to preach the cross" will need to be revised.

Another prominent womanist interpreter, Renita Weems, examines the metaphors in Hosea 1–3 and struggles with how such sexual metaphors

---

[54] For an example of a book that spans Latin American and feminist-womanist issues see Tamez, *Bible of the Oppressed.*

[55] See Phillips, "Feminist Interpretation," 393, and Delores S. Williams, *Sisters in the Wilderness: The Challenge of Womanist God-Talk* (Maryknoll: Orbis, 1993), 178–203.

[56] Williams, *Sisters in the Wilderness,* 62–71, 81–83, 161–67. The quotation is from p. 167.

might produce meaningful and relevant theological themes. She is less willing than Fiorenza to dismiss such biblical themes as violations of the liberation principle and claims that the abuse of women—as terrible as it is—can and does serve as a metaphor for divine love and retribution.[57]

This short introduction into womanist biblical interpretation allows us to stress once again how the liberation readings of the Bible have to do with those humans who stand on the margins of society and whose leaders claim a place at the table of biblical exegesis. Moreover, taken together these two movements vividly demonstrate how the social location of readers can become more than a minor matter of concern; indeed, it can provide interpretation which is primarily focused on liberation. Those who use any method of interpretation need to take note of the importance of the context in which interpretation is done.

IDEOLOGICAL CRITICISM

Ideology, in this case, means the elements involved in the process of creating or discerning meaning. *Ideological criticism* is the investigation of the process by which interpreters create the meaning of a text and the social and political realities that influence that process. Probably more than anything else, it has to do with understanding the roles of power and social position in an interpretative undertaking. However, ideological criticism is not just interested in how the interpreter is predisposed to create meaning but equally interested in investigating the ideology—the process of meaning—encoded in a written text. Some scholars distinguish ideology from what we would think of as beliefs, outlooks, and creeds. Ideology is comprised of the basic perspectives which "emphasize their distinctiveness, resist innovations, and expect consensus and agreement among their adherents." Nonetheless there is an ongoing debate among ideological interpreters as to whether ideologies are intrinsically neutral or naturally oppressive.[58] As a result of Karl Marx's use of the term, ideology is often assumed to be some negative feature, a bias that has oppressive results. However, ideological criticism frequently broadens its meaning to refer to any process connected with the formation of a text or interpreting a text.[59]

---

[57] Renita Weems, "Gomer: Victim of Violence or Victim of Metaphor?" in *Interpretation for Liberation,* 87–104.

[58] Beverly J. Stratton, "Ideology," in *Handbook of Postmodern Biblical Interpretation* (ed. A. K. M. Adam; St. Louis: Chalice, 2000), 122.

[59] Aichele, *The Postmodern Bible,* 272–77.

Suppose, for instance, a biblical interpreter studies Luke 6:20, "Then he looked up at his disciples and said: 'Blessed are you who are poor, for yours is the kingdom of God.'" The interpreter concludes his study by summarizing the meaning of the text: "Jesus declares that those who understand themselves to have no merit before God are actually favored by God and promised a place in God's reign." An ideological critic would immediately ask what the interpreter had at stake in describing the meaning of this passage in this way. The suspicion would be that the interpreter's own economic and social status hindered his assigning the meaning "financially destitute and needy" to the word poor. Instead of having reference to the material status of those who are promised the kingdom, the beatitude is said to have to do with that invisible relationship one might have with God. Why should this interpreter choose this meaning of "poor?"

This is an easy example, of course, but it suggests the way in which an ideological critic might go about digging out of the text its potential for soliciting different meanings, depending on the reader's own context. While power is not the sole concern of the ideological critic, it figures prominently, especially if one is inclined to believe that humans treasure power. Nonetheless, the critic is equally concerned with how interpretation involves particular notions of truth as well as values and action.[60]

As we have said, ideological critics are interested in the text itself as well as how a text is interpreted. That is to say, there is an ideological interpretation of the Bible as well as an ideological interpretation of a biblical interpreter's work. The critic assumes every text contains within it the results of construing meaning, of expressing values, and of preserving power. They accomplish their interpretation by "reading against the grain" or employing a "hermeneutic of resistance." They raise critical questions about a text rather than easily allowing the text to lead them. What is at stake for the third evangelist in writing the first beatitude as we find it in Luke? What matters of justice are at stake and implicit in the beatitude?

Ideological criticism is clearly concerned with the ethics of a text and its interpretation, and so it always appeals to some understanding of what is good, righteous, and just. Hence, ideological critics need a self-consciousness that makes them aware of their own political preferences, positions of power, and so forth. If such a consciousness is not possible, then critics can be expected to do nothing more than impose their own values on the text without realizing that they are doing so.

Liberation interpretations are related to ideological criticism insofar as liberation readings always require a careful discernment of a text's potential

---

[60] Ibid., 272–73.

for oppression as well as liberation. The beginnings of ideological interpretative methods can be traced to the socio-historical liberation criticisms we discussed earlier in this chapter. As a matter of fact, nearly every one of the liberationist interpreters classified in the socio-historical category discussed above could also be categorized as an ideological critic. This is the case simply because both socio-historical liberation interpreters and ideological critics are trying to read through assumptions of oppression sustained by the dominate culture. What feminist liberation interpreters do is also, in part, at least ideological. For instance, they try to find and exhibit the preferences of the author of a text, whatever they may be. The story of the widow in the Temple (Mark 12:41–44 and Luke 21:1–4), for example, betrays an attitude toward women and poverty, suggesting the influence of one's own relationship with women and one's own degree of wealth.

Critics speak of both an *intrinsic and extrinsic ideological criticism.*

> Extrinsic analysis uses the historical and social sciences to help reconstruct or "unmask" the material and ideological conditions under which the text was produced. . . . In an intrinsic analysis, the ideological critic takes up literary critical methods to examine how the text assimilates or "encodes" socioeconomic conditions to reproduce a particular ideology in its rhetoric.[61]

In other words, the ideological critic searches for clues as to how meaning was produced in the text both *behind* the text and on the *surface* of the text.

One of the important forms of ideological criticism today is *post-colonial interpretation,* in which the critic searches out the indications of colonial mentality in either an interpreter or in a text itself. Actually, post-colonial criticism is a large canopy under which a multitude of interpretative methods gather. Stephen D. Moore insists that we should not think of it as a separate method of interpretation but rather as a sensitivity attuned to the relationship between a text and its cultural setting.[62]

Fernando F. Segovia charges that the historical-critical method is itself a colonial import, the assumptions of which are Western modernism.[63] The same assumption can be seen in the work of George E. Tinker, who as a Native American, critiques the biblical story of the conquest and settlement of

---

[61] Gail A. Yee, "Ideological Criticism," *Dictionary of Biblical Interpretation* 1:535–36.

[62] Stephen D. Moore, "Postcolonialism," in *Handbook of Postmodern Biblical Interpretation,* 183.

[63] Fernando F. Segovia, "Reading Readers of the Fourth Gospel and Their Readings: An Exercise in Intercultural Criticism," in *"What Is John?" Readers and Readings of the Fourth Gospel* (ed. Fernando F. Segovia; Symposium 3; Atlanta: Scholars, 1996), 237–77.

Canaan. He points out that the text of this story is inherently imperialist and perpetuates the ideology of colonization. Consequently, Native Americans more readily identify with the Canaanites in their oppression than with the Hebrews in their liberation.[64]

Since ideological criticism is interested in the beliefs, values, and even customs encoded in a text and in interpretations of that text, it is not surprising that it values a multitude of interpretations as true or valuable. Therefore, it contributes to the contention that there is no one, single "true" interpretation of any passage. There is never an interpretation of a biblical text that is not influenced by the ideology of the reader. All readers are bound by their cultural contexts which shape their reading. Hence, ideological criticism affirms the reality and value of *difference* in biblical reading. Modernism has tended to value likeness, and only in this era of dawning post-modernism are there forces undermining that modernist value in favor of the value of difference. Both feminist thought and ideological criticism have been among those forces.[65]

We can better understand ideological criticism by means of an example in which the scholar makes us aware of the steps he or she has taken in the process. David Penchansky begins his study of Judg 2:10–23 with what he calls the "textual story." The passage expresses the Deuteronomic view of history in that it traces a cycle from disobedience, which results in oppression, to obedience, which leads to liberation. Penchansky summarizes the cycle this way:

> Israel commits spiritual adultery
> They are oppressed by their enemies
> They cry out to Yahweh in their misery
> Yahweh raises up a [judge] who delivers them.

However, the story of Ehud and Eglon in Judges 3 seems to teach something quite different. Yahweh's deliverance through a charismatic leader comes without the people's cry for help. Yet this story is included in Scripture. This suggests that while the Joshua text rather than the Judges text became the prevalent Hebraic understanding of history, stories such as the one in Judges 3 continued to be valued. The critic contends that the generalized scheme of J 2:10–23 is deliberate and manipulative. It implies a coercive effort to win approval as *the* model of Hebraic history. The ideological impulse of the text is to force readers to interpret the text and their own history in this one way.

---

[64] George E. Tinker, "Reading the Bible as Native Americans," *NIB* 1:174–80. See also, Aichele, *The Postmodern Bible*, 284–86.

[65] Aichele, *The Postmodern Bible*, 300–307.

Having unveiled what he believes to be the ideological goal of the Judges passage influenced by the ideology of Joshua, Penchansky turns to what he calls "the critical story." Here he offers a critique of his own reading of the passage and admits that he does not "like" the view expressed. While he claims that what he says is actually "in the text," he adds his own views by offering connections, clarifying ambiguities, and concealing other features of the text that might endanger his interpretation. His critical reading of the passage has its own story in his life and consciousness.

In a third and final part of his study, Penchansky speaks of "the meta-critical story" in which he asks in effect, what is an interpreter to do? He answers that, even though his readings will always be determined by his own ideological views, he shares his interpretation with others "under erasure" (what is blotted out). "The erasure therefore becomes a part of what the word, concept or assertion is—erased, . . . as with pen and ink, a line drawn through the erased text, which is still able to be read."[66] In effect, the critic always qualifies her or his analysis with an admission that it is little more than the projection of the interpreter's self onto the text. This view comes close to what we will consider as deconstruction criticism in the next chapter.

Ideological criticism entails the question of the interpreter's posture toward the text. We have noted that ideological criticism favors resistant reading, but it also yields other helpful insights into possible readings. Adele Reinhartz' book, *Befriending the Beloved Disciple: A Jewish Reading of the Gospel of John,* is not strictly ideological criticism as such, although it contributes to ideological and liberation interpretations in specific ways. Reinhartz begins by suggesting that reading entails a relationship between the reader and a text and then goes on to ask how a Jew (like herself) can read the Gospel of John with its seemingly anti-Jewish stance. She investigates three alternative approaches to or postures toward the Gospel. The first is *compliant reading* in which readers intentionally try to conform to the author's (or implied author's) leadership. They "go along with the text," as it were, believing that such submission to the text is the best way to understand what a text says.

At the opposite end of the spectrum from compliant reading is *resistant reading* of the kind we see in ideological criticism and which is often practiced by feminist and womanist interpreters. In this case, readers take the stance as the "other" with regard to the text, standing opposed to it.

---

[66] David Penchansky, "Up for Grabs: A Tentative Proposal for Doing Ideological Criticism," in *Ideological Criticism of Biblical Texts* (ed. David Jobling and Tina Pippin; *Semeia* 59; Atlanta: Scholars, 1992), 35–41. The quotation is from pp. 36 and 40–41.

Reinhartz asks how resistant readers can try to read the Gospel as the Johannine Jews, whom the evangelist attacks, might have read it.

However, Reinhartz goes on to propose still a third type of reading stance, which she calls *sympathetic reading*. "As a sympathetic reader," she writes, "I focus on the matters that might unite the Beloved disciple and myself while ignoring for the time being those that might separate us. . . . I identify various elements within . . . [the text] that resonate positive in some way with the stories, written or lived, that belong to my own tradition and experience."[67]

THE CONTRIBUTIONS OF LIBERATION CRITICISMS TO PREACHING

With Reinhartz's types of reading before us, we can turn now to the importance of liberation interpretation to the preacher. Our examination of some forms of contemporary liberation interpretations of the Bible equips us to ask how all this might be useful to the ordinary pastor in search of a sermon for Sunday morning. We believe that these interpretative methods hold great promise for homiletic use, even though that may not have been the primary purpose in their formulation. For the most part, liberation criticisms (but not necessarily ideological criticisms) arose in the church. They were not the inventions of uncommitted scholars, hiding in their ivory towers. Instead, they originated for the sake of the church and its ministry. That is surely true of Africa American, Latin American, socio-historical, feminist, and womanist liberation interpretations. An argument might even be made that the same is true of ideological liberation, at least in its beginnings. So, when we ask how these criticisms can be used in sermon preparation and congregational Bible studies, we are not imposing a foreign question on them.

There are a number of important generalizations about liberation interpretations and preaching that form a foundation for their homiletic use. The first thing we should recognize is *the centrality of liberation for Christian faith*. God reveals God's self in Christ for the purpose of freeing us humans from all that oppresses us. The Gospel message, in other words, is a liberating message—one that rescues us from our sinful selves and society so that we may enjoy a relationship with our Creator. Liberation theologies, of course, have been critical of the way in which the church in North America has confined the impact of the Gospel's liberating power to our "spiritual" relationship with God. James Cone called the African American churches to take seriously

---

[67] Adele Reinhartz, *Befriending the Beloved Disciple* (New York: Continuum, 2001), 99.

all that the message of liberation means for those oppressed because of race. A good many liberation interpreters would probably agree that deliverance from sin and its consequences is central to the Christian message, even though liberation interpretation focuses much more on the material, social, economic, and political nature.

So, the first task for preachers might well be to ground this sort of "worldly" liberation in the broader message of freedom in Christ. That is really not hard to do, because oppression, poverty, prejudice, racism, sexism, and all the world's injustices are part of the sin from which we seek freedom. These social injustices put faces on sin; they make sin concrete and specific. The sin from which we seek release is not just for the sake of our "souls," nor for the sake of our self-images that represent distortions of the image in which we were created. We need release from our participation—willingly or unwillingly—in perpetuating and widening the gulf between the rich and the poor in our world. We know, too, that we need freedom from our support of social institutions and structures that continue to debase and degrade others in order to preserve our status and power in our society.

The second pillar for the homiletic use of liberation interpretations is that *Jesus' ministry was a form of this social liberation.* Once again, the temptation in white, middle-class, North American churches is to "spiritualize" the meaning of Jesus' ministry. His ministry to the poor, for instance, is understood in terms of those who are *spiritually* poor and in need of forgiveness and love. This sort of reading of Jesus' ministry takes his healings to be symbols for how he heals our wounded spirits. Now, there can be no doubt that this is true, in part. Jesus' ministry reveals God's love for us regardless of our spiritual condition. The problem is that too often we have limited the meaning of God's revelation in Christ to this single dimension of human life. (Equally important is the possibility that we have truncated the meaning of "spiritual.") We preachers can take our share of responsibility for this tendency, because a good many of us have again and again used Jesus' ministry to economic poverty and physical illness as allegories for how he heals our broken relationship with God.

The liberationists help us understand Jesus' ministry in a more holistic way. The Gospel of Luke clearly represents Jesus' words in the synagogue in 4:17–21 as the agenda for the ministry he is about to begin. God "has anointed me to bring good news to the *poor. He has sent me to proclaim release to the captives and recover of sight to the blind, to let the oppressed go free, to proclaim the year of the Lord's favor.*"[68] These are all ministries to the physical,

---

[68] Emphasis ours. Most scholars agree that the "year of the Lord" in this passage is likely a reference to the Jubilee year mentioned in Hebrew Scriptures, for ex-

material, social, and economic conditions of people. Jesus' ministry was holistic and involved deliverance as the liberation interpretations understand it.[69] Preaching liberation and empowering the church today for ministry to the whole range of human needs are faithful responses to Jesus ministry.

The last element in the foundation of liberation preaching is the assumption that *all of us are oppressed in one way or another.* There are some kinds of oppression that are not nearly as drastic and destructive as social, political, and economic oppression, but nonetheless they are truly oppressive. By oppression we mean anything—anything at all—that prevents us from being what God intends and wants us to be. All of us, then, are in need of God's liberating power in several ways. Some are oppressed by psychological realities, such as self-images that are destructive and unhealthy or emotional illnesses rooted in our pasts. Others are oppressed by societal expectations and assumptions. The middle-class family in the USA is often up to its ears in debt, because they erroneously think that "success" involves owning and possessing certain things. And finally, we are oppressed because we participate in and support social structures which oppress others, and we are at a lost to know how to extricate ourselves from the system. Oppressors are themselves oppressed and anyone who supports oppression shares in the responsibility for oppressing others.[70]

A number of years ago a devout Christian family believed deeply that the war in Vietnam was evil. They wanted to withdraw all their support from a government that sponsored such violence, but their income tax went in large part to finance the war they abhorred. They withheld their tax payments for several years, until finally they were threatened with imprisonment and abandonment of their children. What were they to do? It is this kind of complicated and intricate oppression that binds many of us. How does the

---

ample, Lev 25. The concept of Jubilee year entailed a drastic restructuring of society, release of the enslaved, restoration of land to its original owners, and much more. In his synagogue message Jesus invites the group to see the advent of this grand Sabbath of Sabbath years. See Sharon H. Ringe, *Jesus, Liberation, and the Biblical Jubilee: Images for Ethics and Christology* (OBT 19; Philadelphia: Fortress, 1985).

[69] Another interesting passage in this regard is Matt 11:2–6 and its parallel in Luke 7:18–23. John the Baptist sends followers to ask Jesus if he is the long-awaited Messiah. Jesus responds by pointing to the blind, the lame, and the lepers whom he has healed, and concludes his answer with the words, "the poor have good news preached to them." Notice that this story represents Jesus' pointing exclusively to the physical effects of his ministry without a word about its spiritual results.

[70] See the gripping account of how the South African Truth and Reconciliation Commission sought to treat both the oppressed and the oppressors as "victims." Desmond Tutu, *No Future Without Forgiveness* (New York: Doubleday, 1999).

gospel message free us of such entanglements? To be sure, we cannot compare it to the oppression of those living under tyrannical regimes or living from day to day without knowing how they will survive, but it is certainly a kind of oppression.

We wish to establish here that liberation preaching is important and relevant for *every* congregation, regardless of its socio-economic condition. That being the case, the question is how liberation interpretations can help us use biblical passages for sermons that set people free. We need a method of reading Scripture that exposes the emancipating message of a text. We can draw something from each of the methods we have described in this chapter and by doing so be better equipped to exegete and preach liberating texts. It may be more valuable, however, to sketch one interpretative process that employs the most useful aspects of all these methods. Without claiming to be exhaustive, these are some steps which we believe help us to read texts for liberation.

Looking for the Needy or Oppressed in a Passage

In many cases, this will be obvious. When the passage under consideration is about one of Jesus' healings, it is perfectly clear who the needy are. However, in other cases, the needy may be lurking in the shadows or standing on the margins of a story. To bring them front-stage provides interesting possibilities for preaching.

Suppose the lesson is 1 Cor 11:17–26. The usual lectionary lesson is 11:23–26 (the lesson for Holy Thursday all three years), but rather than preaching strictly on the institution of the Lord's Supper in verses 23–26, we might ask *why* Paul includes this memory of Jesus' last meal with his disciples in this letter. It clearly has to do with what Paul sees as the "abuses" of the Lord's Supper of which he speaks in 11:17–22. What is interesting in Paul's effort to set the Corinthians straight on the celebration of the Supper is that there are poor and hungry participants present at the celebration who are not getting fed (v. 21). They are being elbowed out by others. It may well have been that some came to eat what looked like a potluck supper; they came because they needed food. Paul asks, "Do you not have homes to eat and drink in?" Did, in fact, all of them *have* homes?

Bringing these hungry and needy out of the shadows of the story allows the preacher to ask how the hungry and needy today may get elbowed out in our church programs. More importantly, what does the Lord's Supper have to do with physical hunger and need? Paul goes on in this chapter to speak of "discerning the body" (11:29). Of course, the Lord's Supper is the body of Christ, but *that body is the bread and wine taken in the context of a community that is also the body of Christ.* So the question becomes: How do the poor and needy participate in the body of Christ (both in the congregation and in the Sacrament)? Asking these questions of the text brings the needy to our attention and invites us to connect the situation in Corinth with our contemporary practice.

Let us take another example—an easier one. The lesson is Isa 40:1–11 (which the RCL assigns for the second Sunday of Advent in year B). What happens when we focus attention on those for whom God is acting in the passage? Who are they? Yes, they are exiles, but what else does the prophet say about them? He speaks of their having served their "term" (as if they were imprisoned), of paying their "penalty" (40:2), and of their being like lambs, which need to be fed (40:11). What is it like to be exiled, to be forced (by whatever power) to live away from home and among strangers? What is it like to feel that you are being punished for your sins and that your exile is payment for your sins? Indeed, those who are exiled do often feel as if they are suffering the consequences of their sins; they often feel the need to be fed by someone who cares for them. With the condition of the exiles clearly presented, the preacher is ready to move on to draw parallels between the exiles found in the passage and those living in the midst of our own society.

At this point we are practicing a basic principle of feminist interpretation in that we are recognizing what Sharon Ringe calls our "common humanity" with those in the text. When we look for and find the points at which this sharing takes place, we are closer to a liberating message in our sermons.[71]

Another way of identifying the poor and suffering found within a passage is to consider our perspective on the text. Any story depends on "how one looks at it," and often it is the matter of one's perspective that determines meaning (see Chapter Six). We can see more deeply into a story when we try changing our perspective on it. The oppression and need of characters may become clearer to us when we change our way of seeing them. This is particularly true of narratives, where the narrator usually determines the immediate perspective on the events of the story. It is usually true that we hear only the author's side of a story (as in a letter or epistle) while the other side is unconsidered, put down, or condemned. What happens when we reassign the cast of characters,[72] that is, when we change the perspective from that of the author to that of the other characters in the text?

Unfortunately Scripture tempts us to identify most often with the characters presented as "good" as opposed to those presented as "evil." Just the

---

[71] Sharon H. Ringe, "Biblical Authority and Interpretation, "35–38.
[72] See Justo L. González and Catherine G. González, *The Liberating Pulpit* (Nashville: Abingdon, 1994), 81.

fact that we are reading "sacred" Scripture, and not some other secular document, leads us to expect certain actions or speeches to be "good" or "bad." Those of us familiar with the New Testament would never expect one of Jesus' many encounters with the religious leaders of his day to end with his saying to them, "You're right! I never thought of it that way, and I was clearly wrong in what I said about you all." The result of this expectation is what we might call a "stereotypical reading." Many of us tend to identify with the good characters and anticipate a certain kind of conclusion. Doing so limits our insights into many passages.

What happens when we read a story several times and each time identify with different characters? What would we see if we identified with Saul when he offered a sacrifice and was condemned for not waiting for Samuel to arrive to offer the sacrifice (1 Sam 13:5–15)? What would the tale of Isaiah's encounter with King Ahaz (Isa 7:10–17) mean, should we put ourselves in the king's shoes? How would it feel to be one of Paul opponents in Galatia when we read some of the things he writes about us (e.g., Gal 5:12)? Some have even suggested that we identify with the ewe lamb in Nathan's little parable told to King David (2 Sam 12:1–7)[73] or with the fatted calf in Jesus' parable of the prodigal son (Luke 15:11–32).

This re-reading through the eyes of different characters is useful no matter what sort of a sermon you plan to prepare, but it is especially so when we are trying to find the oppression and liberation in a particular story. Switching identifications often unveils the power plays taking place in the Scripture and helps us name both those who are being oppressed and those who are oppressing. In this sense, the process is similar to an ideological reading. By reassigning roles we may find ourselves identifying with a character whom we discover is like us—who shares our common humanity—and that character may not always be the protagonist. We may discover our own role to be more like that of the powerful and wealthy than like the poor and oppressed.

Justo L. González and Catherine G. González suggest that, if we try taking the role of Simon Magnus in Acts 8, we may find ourselves to be the powerful and influential set against the despised circle of Christian disciples.[74] The key to such an insight comes, however, when we honestly attend to the social and political situation of the character as well as to our own situation.

To take another example from Acts, try switching roles in the story of Philip and the Ethiopian Eunuch (Acts 8:26–40). First, take the role of

---

[73] Robert McAfee Brown does this very thing in *Unexpected News,* 52–56.
[74] González and González, *The Liberating Pulpit,* 82–83.

Philip, a simple Galilean who dares to offer the gospel message to one who is important by virtue of his place in the royal court. How does it feel to reach out to one whose sexuality may be very different from your own and who has suffered exclusion because of his sexuality? Now, jump into the skin of the Eunuch. The court official is riding along in his chariot and here comes this strange man out of nowhere, but you ask him to help you understand the Scriptures and then allow him to baptize you in a new faith. The Eunuch is a complicated character because, on the one hand, he has been forced by political power brokers to lose his sexual identity but, on the other hand, he has now earned himself a place of prominence and power. Moreover, more than likely the implied author of the story invites us to think of the Eunuch as African American. (The word "Ethiopia" possibly means "the land of the people of burnt faces."[75]) Philip dares to cross social lines of division, because a eunuch would be unclean by the Jewish standards of that day and therefore excluded from participation in his faith community. He dares to instruct one more powerful than he. The eunuch, on the other hand, holds a precarious position of power but seeks instruction from the powerless and poor. There's a sermon there!

Making Connections with Contemporary Situations

Having dug the poor and needy out of the shadows of the text by reassigning the cast of characters, the preacher then needs to ask how their situations and what is happening to them is comparable to something in the contemporary world. Who are the hungry and the homeless today who are squeezed out of the Body of Christ? Who are the exiles today who may feel they are being punished for their sins? Who are the contemporaries to the Ethiopian Eunch and Philip?

An easy example of making a connection between a biblical story and a contemporary situation might be the story of the rich man and Lazarus in Luke 16:19–31. First, it is easy to identify the poor in this story, for Lazarus is nothing if not poor. That is what we are told about him. Changing roles in this story is important, because the good and bad characters are so stereotypically evident. Still, it might help us to take Lazarus' role so that we can better understand what it feels like to be ignored even when we are in need of help. We might also find it helpful to take the rich man's role and watch ourselves as we dream up excuses for not paying any attention to Lazarus. This

---

[75] See Robert Houston Smith, "Ethiopia" and Beverly Roberts Gaventa, "Ethiopian Eunuch," *ABD* (ed. David Noel Freedman; New York: Doubleday, 1992), 2:665–67.

latter identification would help us to understand how we act as the rich man did for sundry reasons, not least of all that we are far too busy to stop and aid such a pitiful creature.

The preacher must next ask how this story of Lazarus and the rich man parallels a contemporary situation. The specificity of Lazarus' lying at the rich man's doorway conjures up images of the homeless we see on our city streets, stretched out in the doorways of stores trying to stay warm. The need of the poor and the responsibility of those who have some wealth is crystal clear, but so too is Jesus' teaching that the way we respond to human need has eternal consequences.

A clear connection with the Isaiah passage concerning the freeing of the exiles considered earlier comes to mind. One of the harsh realities in North American society is that there is a lingering sense that the poor are poor because they have failed to work. There is still an implicit presupposition in our success-oriented society that anyone can succeed if they just try. The victims of poverty may be falsely haunted by the sense that they have been sinful and are being punished. Like exiles, they assume that they are imprisoned for their wrongdoing. The liberating God wants to comfort them and "gather the lambs in his arms and carry them in his bosom" (Isa 40:11).

Jesus' parable of the Pharisee and the tax collector (Luke 18:9–14, the Gospel reading for Proper 25, year C) provides a very different kind of liberation text. Ask who the oppressed are in this parable, and it appears that both characters have been caught in unhappy situations. The tax collector was just trying to make a living for his family and was caught up in a corrupt system of taxation that he found hard to resist. He is a victim of a political system that ruled the country. And, as his prayer indicates, he knows all of this.

But how about the Pharisee? We would not usually think of the Pharisees as oppressed, would we? What is striking about his prayer in this parable, however, is that it is done exactly the way a pious Jew of the time would have prayed. Contrary to popular interpretations of this parable, there is nothing prideful or boastful about his prayer that is not part of the religious piety of the time. The Pharisee is being a good Jew, praying a prayer of thanksgiving. We should remember that, in spite of their almost totally negative portrayal in the Gospels, the Pharisees were a movement of respected lay people who had banded together and pledged themselves to be faithful to all of God's Law as understood in their Scriptures, including the laws usually applicable only to the priests. This Pharisee is a member of a group that seeks to be fully faithful to God. He is not a hypocrite or self-righteous. He is a good Jew practicing the most strenuous application of the Law. We may believe the Pharisee was wrong in his commitment and understanding of the purpose of the law. Jesus clearly declares that the tax collector "went down to his home justified rather than the other" (18:14). Nevertheless, we need to recognize that the Pharisee was in a sense the victim of a system just as the tax collector was. The Pharisee was victimized by a well-intended religious system and prevented by it from praying the tax collector's prayer with him.[76]

One very difficult text is a rich resource for preaching liberation. The story of Jesus and the Syrophoenician woman in Mark 7:24–30 (part of the Gospel lesson for Proper 8, year B) poses many problems for a preacher. We suggest preachers turn those problems into a liberating message. A desperate mother comes looking for healing of her demon-possessed daughter. Jesus' response is curt and appears to be bigoted: "Let the children be fed first, for it is not fair to take the children's food and throw it to the dogs." He said this to a foreigner and a *woman!* She is doubly oppressed, and Jesus treats her as she was probably used to being treated—like one would treat a dog! The English translation, "dogs," is not quite accurate, since the Greek word (*kynes*) actually means "little dogs." (Several centuries earlier in Greece the term was used mockingly of those who eventually took the label as their own, "the Cynics.")

The woman acted in an unconventional way and violated social custom. First, as a woman she should not approach a strange man. Nor should she have assumed the task usually taken by the male head of the household, namely, the protection of the family. Her request, then, was "shameful, drawing both Jesus' refusal and his disdain."[77] (In its Markan version, this story sounds as if Jesus was limited in his vision of his work, believing that God had come to save the Jews, but not others. This woman opens his mind and heart to others.[78]) We can imagine that this mother had learned to stay in the shadows, to remain silent, and above all never to seek privilege. In this case, however, she is frantic to save her daughter and accepts Jesus' label for her ("dog"). But then she turns it around on him: "Sir, even the dogs under the table eat the children's crumbs." Okay, this puppy is ready for only the crumbs if that's all there is. Jesus' new admiration for her is found in his response in v. 29. Note that his response does not say that the woman's faith has brought the healing but that her *word* ("saying") has done it.

---

[76]See Bernard Brandon Scott, *Hear Then the Parable: A Commentary on the Parables of Jesus* (Minneapolis: Fortress, 1989), 94–96 and Joachim Jeremias, *The Parables of Jesus* (2d rev. ed.; New York: Charles Scribner's Sons, 1963), 142–43.

[77]Mary Ann Tolbert, "Mark," *The Women's Bible Commentary,* 269. Much of this discussion of the story draws on Tolbert's remarks (268–69).

[78]Joanna Dewey writes of this story, "The Syrophenician woman has led the Markan Jesus to enlarge the boundaries to include even Gentiles: in the next episode . . . he feeds four thousand Gentiles. A great abundance of crumbs!" "The Gospel of Mark," in *Searching the Scriptures: A Feminist Commentary,* 485.

Here is a model for the boldness and bravery of oppressed women who refuse to kowtow to the patriarchal system. A reader of Mark cannot help but compare her to Jairus whose request of Jesus is fulfilled (5:21–43)—but he was a man, a Jew, and a prominent leader. We remember, too, that Jesus healed the demoniac at Gerasenes, and he was surely a Gentile—but also a man! We cannot avoid the possibility that Jesus refused this mother more because she was a woman than that she was a Gentile. She was a woman, moreover, who had broken social custom and violated social propriety. While she assumed an inferior role, she was actually undercutting the basis on which Jesus had expressed his denial of her request. Turning his saying upside down, she turned the social system oppressing women upside down. The liberating Jesus saw and affirmed this foreigner's assertion. The church, likewise, is called to affirm and support those who challenge oppressive and tyrannical systems.

Who are those oppressed by the system—whether social, political, or religious—today? It could be those who have bought into a religious system that teaches them that faithful Christian practice results in financial wealth. It could be those who are entangled in a religious system that entails their absolute loyalty to a charismatic leader, even when that leader calls on them to take their own lives. It could be a religious system that teaches that your infant died because it was God's will. What religious systems are destructive in our day? In our denomination? In our congregation? How does the Gospel offer liberation from such systems?

Liberation interpretations almost all agree that Jesus identified himself with the poor and the needy of his day, and in fact was one of the poor. Yet the church seems to stand aloof from the poor, whether they be in the cities or in rural areas. What does Jesus' life of poverty mean for the church today?

Designing a Liberating Sermon

Finally, having identified the poor and needy in a passage and having made a connection between their situation in the text and in a contemporary situation, we are tasked to design a sermon intended to offer liberation to the oppressed—in whatever form that oppression may take. The process of designing a liberation sermon is no different from the steps through which we go to prepare any sermon. What we seek to do here is to offer two simple steps which might be added to one's usual process of sermon preparation when the goal is liberation preaching.

First, designing a liberation sermon requires that we identify the social and political dimensions of a text and of the congregation and do so as specifically as we can.[79] In some cases, the preacher will be asking the congregation to think very differently about a biblical passage as in the example discussed above, that of the Pharisee and the tax collector. While our congregations probably know the Exodus story as part of the story of the beginnings of the nation of Israel, and will remember the crossing of the Red Sea as a wondrous miracle, they may need help in seeing the story as a political power struggle between powerless slaves and the Pharaoh's immense power. They may hesitate to go along with the preacher's exploration of who might be political slaves today and of how God is seeking to free them. Many congregations may have never thought of the Jesus movement as a political revolution with a call to social upheaval. One may, however, find more acceptance and appreciation of such readings than expected, because among some congregations there is a keen sense of the injustice in the distribution of wealth in the USA.

The identification of the social and political dimensions of a text and of the current situation of a congregation needs to be as specific as possible. It may help to name the social and political realities of the text with contemporary language. The complaints of the dissatisfied workers in the vineyard in Matt 20:1–16 are much like modern workers' filing a complaint with management and are similar to the modern beginnings of a process of unionization. The question to Jesus about paying taxes (Matthew 22:17 and Mark12:14) may indicate similarities to the modern beginnings of a taxpayers' revolt. The Psalms often speak of the poor and thereby imply class differences among the Hebrew people. One wants to be as specific as possible in naming the social and political oppression in the text. In a similar fashion one needs to do the same with regard to the contemporary situation that we believe is comparable to the one in the text of the Scripture. How would North American women feel today if they were forced to veil themselves in public, as the Corinthian women had to keep their heads covered when they worshiped (1 Cor 11:4–6)? How are the poor exploited today in a way comparable to Amos' condemnation of Judah (2:6–7; 5:10–12; 8:4–6)? How does the effort to move the poor out of the way for a freeway by eminent domain compare to the situation in Amos? How does shipping all of the homeless out of center city when a large convention is coming to town compare to the exile? Identify the social and political dimensions of a text and of the congregation and do so as specifically as possible.[80]

---

[79] Ronald J. Allen gives an excellent example of the way in which preachers quiz the text to add specificity to a liberation sermon on Jer 22:13–17. *Contemporary Biblical Interpretation for Preaching* (Valley Forge, Pa.: Judson, 1984), 100–102.

[80] See Robert Kysar, *Called to Care: Biblical Images for Social Ministry* (Minneapolis: Fortress, 1991), 44–51.

Second, designing a liberation sermon entails announcing the liberation of the present congregation in order to empower them for a ministry of liberation. Preaching liberation does not mean beating the congregation with what they should be doing for the poor and oppressed in the world. While that sort of a sermon usually stirs a good deal of guilt, guilt is probably not a sufficient motivation for action, at least not for a lasting commitment to action.[81] A congregation may express their appreciation to you for "preaching the law," for "telling it as it is," and for "giving them hell." When we know we are guilty of neglecting some action, it actually makes us feel better to be charged with that neglect. But the guilt soon wears off and fails to produce lasting action.

Congregations that understand their own liberation from oppression in Christ are more likely to act to liberate others than those who simply feel guilty for their neglect of social needs. This means that preaching the good news of God's liberating act in Christ becomes the foundation for fostering agents of liberation today. Some have discussed this preaching of the good news in terms of the *indicative* and the *imperative*. The indicative is the declaration of what God has done for us, and the imperative is what we are asked to do in response. The imperative is more effective when it is rooted in and arises from the indicative. Announcing God's liberation of the congregation is the basis on which the preacher asks the congregation to be active in causes that liberate others.

Suppose we are preaching from the story of the tax collector, Zacchaeus, in Luke 19:1–10. The story offers us an example of the relationship of the indicative to the imperative. Notice that Jesus takes the initiative to approach Zacchaeus and announces that he will come to the tax collector's home for dinner (v. 5). Verse 7 makes clear the disdain the villagers have for this cheating little man. He is a social outcast, who lives in isolation from all but those of his own kind. That does not bother Jesus. In the eyes of some, Zacchaeus' sinfulness will rub off on Jesus if he dines in the tax collector's home; but dine he does.[82] Jesus acts in friendship toward this friendless creature, and Zacchaeus spontaneously and unsolicitedly makes his pledge: "Look, half of my possessions, Lord, I will give to the poor; and if I have defrauded anyone of anything, I will pay back four times as much" (19:8–9). Jesus then declares that salvation has come to Zacchaeus' house because "he too is a son of Abraham" (v. 9).

---

[81] See the important little book by George S. Johnson, *Beyond Guilt and Powerlessness* (Minneapolis: Augsburg Fortress, 1989).

[82] See Fred B. Craddock, *Luke* (IBC; Louisville: John Knox, 1990), 218–20.

The social situations are clear. Here is a social outcast, a little man who again and again is lumped in with sinners (Luke 15:1–2), yet Jesus befriends him even to the degree of eating in his home. Jesus' act is pure grace—unmerited, unearned love and acceptance. This is the indicative of the passage. Zacchaeus responded and drew the imperative for himself. He did not even have to be told what he should do! He had cheated many people in his role a chief tax collector—not only the common people but also probably the tax collectors under his supervision. Now he will support the poor and right his wrongs by serving others. This is a powerful passage of liberation. It tells us of God's liberating action on behalf of Zacchaeus and of Zacchaeus' becoming the liberator of others as an act of gratitude and faith.

The precedent of the indicative that leads to the imperative assumes that God's action in our lives makes us *want* to act toward others as God has acted toward us. Preaching in that order will prove more effective in empowering a congregation to become agents of liberation than preaching about guilt.

Of course, how one preaches liberation depends a great deal on one's congregation. Do they experience first hand the racism and deprivation that calls for the assurance of God's liberating presence in our world? Are they victims of sexism or economic loss? What are the issues faced by members of the congregation? Unemployment? Poverty? Homelessness? Sexual abuse?

One of us once served as pastor of a congregation in an economically depressed region. The old coal mines that once made this a prosperous region had long since been shut down. There was no attraction for new businesses. The young people were leaving the area in droves. Two-thirds of the men over fifty suffered from "black lung" and were on disability support. Equally important was the fact that the economic depression brought about a kind of social and individual depression. Many parishioners thought very little of themselves. They were unworthy of any of the attention we wanted to give them. Our preaching in that situation had to address this difuse and pervasive despondency and despair. All of the efforts to right the injustice done to them by the coal barons had long ago been exhausted—that was no longer an issue. Now this congregation needed liberation from the social hopelessness that had overcome them. The circumstances peculiar to this region determined the kind of liberation preaching we were called to bring to the pulpit.

Like all good preaching, liberation preaching requires preachers to know their congregations. Liberation interpretation, moreover, must be linked to committed action in the community. The issues in the community provide the context by which the interpreter comes to the text. Liberation preaching calls for a pastor and a congregation to be engaged in their community, to struggle with whatever is of vital importance in that community, and to be willing to read and preach texts the meanings of which are shaped by those struggles. Good preachers are usually good pastors. To preach effectively and to be relevant to the lives of the parishioners, clergy must be attuned to the congregation's and the community's needs. Good preachers need to exegete their congregations and communities as well as biblical texts.[83]

A SAMPLE SERMON

The following sermon was preached at a workshop for pastors and laity on sexual abuse. The simple worship service was the opening event for the workshop, and the reading for the day was Mark 5:21–34. The preacher sought to characterize the oppression of abused people with the oppression of the woman with the hemorrhage, whose story Mark sandwiched between his telling of the healing of Jairus' daughter. The goal of the sermon was to empower the congregation with confidence that they could be the agents of healing for the abused. Clearly the end of the sermon attempts to declare the good news of Jesus' suffering and death for us as the basis for the imperative to offer others Christ's healing.

---

[83] One of the best books on this topic is Leonora Tubbs Tisdale, *Preaching as Local Theology and Folk Art* (Fortress Resources for Preaching; Minneapolis: Fortress, 1997).

"A Touch"

Mark 5:21–34

SHE WAS MADE TO FEEL SO SHAMEFUL—THIS HEMORRHAGING WOMAN! TWELVE LONG years. An outcast. Unclean. Made dirty. The shame she was made to bear, because of what had been done to her body. Not for what she had done, but for what had been done to her and to her body. It was bad enough having been born a woman. But now this—this demon that haunted her within, that sapped her of her life blood. The shame she was made to feel because of it.

And the misunderstanding of it! She suffered still more because of those who would not understand, who could not allow themselves to understand— those so-called healers! Dismissed. Ignored. Incurable. "It must be your fault— your fault that this has come upon you!" She had endured much at their hands, at their misunderstanding.

And the silence of it! Like a death shroud, it slipped over her. No one would even speak it, so she dare not speak it. It was made unspeakable. Too horrible to mention. Too threatening even to put into words. Silent. Hidden away. Concealed in the darkness of wordlessness.

And the desperation of it! Could she never speak it? Could she never be understood? Was there no healing? It grew worse day by day! Would she for her whole life carry within her body this unspeakable secret, this shameful reality?

Driven to desperation, she wiggled her way through the crowd, hoping no one would recognize her. No one must know. Not even him! For he, too, might not understand.

She could not face him and ask it of him. Not like Jairus—Jairus, the man! Jairus, the leader of the synagogue! Jairus, the respected and honored! No, she must approach him from behind, from behind—where she would not be seen. As invisible as she was silent. She could ask nothing of him. She must simply touch him.

He was on his way now to Jairus' home. His attention fixed on what he must do there. He would never know. Never notice. Just a touch. Not a word. Not a plea. Just a touch. A touch arising out of the tiny embryo of faith. A touch arising from an unspoken confidence: "If I but touch his clothes, I will be made well!" After all, he had healed others with *his* touch. Now perhaps *her* touch of just the hem of his garment would be enough.

The trembling hand went out and touched. And with a touch, a surge of power, a charge of empowerment, a spark of strength.

"Who touched my clothes?" he asked.

She cowered in the crowd, wanting not to be discovered, not to be known. But her new power emboldened her to speak, to confess her offense.

Still trembling from head to toe, she fell at his feet, her eyes fixed on the ground, frozen in fear. She had done it—she the unclean one, the dirty one—she had done it!

And without hesitation, he spoke to her. Spoke and broke the awful silence. Spoke without shaming! Spoke without misunderstanding.

"Daughter, your faith has made you well; go in peace and be healed of your disease."

He called her *daughter!* And with that single word shattered the prison of silence. And with that single word embraced her in the arms of love, and claimed her as his own. His word declared her well, healed, whole! And the silence was broken. The shame lifted. The misunderstanding dissolved. And a daughter went her way in peace, in wholeness.

With this remarkable story Mark represents all those who feel the shame, who are ignored. All those driven to silence. This woman is anyone who cannot speak their secret, even to Christ. This one woman, who does not even merit her own story. This one woman whose story is sandwiched between episodes in the healing of another. This one woman, who is not allowed to speak in her own story, except as she speaks to herself. She is all those who are silenced by the tragedy of their lives. All those who feel they must approach Christ from behind are this hemorrhaging woman. All those who feel they must hide in the crowd are her sisters and brothers.

Yes, all those, whose lives have been raped by abuse, whose souls are scared by terrible offense. Yes, all those—Let the silence now be broken—who have suffered sexual violence, ravaged by the madness of others, violated by twisted souls. They are this woman. They are this woman to whom Christ spoke the healing Word.

And there is still a healing Christ-Word. There is still a Word that still breaks the silence, even as it broke the silence for that woman. There is a Word that still shatters the shame, lifts the burden of misunderstanding, and overcomes the desperation.

It is that suffering, hemorrhaging, dying Word. That Word, who himself went into the shadows of shame, and was broken under the weight of misunderstanding and injustice. That Word who was silent, silent, except for a cry of abandonment. The same cry that explodes from every abused soul: "My God, my God . . . why?"

That Word still heals and makes the brokenness whole. For he was broken for every one of us. He was silent for every one of us. He was shamed for every one of us. And from the garments of that Word still flow the power—the power of God's peace-making care and compassion. For those who approach him from behind in the crowd there is still the embracing word. "Daughter . . . son, your faith has made you well; go in peace and be healed!"

But where in the crowd today are they to find that Word? Where among the throng today is the garment to touch? Where is the healing Word found for the hemorrhaging, the silent, the shamed, the desperate? To whose garments can they reach out?

Might they touch our garments? Might they touch our water soaked garments and find their wholeness there? Our garments soaked in grace with which we have been clothed by the grace of God. Our garments put on with a splash of water and silence-breaking words, "I baptize you . . ." Our garments put on in the address, "child of God," put on with the seal of the Spirit. Put on with the sign of the cross.

Baptized into Christ, we have put on Christ. Might our garments, then, become the garments of that Word, the empowered Word, the health-giving Word? Our garments washed in his hemorrhage on the cross for all the hemorrhaging of the world.

Might they touch our garments?

Chapter 5

What Difference Do Deconstruction Theories Make?

Few hermeneutical constructs or theories from the past couple of decades have been so energetic or more enigmatic than those associated with the notion of *deconstruction*. The word itself gives the clue to its larger framework, a framework against which the theory is a kind of rebellion. That framework was known throughout the twentieth century as structuralism. (See Chapter Three for an introduction to structuralism.) As many have pointed out, the word deconstruction, then, means to "de-structure," or to "de-struct." Others have simply used the term *post-structuralism,* intending by it to take in various related forms of "de-structuring."

While during the first half of the Twentieth Century literary scholars were occupied with describing the nature and intricacies of textual "structure," appreciating both its order and beauty, the second half of the century changed all that. Beginning in the 1950s in Europe but spreading to the United States through the 1960s and 1970s, a literary rebellion began. It was, to be sure, a part of the larger currents of the age. At its root, its anti-rationalism was an outgrowth of the profound European revulsions against the Nazi holocaust, quickly supplemented by American upheavals for racial justice and uprisings against a war in Southeast Asia. Everything intellectual, aesthetic, and spiritual was affected, if not changed, by a kind of global turmoil. Reason, order, beauty, logical structure—all were severely challenged, including language and literature. Instead of celebrating what appeared to be clarity and structure, it was necessary to challenge it, even rebel against it, to "de-structure" it. No one understood the effect of this kind of thinking on literature more keenly at the time than the French scholar and critic Jacques Derrida. It was he who announced in the late

1960s what amounted to a celebration of de-structuralism; or, in his memorable word, "deconstruction."[1]

Because of the peculiarities of this movement and its complexities, we have chosen to deal with it in a way different from the previous chapters. It seems best to probe the meaning of the movement by seeking to understand its founder. Homiletical observations will be scattered throughout the exposition of Derrida's work.

THE ROOTS OF DECONSTRUCTION

Behind the work of Derrida—and others who have given themselves in recent years to deconstructing textual materials—lay a much deeper current. It is important that we understand this deeper current in order to put the deconstruction hermeneutic into its proper framework. In the opening years of the twentieth century, significant human research done particularly by social scientists, anthropologists, and linguists began to redefine the very nature of language itself. So pervasive and far-reaching did their work on the nature of human language become that they are the ones who created the groundwork out of which the explosive work of Derrida and the deconstructionists emerged.

The Language Revolution

To summarize briefly, that language revolution argued—and continues to argue—that a word has no logical or inherent connection to any particular "referent" outside of itself. The word "cat" is in no way related to a cat. That

---

[1] Derrida is not, to be sure, easy to read. His books are numerous and complex, utilizing language and language constructions that, even in translation from French, are never easy to follow. The reader seeking a good introduction not only to Derrida, but to deconstructive theory, would do well to begin with the 600-plus page collection of Derrida's work edited by Peggy Kamuf, *A Derrida Reader: Between the Blinds* (New York: Columbia University Press, 1991). All citations in this chapter will indicate pages drawn from that book, to be referred to as *Reader*, even though in most cases an indication of the source material itself will be given as well. Four books by Derrida, in particular, provide what we believe to be the best way into Derrida's work: *Of Grammatology* (trans. Gayatri Chakranorty Spivak; Baltimore: Johns Hopkins Press, 1976); *Dissemination* (trans. Barbara Johnson; Chicago: University of Chicago Press, 1981); *The Post Card: From Socrates to Freud and Beyond* (trans. Alan Bass; Chicago: University of Chicago Press, 1987); and *Glas* (trans. John P. Leavey Jr. and Richard Rand; Lincoln: University of Nebraska Press, 1986).

animal could be called "anything" and as long as everyone who had one knew what it was called, the word would "refer" to that animal. Objects are called what they are not because there is some irrevocable or innate linkage between word and object. People "agree" together to call something by one particular name instead of some other. When people decide to call it something else, the meaning of that particular word can, and often does, undergo change.

That a word *did,* in fact, have a binding, even universal, relation to the object to which it referred is the idea of the older *referential theory of language.* (See the next chapter.) However, it gradually gave way as social research began to understand language and its usage in a new way. Ever so subtly (as far as the public was concerned) what emerged was a very different and more relativistic understanding of words, of language, and, of anything textual. It is true that the mental mechanism for learning language appears to be species-specific, meaning that all humans appear to have an innate capacity for language learning. However, the language that is actually learned by a human being is the one that is used within the particular cultural group, or sub-group, in which one is reared. Consequently one group calls an object one thing while another group (even one using the same language) may refer to the same object with a different term or expression. This explains, for example, the long-standing problem of why different people can look at the same thing and call it by different names, or understand it differently.

Results of the Revolution

The most profound effect of this change was that it broke down the notion that there was one "correct" or "true" name for something, which everyone should use. The question now became whose name for this or that was indeed the "correct" one that everyone who sought "truth" should actually use. Everyone involved in such an enterprise was sure that the name employed by his or her group was the true name. They therefore assumed that, for harmony to exist, all others should accept that they should drop their own designation for something and adopt "ours." In biblical studies, as we have seen earlier, this meant that we have been forced to surrender the notion that there is one true interpretation of any text.

It did not take very long for many to appreciate the validity of the new orientation to words and language. Indeed, it was very difficult to dispute the emergent premise that, at its root, language itself is relative. The words we use and what we mean by them—and even how much emotion we invest in them—are largely passed along to us by the groups and the cultures in which we grow up. Their words become our words; their emotions, wrapped in language, become our emotions; their ways of cursing and praising become our ways of cursing and praising.

This new view of language gradually affected virtually everything involved in the process of creating and reading texts of all kinds. Language was no longer viewed as neutral or objective in any way. Texts reflected the cultures and the power relations within the cultures from which they sprang. In a sense, one had to be suspicious of texts, since it was not always possible to readily detect the "icebergs" that lay hidden beneath their surface. Moreover, since every reader came to a text with his or her own cultural sets of words, meanings, and feelings, what the reader "found" in a given text was not so much a result of what the author had put there as it was a result of what the reader brought to it (see Chapter Three). Moreover, since writer and reader no doubt had different meanings for the words that were on the page, the idea of where the "truth" of those words actually lay had to be found in a middle ground. Or, perhaps there simply was no truth in the words! For centuries the dominant question in the interpretation of texts was "what is the truth of this writing?" Now, however, the new questions were: "Why has this writer written these words?" and "What does this writer hope to accomplish by writing this particular text?" The hunt was on for the viewpoint and the motive behind or under any given text.

Texts are "structured" to accomplish particular goals more than they are to elucidate "truth," which can no longer be readily discerned in some objective, once-and-for-all sense. Even the search for a text of beauty is suspect, since it is presumed to reflect hidden understandings, assumptions, and even culture-specific ambitions, no matter who the author is. In fact, from this perspective, the writer becomes relatively insignificant. What must now be given the highest priority in the examination of a text is how it is used as the writer's "weapon" on behalf of a particular cultural, political, or even religious perspective.

Fruits of the Revolution

All of this represents the intellectual soil from which the work of literary deconstructionists like Derrida emerged beginning in the late 1960s. This was their view of language and literature, one that was profoundly different from the understanding of language and text that had prevailed for centuries. Led by Derrida, the deconstructions began with a clear set of notions about what they had to do with texts. Three of their main concerns can be summarized in the following way.

First, the idea of "what is true?" was simply an irrelevant question, because it was no longer answerable. Why should one even try to pose it?

Second, since writing was envisioned as embodying complex histories, power struggles, and the use of language to accomplish goals or ends, it became important—even urgent—to get into and behind the writing to uncover what goal was hidden throughout and under the texts themselves. It was necessary to bring those latent and very powerful dimensions of past and power out into the open.

Third, all of this was necessary so that any dialogue that readers have with a text could be a fully *informed* dialogue. To be informed means that readers have to be able to "come clean" with a text, and that the text needs to "come clean" with readers. We need those textual dialogues—particularly with biblical texts—but we need our dialogues to be fully exposed and honest, so that any "new meanings" we struggle with are based on an unmasking (as it were) of hidden messages from the past.

To accomplish this, Derrida argued, one has to "de-construct" the text. At its most basic level, as we shall see, that process is a highly skeptical form of textual analysis. Many books have been written by theologians and scholars of biblical literature who were impacted by deconstructive work. Preachers are faced not only with reading and assessing the work of such scholars, but also with the implications of reading a text through their own deconstructive eyes. We know very well that the results of such reading will probably not be what most clergy learned in seminary. What are we who are interested in "sacred text" to do with deconstruction? Does it affect us? What are we to do with it in our week-in and week-out studies of biblical texts for preaching?

Constructive Deconstruction

What needs to be said about textual or literary deconstruction is what has to be said about the larger umbrella under which it resides, postmodernism: everything in moderation. There are, as some have called them "skeptical postmodernists," who reject any assertions of ultimate truth, and "affirmative postmodernists," who are "constructive" in that they affirm certain norms. That same distinction applies to deconstruction. Deconstruction itself has gotten a bad name, largely because of scholars for whom the best synonym for deconstruction is "destruction." These, whom Rosenau calls the "skeptical" postmodern, we might call "destructive deconstructionists,"[2] who deconstruct in order to destroy. Strangely, this has become the popular view of deconstruction. Without question, there are many scholars in numerous

---

[2]Pauline Marie Rosenau, *Postmodernism and the Social Sciences: Insights, Inroads, and Intrusions* (Princeton: Princeton University Press, 1992).

fields (including theology and biblical studies) who practice destructive deconstruction and who believe that a kind of textual annihilation is precisely where it is supposed to lead.

Not all deconstructionist scholars believe this, however. There is a deconstruction that is *not* fundamentally destructive at all, or at least that does not set out to be. Following Rosenau again, we might call these critics affirmative, positive, or even constructive deconstructionists. Even Derrida believed, somewhat passionately, that the deconstruction he practiced as a literary critic was a positive act when used to understand or come to terms with a text.

The difference between destructive and constructive deconstructionists seems to be much more a matter of the "intention" of the interpreter, rather than their methodological orientation or procedure. If one wishes, it is possible to use deconstructive procedures to destroy a text. However, most critics use deconstructive procedures to *open* a text to fresh scrutiny and insight. They seek to know the text anew in an effort to affirm it in some way. For preachers and biblical scholars, who wish to affirm a text, deconstructive methods can provide a remarkable way to study the text with an eye toward that affirmation.

OPENING THE DOORS TO THE TEXT

Having reached this point, then, we wish to turn specifically to the work of Derrida himself, since a survey of all those who have learned from him, reacted to him, or tried to build "artifices" of their own work atop his, would be far beyond the scope of this brief chapter. What we wish to do, instead, is to provide some strands of Derrida's ideas and insights that we believe open doors onto textual analysis and deconstruction for those who study and preach from biblical texts. We wish to provide a sense of the texture of Derrida's work for those who have not read him, so that preachers might be able to decide whether they wish to delve more deeply into the veins than Derrida has unearthed. On a different level, our task is to lay out a few of Derrida's ideas about text, some of which are far more constructive than many credit Derrida with being. We do so in order to help preachers develop a "constructive" eye toward the textual work of deconstruction.

When Derrida began his work in Europe in the mid-1960s, it was with a clear desire to "change the rules," to "deconstruct" the old, "out-of-date" ways of thinking and to replace them with new premises and goals.[3] Ac-

---

[3] Accounts of Derrida's origins and general historical/literary orientation can be found in many places. One that is particularly useful and readily accessible is Robert

cording to Derrida the times called "for a new theory and for the constitution of new statutes and conventions that, capable of recording the possibility of such events, would be able to account for them."[4] Derrida's stance was that of a *critic,* and he contended that criticism was not a "reactive" form of writing, secondary to literature. Criticism itself, he argued, is a primary "strategy of intervention" in the affairs of society. His orientation to critical thinking and writing was an "activist" one, designed to change outlooks and orientations.

It is difficult to overstate Derrida's influence not just on Western literature but on Western philosophy during the second half of the twentieth century. From his seminal articles in the 1960s on critical method—the work in which he developed the concept of "deconstruction"—to his books of the 1970s and 1980s in which he not only explained what he meant but actually *demonstrated* it, Derrida became a virtual symbol of postmodernism himself. As such, his writings are difficult to grasp, requiring that the reader not only read in a different way but come to terms with the meaning and nature of language itself in an unexpected fashion. With practice, though, a reader can become somewhat adept not only at fathoming but even appreciating Derrida's uniquely disjointed postmodern expression.

Making Way for a Future

Why deconstruction? As we indicated earlier, for Derrida, it was not a negative program; it involved some negative actions and dimensions, but behind it lay a need to create something new from old texts. For Derrida, these ongoing tasks of re-construction could not proceed without deconstruction taking place first. In his famous *Letter to a Japanese Friend,* he wrote that,

> the undoing, decomposing, and desedimenting of structures, in a certain sense more historical than the structuralist movement it called into question, is not a negative operation. Rather than destroying, it was also necessary to understand how an "ensemble" is constituted and to reconstruct it to this end.[5]

Moreover, for Derrida, deconstruction is not something that one imposes on language or any other system. Deconstruction is, by its own nature,

---

Con Davis, *Contemporary Literary Criticism: Modernism through Post-Structuralism* (New York: Longman, 1986). Derrida is the concluding section of the book. His place in the history of French philosophy is found in Robert Wicks, *Modern French Philosophy: From Existentialism to Postmodernism* (Oxford: Oneworld, 2003).

[4] *Reader,* 207, 208.

[5] *Reader,* 41, from *Of Grammatology.*

a "normal" process, and to become involved in deconstructive work is merely to follow, or to become involved, in a natural phenomenon. "Deconstruction takes place," he wrote to the Japanese friend. "It is an event that does not await the deliberation, consciousness or organization of a subject, or even of modernity. [Everything] deconstructs itself."[6] Derrida's view was that to deconstruct is to participate in the active, productive process of "disengaging the past." However it was not a way of getting rid of the past, but a way of constantly reconstructing it. At one point, he described deconstruction as a "responsible" way of "distancing" oneself from the past. Nonetheless one could distance oneself from the past only by having lived that "past" from the inside, from within its language, philosophy, and structures.

> The movements of deconstruction do not destroy structures from the outside. They are not possible or effective, nor can they take accurate aim, except by inhabiting those structures. Inhabiting them in a certain way, because one always inhabits, and all the more when one does not suspect it. Operating necessarily from the inside, borrowing all the strategic and economic resources of subversion from the old structure, borrowing them structurally, that is to say, without being able to isolate their elements and atoms, the enterprise of deconstruction always in a certain way falls prey to its own work.[7]

Why does one subvert as a part of deconstructing? Derrida's answer was that only in so doing do we make possible the process of "invention," a concept that he likes very much. "It is inventive, or it is nothing at all," is the way he phrased it at one point. Every invention builds on what preceded it; yet, at the same time, it wipes it out and replaces the previous invention. "Out with the old; in with the new," we might say. For Derrida to create a new invention always produces a "disordering mechanism that, when it makes its appearance (opens) up a space of unrest or turbulence to every status assignable to it." Derrida asks: "Is not (an invention) then spontaneously destabilizing, even deconstructive?" He continues: "In what respect can a movement of deconstruction, far from being limited to the negative or destructuring forms that are often naively attributed to it, be inventive in itself, or be the signal of an inventiveness at work in a sociohistorical field?"[8]

His response to those questions is that deconstruction is endlessly "inventive," because it alone "opens up a passageway" into a new way of seeing and thinking. It "marks a trail." Thus, deconstruction itself is an "affirma-

---

[6] Ibid., 41.
[7] Ibid., 41.
[8] This discussion begins on 217 of the *Reader* from *Psyche: Inventions of the Other*.

tion" of something, an event, an "advent," an "invention."[9] What is "invented" by linguistic and literary deconstruction? Always, says Derrida, such deconstructions invent—or "re-invent"—a new "future." More than that, deconstruction invents a future that cannot be designed in advance, but one that constantly seeks to "de-invent" the merely "possible" and make way for the "impossible." "For a deconstructive operation," Derrida writes,

> possibility would . . . be the danger, the danger of becoming an available set of rule-governed procedures, methods, accessible approaches. The interest of deconstruction . . . is a certain experience of the impossible, in other words, as the only possible invention.[10]

In many ways, Derrida's handling of the concept of "deconstruction" is haphazard. Still, its outlines are not difficult to find: deconstruction is the positive means by which new futures are "allowed" to come into being. These are futures containing what is thought to be impossible. That is how he framed the underpinnings of the deconstructive program.

Four Approaches

So how, for Derrida, does deconstruction work? Ironically, nowhere in his numerous books does Derrida actually come right out and answer that seminal question: How does one do this?[11] Instead, at various places, he

---

[9] Ibid., 218.

[10] Ibid., 209.

[11] In his *Letter to a Japanese Friend,* Derrida says emphatically that deconstruction is "not a method and cannot be transformed into one"; neither is it, he adds, "an act or an operation." Then he says this: "Deconstruction is neither an analysis nor a critique and its translation (into Japanese) would have to take that into consideration. It is not an analysis in particular because the dismantling of a structure is not a regression toward the simple element, toward an indissoluble origin" (*Reader,* 274). What becomes clear in his discussion, though, is that he is trying, for the most part, to explain why deconstruction is so difficult to define, summing it up like this: "All the predicates, all the defining concepts, all the lexical significations, and even the syntactic articulations, which seem at one moment to lend themselves to this definition or that translation, are also deconstructed or deconstructible, directly or otherwise. And that goes for the very word, the very unit of the word deconstruction, as for every word" (*Reader,* 274). At one level, what Derrida writes here must be taken seriously, since he is merely trying to carry his concept all the way out to its logical conclusion. Yet, one does not read very far into his work without discovering that he is, indeed, very concerned at a number of points with the "how" of the process of deconstruction. Derrida's *Letter to a Japanese Friend* can be found in a variety of places (*Reader,* 269–75). Others have criticized Derrida's deconstruction on the basis that it

engages in extended discussions of what can only be understood as "methods," though something in him does not want to call them that. Even so, to actually focus on what we will designate as "method" is itself somewhat of a stretch, since they are not what we are used to understanding as method or procedure: Do this—and that will follow.

What Derrida gives us, instead, are ways to let a text bestow on us what we can best call a "new consciousness." By new consciousness he seems to have meant a new way of understanding what we are reading and what is *behind* what we are reading. Beyond that, it is a new way of understanding ourselves in the world as a result of what we discover about this or that text. This, we hope, will become clearer as we articulate four of his "approaches" to "constructively deconstructing" a text. Using Derrida's own language, we will sketch our understanding and apply it to the preacher's task of study and preparation for a sermon.

Word-consciousness. The first approach that one can learn from Derrida is what might be designated as the development of an intense "word-consciousness." Before we think about how one becomes "word conscious" in a practical and useful way, it is necessary to understand something of the richness and complexity of how Derrida understands the nature of language. For Derrida, as for all deconstructionists, at one level words are heavy with the freight of all that they have been through. They do not have "meaning," as such. They have many meanings—even countless meanings—depending on who has used those words in the past. Words also have a kind of collected "hierarchy," which means that many words have been used for the establishment and maintenance of power relationships. They have been used for subjugation, or sometimes ridicule and even banishment. Words have been used to show homage, praise, or even worship of a master, a king, or a god, or God. The fine distinctions of time, place, and use may be lost, but the emotional and cognitive residues adhere to the words.

Trace. As a result of his view of the nature of language and words, Derrida does not like to talk about "words" or "signs." Instead, he utilizes the notion of the "trace" as a way of talking about the word or the sign. Moreover, one would expect him to talk about the problem of "meaning" in language as well, and yet his view of "meaning" is even more elusive than his view of "word" or "sign." It does, however, emerge from a discussion of the issues surrounding the "trace."

---

is self-defeating. If deconstruction is effective on all kinds of statements and methods, then it is itself subject to that claim. "[The] deconstructionist perspective applies to all perspectives, including itself, and is thereby self-referentially consistent" (Wicks, *Modern French Philosophy,* 209).

Derrida acknowledges that a word is a "thing," in a sense; some identifiable object. But it is ephemeral; it cannot be possessed. It can never be pinned down. One grabs for it for a flashing instant, and even tries to capture it on paper, but that, itself, is a strangely futile undertaking. Even on the page, the word is not trapped. To have it is to turn loose of it; to have it, in fact, is for an instant to "effect" it, to "scratch" it or even to "smudge" it. To have it is to "disturb the order of the world," as Derrida at one point puts it. When a word appears, moves away and passes by, it exists as only a "trace," an invisible "mark," leaving behind only the "scar" of where it has been. That mark may indicate a fleeting presence, or even a fleeting absence. Still, after leaving the "mark," the "trace" itself disappears into the formation of the unconscious. After a moment of consciousness, it becomes part of that "other" human realm. The "resonance" of the trace may linger indefinitely, even when the time and place of the encounter are long forgotten.

In various ways throughout his writing, Derrida says the trace is also what establishes "intimate relationship" between that which connects the human "inside" to everything exterior to itself. This is a "spatial" connection, as it were, tying together "living present" with the "outside." Derrida thus refers to the "trace" as the "opening to exteriority in general." It is also the trace, Derrida says, that engages the human struggle over the concepts of past, present, and future; i.e., the problem of time, the temporal. Do words appear? Are they part of the present? How do they connect past and future? For Derrida, the present is the most elusive category of all. It is the "future" until the moment it emerges, and then, as soon as it emerges, it becomes the past. This makes of the present, in Derrida's deconstructive framework, a "false appearance." Traces move by us so quickly that the idea of something "remaining," becoming fixed in a present, probably cannot be. "There remain only traces," he says, "announcement (future) and souvenirs (past), foreplays and aftereffects which no present will have preceded or followed and which cannot be arranged on a line around a point, traces here anticipating, there recalling, in the future, in the past, under the false appearance of a present."[12]

This sense of "word" or "trace" is important to Derrida because it emphasizes the utterly fleeting nature of language and social activity, its transitoriness, and its constantly shifting nature. And yet, in all of the movement, in all of the shifting, the traces are left. The marks of the verbalizations remain, however faintly. What we as individuals are at any given moment, constantly fading from past into future, is a cumulative compilation of those traces. Every element, or "trace," that passes across the "scene," or our "present," not

---

[12] The discussion of the "trace" is described in *Reader,* 185 and in "The Double Session," *Dissemination,* 173–286.

only has the mark of past "traces," but every trace carries within it as well all of the "traces" of a future that has not even opened up before us yet.

Thus, for Derrida, words are not "fixed" on a page, despite their writtenness; they are ephemeral. They cannot be pinned down. In a sense, as Derrida points out with such care, they hardly exist at all in the present. So what "marks" or "scars" do the traces (the words) leave? Derrida's underlying question, therefore, is how those of us who read and become fully and deliberately conscious of words that are on a page are then able to treat them as important and yet as "only" traces left behind, like scratches on an ancient cave wall that are (at the same time) not important either.

Spacing. There are two other dimensions of word-consciousness for Derrida. The first he discusses using the strange, but again fascinating, notion of "spacing." Between every trace, he says, (every word?) there is a space, a distance, a separation, a sense of otherness. This is the counter-side of the paradox of how everything tends to "flow together." Not only is there a "space" between every trace, but there is also "spacing" between the human being who uses the trace and the trace itself. In short, we are not the traces, and they are not us. There is always that otherness about the traces that comprise us. At one point, Derrida does an extensive analysis of one of Van Gogh's peasant shoe paintings. One expositor, discussing Derrida's commentary, states:

> It is the detachability of the work from any context, all the ways in which the painted shoes are not tied up with or tied down to any subject, that impels this polylogue, for more than a hundred pages, in a back and forth movement, like laces crossing over the tongue of shoes . . . Derrida does not so much fill Van Gogh's shoes with his words as restore to words their condition as detachable things, abandoned, unlaced shoes.[13]

Différence and Différance. The other aspect of the word or "trace" relates to Derrida's well-known discussion of the words *différence* and *différance*. These words are translated the same in English, but in French a single change shifts the concept. What emerges is a root word for "to differ," which is a spatial differentiation, and a root word for "to defer," which is a temporal differentiation.[14] One philosopher explains the use of these words this way:

> [T]he difference between the two words ("*différence*" and "*différance*") amounts to no difference at all when the two words are spoken; whatever difference

---

[13] See Kamuf's notes in *Reader,* 278.

[14] Again, this is one of those ideas that runs throughout Derrida's writing. One can find it explained in a basic sense in the section on "Difference," from *Difference at the Origin, Reader,* 60–79.

there is between them is a silent difference, since this difference appears explicitly only when the words are written.[15]

For Derrida, and deconstructionists, every word, every "trace," is different from every other word; every word is set in contrast to every other one by some kind of "difference." No synonyms exist. However, the unique feature in traces is silent and elusive. The emphasis, in fact, is on "difference"; and what is abolished in Derrida's extensive analysis using these concepts is the notion of any similitude whatsoever in any language or "trace" system. In language, there are only differences, and the nature of the differences can be nearly inexhaustible. Words may, of course, infer each other, and be set alongside each other. However, their very movement as "traces" from future to past means that one never returns to the same word or "trace" in the same way ever again.[16]

THE CONTRIBUTIONS OF DECONSTRUCTIONISM TO PREACHING

We stop here, then, to ask what all this might have to do with the systematic, regular study of Christian Scripture for sermon preparation. The answer, in short, is that it offers a relatively simple and straightforward way to increase the appreciation of biblical text. We can demonstrate this by outlining five sets of questions that, if taken seriously, will impact how a preacher understands a given text.

Homiletical Implications of Word-consciousness

The goal of deconstructionism, of course, is to become profoundly language-conscious and word-conscious. Each of these questions is designed to elicit an increased consciousness. To ask these five questions, one must choose a text and select a series of key words. They should not be only what are presumed to be the text's most important words. They should instead be those that are pivotal or even disguised in some way, including words that seem unusual either by their selection or their placement.

The first set of questions is, "Where did this word—the specific word that I am reading right now—come from? Why is it here?"

If you have a Greek text, or a Greek-English Interlinear text, look up a word there and ask the same questions. After you do, compare the two—the

---

[15] Wicks, *Modern French Philosophy,* 183.
[16] *Reader,* 63.

English and the Greek. Ask yourself how the translator of the particular English text you are using came to use this particular word at this particular place. You may recognize that this involves you in what you may have learned to call "word study." It is exactly the foundational kind of word study that starts you down the path toward a well-honed word-consciousness. This kind of word study, however, is only the very beginning of the process according to deconstructionists.[17]

Think, for instance, of the rather controversial translation of Matthew 2:2 in the New Revised Standard Version where the wise men respond this way to the question of how they found their way to Jesus' birth place: "For we observed *his star at its rising,* and have come to pay him homage." The famous and dear translation in the past has read "For we have seen *his star in the east.*" An interlinear translation will show you that the Greek phrase in question is *autou ton astera en tē anatolē.* What would lead the translators to change such a traditional expression? Are linguistic studies enough basis on which to disturb the older view?

The second set of questions begins with "How would different people, past and present, have used this particular term? What would they have used it for?"

If you find the word used to describe some particular person or group of people, would those individuals have used the word for themselves? Do you think that others in the same scene have used it for themselves? If you move the word around, giving it to others in the story, what would they have meant by it? Can you know for sure? Of course not. But go ahead and try. Be empathetically imaginative and see what you think. Remember, of course, just how elusive the words are. We are doing this in order to become more sensitive to the "traces" of the past, from whatever source, that now inhere in words before us in a text. The words of the text are slippery, wispy, palimpsestic (written on several times), worn by time and circumstance. Most importantly, we are seeking to become keenly aware of all that we can; and the payoff in our study of biblical text may be surprising.

A useful example might be Paul's cutting question in Gal 3:1 to his readers: "O foolish Galatians! Who has bewitched you?" Would the Galatians have used that word "bewitched" as a description of what had happened to them? What exactly does Paul mean? Would the Galatians use that word to describe Paul? He has just accused Peter of cowardly behavior (Gal 2:11–14). Would he have used this word of Peter as well? How would we today respond should others say we were bewitched by the church?

---

[17] Joseph M. Webb and Robert Kysar, *Greek for Preachers* (St. Louis: Chalice, 2002).

The third set of questions revolves around asking not about meaning, but about emotional content. What kind or kinds of emotional "baggage" is, and has been, invested in this particular word?

Now the process becomes even more complicated. Now we are hunting for more than word meaning. We can begin by trying to fathom our own personal emotional response to a term. Then we have to be able to get outside of ourselves enough to grasp how others, particularly those different from us, emotionally respond to it. After that, we are faced with seeking ways to get some glimpse of how people of biblical times might have emotionally responded to the term. That is, of course, very difficult and perhaps impossible. But it is only in taking seriously this set of questions that we can grow in word-consciousness.

A possible example is the emotion packed into the word "hate" (Greek: *miseō*) in John 12:25: "Those who love their life lose it, and those who *hate* their life in this world will keep it for eternal life" (NRSV). How do you respond emotionally? How will your congregation respond? What examples of responses from those in the past do you think of? Try to imagine what emotional responses to these words would have been before the rise of the contemporary emphasis on loving one's self.

The fourth set of questions concerns turning words over to expose their underside. What is the opposite of this word, or its polar counterpart?

This is exactly what Derrida does. We would gain some significant perspective on the text if we were to try replacing this word with the one that stands counter to it. If it is the word *proud*, what would it do to the text, to its story, characters, and even teaching, if we were to substitute the word *humble*, for example? Or, more dramatically, as Derrida sketches it, what would happen if we were to substitute the word *male* for *female* or vice versa? Or what if we were to substitute a word like *outward* for *inward*, or *weak* for *strong?* Ironically, when we start this kind of process, we cannot help but become aware of how radically the New Testament itself seems at least subconsciously built on just such substitutions. Doing this deliberately and consistently, however, results in our perspective being challenged. We may then feel forced to look at what we are read in a different manner.

Think, for instance, of how Paul does this very thing in 1 Cor 1:18–25. He substitutes *foolish* for *wise* and speaks of the crucifixion as foolish. How would that play out today? What does God's strength look like, when we do as Paul did and speak of God's weakness?

Finally, the last set of questions has to do with what we like to call synonyms. What words are like this word? What other similar words could the author have used?

As we have seen, for Derrida and the deconstructionists, synonyms do not exist. Every word for them is unique, containing slightly different meanings and feelings for everyone who uses the word. We may think that words can be substituted for each other, but there is a rather easy way to demonstrate that that is not the case. Take a word from a biblical text, like the word *announced,* as in Rev 10:7, "as he announced to his servants the prophets." Now make a list of synonyms for that word. What other words could the writer have used to make that same statement? Create a list of such possible synonyms, such as *proclaimed, asserted, said loudly, preached, delivered,* and so on. Now read each word in the statement, "he announced to his servants the prophets," and try to think about what general feelings, emotions, and meanings are conjured up with each change of word that you make. You will quickly get a sense that these are definitely not synonyms.

With each word that you have in your text, isolate some of them, and ask what other words might have been "substituted" so that you can get a sense of just how unique, how fleeting and evanescent, and even how powerful, the word is that you are examining. In all of this, you will begin a process of becoming word-conscious.

Homiletical Implications of Literary Structure

The second value to the preacher that arises from deconstructive theory has to do with the nature of literary structure itself rather than with words or traces. The length and breadth of Derrida's deconstructionism is intended to move the understanding of literary production from what he (and others) saw as an outdated "linear model" to one that he most creatively calls "pluridimensional." We are now leaving, he argues, one "age of writing" for a new one, and because "we are beginning to write . . . differently, we must re-read differently." In short, Derrida says: "All the revolutions in these fields can be interpreted as shocks that are gradually destroying the linear model" or "the epic model."[18]

What Derrida argues for as pluridimensionality in every kind of written material is a model based on something that resembles montage in film. The idea, in brief, is that relationships between things—words, ideas, concepts, sentences—are not established by logical connections, and that written materials are seldom, if ever, created in some kind of smooth flowing progression of the mind. Even stories or narratives which seem to unfold "logically," moving neatly from scene to scene in the telling, are deceptive in that they are always part of a complex process of internal "editing." Actually works are cre-

---

[18] *Reader,* 50, 51, from *Of Grammatology.*

ated by an unending process of what Derrida calls "juxtapositionings." In his inimitable fashion, he describes the process at one critical point like this:

> The art of the text is the air it causes to circulate between its screens. The chainings are invisible, everything seems improvised or juxtaposed. The text induces by agglutinating rather than by demonstrating, by coupling and uncoupling, gluing and ungluing rather than by exhibiting the continuous, and analogical, instructive, suffocating necessity for a discursive logic.[19]

In a sense, this is a variation of composition, or discourse, as a "cut and paste" operation. Things belong together simply because they are placed together, and not because of any "logical" or "linear" argumentation that wants them together. For Derrida and the deconstructionists, this is the way the psyche works. It is the "normal" movement of the mind, and for them the old sense of a mind's operating with a kind of straight line thinking does not reflect the preponderance of human mental activity, and certainly not literary activity. Put another way, Derrida contends that the mind works by a process of what, at one point, he calls "overlapping, of finding pieces and creating new connections and systems from those pieces." And when those pieces come "unglued," we take the remaining pieces and construct something else again—not in any "logical" manner, but by some intuitive inner motive of connectedness. "In little continuous jerks," he writes, "the sequences (of our lives) are enjoined, induced, glide in silence." Speaking of literary creation as "agglutinization," Derrida says:

> No category outside the text should allow defining the form or bearing of these passages, of these trances in writing. There are always only sections of flowers, from paragraph to paragraph, so much so that the anthological excerpts inflict only the violence necessary to attach importance to the remains. Take into account the overlap-effects, and you will see that the tissue ceaselessly reforms itself around the incision.[20]

For Derrida it is not that there is no more "logic"; it is, instead, that the nature of "logic" has changed. Texts are, by nature, interrupted, if not by the writer (which is usually the case), certainly by the reader. Texts interrupt themselves. A writer brings together in one place different languages, different ways of thinking, and creates something entirely different. This is how writers creates a fabric of their work,

> interrupting the weaving of one language and then by weaving together the interruptions themselves, another language comes to disturb the first one. It

---

[19] While a part of this quotation is used in the *Reader*, it is found in *Glas*, 75.
[20] *Reader*, 25, from *Glas*.

doesn't inhabit it, it haunts it. Another text, the text of the other, arrives in silence with a more or less regular cadence, without ever appearing in its original language, to dislodge the language of translation, converting the version, and refolding it while folding it upon the very thing it pretended to impart. It dissimilates it.[21]

The point for Derrida and the deconstructionists is that writers "build" their works. They knit them, weave them, and they draw their "languages" and materials from anywhere they wish. The metaphors likewise may change. But then, by following something within themselves, an idea or a piece of an idea, a general impression of something they say, an intuition or some "gut" notion that catches and drives them, they build with words.

With this as the process, the question of what the writing "means" becomes complicated almost beyond belief. Who can say what the essay, the story, the historical sketch, "means?" Can the one who wrote it? In a sense, yes; but in another sense, not really. Can the reader? This one can, yes, and that one can, yes. However, it quickly becomes apparent that no two readers are going to answer the "what does it mean" question in the same way. Who is right? Things become imponderable fast. As one reads it, does the writing actually "mean" what it says, or, in other words, what lies there on its surface? Seldom, if ever. What one does not know, of course, is the set of underlying decisions or intuitions that caused the writer to select these particular pieces and then string them together in this particular fashion. For the deconstructionists what eventually becomes clear is that there is not one meaning. There are countless meanings, and some of the most important ones are often hidden in the cracks and crevices out of the main line of "reading" sight, if we may put it that way. (See the next chapter.)

It is this orientation to the production of written texts that causes Derrida to reject the common "wisdom" that guided the now passing "linear age of writing." That era called for criticism to focus on the "main line" or center of a text, its thesis or proposition. Instead, what the deconstructions want to do is to break through that neat, clean surface operation in order to ferret out the twists and turns, the materials and decisions, out of which the words were chosen and then strung together as they are. Derrida has, in fact, devised what amounts to a methodological perspective from which to approach this task. It is a perspective of *decenteredness*. Given his view of how texts are actually created, he argues that texts have no "centers" as such. At least they do not have the kind of easily discoverable, "logical" centers or "central points" that "linear writers" have assumed they have. He does believe there are "guiding principles" at work when a writer produces a text. Yet he

---

[21] Ibid., 214, 215, from *Psyche: Inventions of the Other.*

believes that what the writer assumes those principles to be is often *not* what is at work in what the writer actually *does* in producing a text. Moreover, he argues that texts have no "borders," because any given text is made from countless pieces of other "things," such as ideas, texts, reactions to this, that, or something else. Hence, the edges are always blurred, with one writing "merged," as it were, into who knows how many other pieces of writing and experience.

At one level, then, this is the pluridimensional nature of both the *production* of texts, as well as what they *resemble* in their final form. Yet when all is said and done, the "form" is never "final." It also demonstrates what Derrida means by both the "decenteredness" of texts and their "borderless" nature. On these bases, Derrida and other deconstructionists have contended for a completely different orientation to the criticism, or the hermeneutic, of texts. In a nutshell, they contend that in order to break open a text for analysis in order to gain some understanding, it is necessary to skip over the "main point," the "center," the "proposition" of the text, at least initially, and "begin" at the edges, the borders. *Work not from center out, but from the borders in.* That is the principle, even though Derrida himself does not offer much in the way of "how to do this."

If we consider what this means for the study of biblical texts, we can come up with some interesting and potentially useful observations. They do not amount to methodology as such, but to a perspective. They suggest "where to look and what to look for" in a biblical text in preparation for a sermon.

First, Derrida would advise skipping over the "heroes" (the main characters in the story) and searching out the "bit players." These are not just the minor characters, but those who are barely visible in the scene. They are the observers, as it were, in the shadows. Start there. The heroes are always fawned over. In biblical texts they have been puffed up, and praised, and even criticized so often that there is probably nothing that could be said about them that has not already been said. Start with the "supporting" cast rather than the stars, since the supporting cast does just that—they "support" the main characters. To call them supporting is a way of saying that without them, the main characters would be less than they are.

Who are the supporting players? What would one say if one were to select one of them and write her or his biography? What is the nature of the "support" provided by that cast member? Who is that person, and what would happen in the scene were that individual not there? We may not think about such matters regularly when we have the "heroes of faith" in mind; but there are literally dozens of minor characters who live "in the margins" of biblical text. Deconstructionists would argue they are characters who are there for a reason. Often they are there for a profoundly important and complex reason, and by probing into those characters we may gain new understandings of the situation in the story, the "main" characters, and even biblical meaning (see Chapter Four).

As an example, think of those who supported Paul in each of the communities where he planted churches. He occasionally names them, but that is about all we know of them. The longest list of these supporting persons is found in Rom 16, but for many of them we have little more than a name. What happens when we bring them out of the shadows and reflect on how Paul depended on them?

Second, if we take Derrida's concept of literary structure seriously, we will focus not on the main lines of biblical events, but on what we might call the "intersections" of the events. Those places are where (in Derrida's language) events touch or "space," where the rough edges of transition can be detected. How does one scene become another? Where are all of the varied scenes, the bits and pieces from which the text is created? Or is that just not possible to know? If that is the case, then let us follow our imaginations and see where we come out. Granted, at this level we know that many good biblical scholars have come very close to treading this ground, too. But our question will be slightly different from theirs and will go somewhat beyond theirs. We are not as interested in the origin of the various isolated pieces, although that is not entirely outside our frame of reference. We are interested in what happens when one "piece" is actually laid next to a very different "piece." Granted this sounds somewhat abstract, but in actual practice it is not, and it may provide a new insight into the nature of almost any text, including a biblical one.

A biblical example is the scene in which Jesus' brothers try to persuade Jesus to go to Jerusalem for the Feast of Tabernacles in John 7:1–4. He refuses to go because his "time has not yet fully come." Yet 7:10 announces that as soon as his brothers are gone, Jesus takes off for Jerusalem. What is the relationship (if any) between these two scenes? The intersection is the departure of the brothers. What would happen if Jesus had been persuaded by his brothers and went to Jerusalem *because* of them and not *in spite* of them? The implication in the story as it now stands is that Jesus will not be persuaded by anyone to do anything. He is dependent entirely on the Father's will for his life.

Third, look for and tease out the details of the scene you are studying. How does the writer "set the scene?" What little things, even unimportant things, does the writer see fit to mention? Is the selection of a certain thing out of all the possible things that could have been mentioned made at random? Where in the text are the "side glances" of the text? Where are the "observations" that appear to be throwaways; but which, for deconstructionists, never are? Such details, while residing in the margins of a text, are never, of themselves, random or "just there." The question, for the student of the text, is why are these things pointed out?

For example, interpreters have pondered a small detail in the story of Elijah' victory on Mount Carmel. After subduing the prophets of Baal Elijah goes to the top of Mount Carmel.

> [T]here he bowed himself down upon the earth and put his face between his knees. He said to his servant, "Go up now, look toward the sea." He went up and looked, and said, "There is nothing." Then [Elijah] said, "Go again seven times." At the seventh time [the servant] said, "Look, a little cloud no bigger than a person's hand is rising out of the sea." Then he said, "Go say to Ahab, 'Harness your chariot and go down before the rain stops you.'" In a little while the heavens grew black with clouds and wind; there was a heavy rain (1 Kgs 18:43–45a).

What role does the posture of Elijah play in this story? Why the detail of his putting "his face between his knees?" Is it accidental that Elijah puts himself into the shape of a cloud, and that his posture is part of his prayer for rain? What a powerful detail.

Some will object that this method amounts to admiring the flowers around the tomb of Jesus, instead of contemplating the empty tomb. But that is not really the case. If a writer chooses to tell the story of the empty tomb and adds a reference to those flowers, then, for purposes of studying that text, the flowers will play a role in how one is to respond to the story. For deconstructionists the reference to the flowers may be (repeat, "may be") the most important key for opening up the story itself. Details and side glances that appear to be insignificant references may not be important in and of themselves. For Derrida and other deconstructionists, however, they become very important to the overall story if the writer has seen fit to include them in the poetry or prose of the narrative. There are other ways, of course, to work "from the margins to the center" of a text, but these are examples of how deconstruction theory aids in our work on biblical texts. (Two other examples are found in John 6:10 and 20:1).

Homiletical Implications of Poetics

There is a third orientation to text that arises from Derrida's constructive deconstruction that the preacher needs to know about, and it has to do with the nature of "poiesis" or poetic. Poiesis is done, Derrida says, "by heart" and this involves one of his richest explorations. The common term, "by heart," becomes, in his hands, another rich metaphor for a complex process of giving form to a creative impulse. Derrida treats poetry in a larger, more encompassing sense than is usually meant by the term "poem." Poetry is poiesis, the process of creating a text or a discourse. It entails the "choosing" of language as a means of giving form to oneself and the world. It is "another word for voyage," or the random rambling of a trek. The strophe is the means of creating a past and a future and trying to lay hold, as impossible as that is, of a present. Poiesis is giving form to one's heartbeat, to one's "downbeat, the birth of rhythm, beyond oppositions, beyond outside and insight, conscious representation and the abandoned archive." Derrida puts it succinctly like this:

> I call a poem that very thing that teaches the heart, invents the heart, that which, finally, the word heart seems to mean, and which, in my language, I cannot easily discern from the word itself. Heart, in the poem, "learn by heart" (to be learned by heart), no longer names only pure interiority, independent spontaneity, the freedom to affect oneself actively by reproducing the beloved trace. The memory of the "by heart" is confided like a prayer—that's safer—to a certain exteriority of the automaton, the laws of mnemotectics, to that liturgy that mimes mechanics on the surface and bears down on you as if from the outside: *auswendig,* "by heart" in German.[22]

Three things develop from Derrida's notion of the "heart" as the "essence" of the making of texts and discourses and the constructive deconstruction of them. The first is the "immanence" of what must finally take form in the ongoing process of creating word-statements and images. But it is an immanence of the "invisible," of the "hard to find."

> Someone writes you, to you, of you, on you. No, rather, a mark is addressed to you, left and confided with you, is accompanied by an injunction; in truth, it is constituted in this very order which, in its turn, constitutes you, assigning your origin or giving rise to you; destroy me, or rather, render my support invisible to the outside, in the world, in any case do what must be done so that the provenance of the mark remains from now on unlocatable or unrecognizable.[23]

The language of poeisis is elusive. It arises from human recesses and wants desperately to resettle in human recesses. It provides the smallest pieces from which we are made. They are pieces so small that, despite their formative power, they are buried to the point of being overlooked. With poiesis, there are no "histronics," no "phoenix," no "eagle," but only the herisson, "very low, low down, close to the earth. Neither sublime, nor incorporeal, angelic,

---

[22] Ibid., 231.
[23] Ibid., 227.

perhaps, and for a time."[24] The "herisson" is a hedgehog, a lowly animal, hard to see, particularly at night, an animal that seems to be constantly in hiding; it is one to which humans seldom, if ever, pay attention. It is the anti-eagle. That shy, ugly animal is Derrida's remarkable metaphor for poiesis, an invisible kind of poetic that one must consciously and deliberately look for in order to become aware of it—or appreciate it.

A second aspect that develops from Derrida's notion of "heart" is that, for Derrida, it is only in poiesis that both wounding and healing take place. It is only poiesis, "arising from the heart," that exposes us to life's most intense dangers and vulnerabilities, the ones that make us, in a sense, human.

> No poem without accident, no poem that does not open itself like a wound, but no poem that is not also just as wounding. You will call a poem a silent incantation, the aphonic wound that, of you, from you, I want to learn by heart. It thus takes place, essentially, without one's having to do it or make it: it lets itself be done, without activity, without work, in the most sober pathos, a stranger to all production, essentially to creation. The poem falls to me, benediction, coming of (or from) the other. Rhythm but dissymmetry.[25]

With poiesis, the wounds of the heart are inflicted, they become visible, sharing other wounds, wounding; with poiesis, too, the "benediction" with which one's "heart" deals with the wounding is brought to the surface, offering that benediction for sharing, being a benediction for other wounded "hearts."

The third aspect that develops from Derrida's "by heart" metaphor is that poiesis renders a certain anonymity to everything that springs from the "heart." It represents, in a sense, the willingness of a "heart" to lose its own identity in the process of expression. At one point, Derrida says that the poiesis

> event always interrupts or derails absolute knowledge, autotelic being in proximity to itself. This "demon of the heart" never gathers itself together, rather it loses itself and gets off the track (delirium or mania), it exposes itself to chance, it would rather be torn to pieces by what bears down upon it.[26]

To create text or discourse—as well as to deconstruct it—in a poetic manner is to "give oneself up," as it were, to merge one's "heart" with every other

---

[24] Ibid., 227. Derrida has great fun with the metaphor of the herisson, which he describes as a strange, ancient type of spiny animal that wraps itself into a ball in order to protect itself on the highways of France. The metaphor is in the sheer lowliness, and yet ingenuity, of the animal.

[25] Ibid., 233.

[26] Ibid., 236.

"heart," or at least to hold out the possibility of such a "merging" taking place. Derrida, even here, must be allowed to speak for himself:

> Without a subject: poem, perhaps there is some, and perhaps it leaves itself, but I never write any. A poem, I never sign(s) it. The other sign(s). The *I* is only at the coming of this desire: to learn by heart. Stretched, tendered forth to the point of subsuming its own support, thus without external support, without substance, without subject, absolute of writing in (it)self, the "by heart" lets itself be elected beyond the body, sex, mouth, and eyes; it erases the borders, slips through the hands, you can barely hear it, but it teaches us the heart.[27]

Largely through Derrida's own language and patterns of thinking we have discussed his perceptions about the "state of mind" or the "orientations" that are necessary in order to do the difficult work of textual deconstruction. Through it we have seen that this work is not essentially destructive, but that it attempts, with honesty and sensitivity, to imbue itself with a text in order to call it into new speech, for a new time and place. What becomes apparent in studying Derrida's books on deconstruction is that, while method is not of great concern to him, his work resounds with creative ideas about how to look at and peel back texts in innovative and exciting ways. These are ways that can be of considerable service to those of us who work regularly in biblical texts.

There are two major ways in which Derrida's moving discussion of poiesis can speak to those of us who work with biblical texts. First, it speaks to the nature of the interpreter in the interpreter-text interaction. In a sense, it implies and is a method. The interpreter must learn to study with his or her "heart." Consider that Derrida speaks primarily of those who study great secular texts when he advocates the use of the heart ("by heart") in text work. However, in taking our cue from him, how much more might we see the role of our hearts as an important dimension when we turn to our sacred texts in preparation for the pulpit. We of all people should learn to study not just with our heads, but with our hearts.

But what does that mean? It means that we come to the study of texts with an enthusiasm that can only arise from within us, a sense that in our work we are going to give birth to something. We are not just scholars or students, not just going through motions, or even an enterprise for which we shall be compensated. We are, instead, turning to our texts because we are drawn there, and we come with minds, eyes, ears, and hearts that are eager to know and experience. The text then becomes the door through which that

---

[27] Ibid., 237.

experience comes alive in our hands. When we preach sermons about texts that have been through us and when they arise from the very depths of our hearts, our congregants know it, and often they are moved by what we do. It is essential that we learn to preach "from our hearts." If we do not, it is fair to say that our chances of success in the pulpit will be limited at best. On the other hand, if we do learn to study and preach "from our hearts" our chances of failure in the pulpit are vastly diminished.

There is a second way in which Derrida's rich notion of poiesis speaks to preachers concerning deconstructive work. It is the process of reading all biblical texts as poetry (including prose or narrative ones). Poetry is language of the heart: that is at the center of Derrida's entire discussion. Although there are exceptions, for Derrida anytime a serious writer sets thoughts down on paper or reports on matters of life and death, love and loneliness, fear and hatred, and matters charged with eternity, the heart of the writer undergirds it all. These are all things that populate biblical texts. When these are the subject of the text, the writing invariably is poetic in intent, style, and even in the ways in which stories themselves are told. That is what is embodied in the complexity of poiesis.

As you study a biblical text, in short, think of it as poetry, whether or not you recognize it as such. As Derrida says at one point, think of the text as something that "teaches the heart, invents the heart." It is more than a great idea, more than a moving story, more even than a divine spiritual insight. In effect, it is all of these things, but given form in a way that, when the preacher's heart is open to it in study, it is most likely the congregant's heart will be open to it when it is embodied in the pulpit. Strangely, merely saying that the preacher should learn to study with his or her heart sounds abstract and even somewhat awkward in a book on the academic disciplines of interpretation. Yet until one has actually taken a text and meditated over it, as well as studied it, one cannot fully appreciate the wisdom of "learning a text by heart," an admonition that comes from one of the most unlikely of literary sources and scholars.

The Meanings of Play

One other orientation that Derrida provides for deconstructive "moves" revolves around his well-developed notion of "play," as in "playing with words," or "playing with texts." However, his sense of "play" means something different with each of the dimensions of "words" ("traces") that we have attempted to explain. Each is worth a second look within the context of "play."

First, for Derrida if something has "play" in it, it has a quality of movement. It is play in the sense that the mechanic might say that there is play in the wheel of our car that needs to be tightened. In this case, play means that it is not fixed; it is not secured; it is not "true." There is an ambiguity in the "joint," in that it can turn at will, that it can be one way one moment and some other way the next. This is the notion, again, of "undecidability" in language. Undecidability is the result of words that are never "fixed," of traces that are elusive, that have a kind of blur about them. They are glimmers out in front of us and shadowy marks once they are past. Meaning is not something that is "true." There is always play in it, which is to say, an element of pushing and pulling, an element of "give." To sense the play in words is to sense that nothing related to language can ever be "held down" or even called "true" in a metaphysical or an epistemological sense. To grasp the play in words is also to realize the futility of ever trying to hold meaning or usage in place. To understand requires that we realize the give of words or traces is their very nature. For Derrida and deconstructionists, this is what language is.

The second way in which Derrida uses the notion of play is in the sense of being "performed," or of being involved in a kind of ongoing masquerade: to be "in" a "play." This orientation tends to conform to the second quality of the trace; that is, its sense of moving constantly from future to past, of being "acted out" as it passes through our consciousness. There is, for Derrida, a game-like element to our attempt to hold onto a present that is never present. Moreover, both our future and our past are "acted out" at the intersection of consciousness and unconsciousness. This is the case whether we "act" alone or in conjunction with others. Our language, then, he says, "plays a double scene upon a double stage, even if these are only separated by a veil, which is both traversed and not traversed."[28] By that he means that whenever we use language, we act doubly. We act alone and we act with others. This is the nature of "being in a play." Even when we are alone, others are present; and even when we act with others, we still act alone. In a sense, for Derrida, because of this "play" we are constantly "in." It is impossible ultimately to tell what is "real" from what is not. In the end, it is only the play that is real, and there is only the language, the "lines" to carry us from the past into the future, from our origin to our point of "arrival." How we say our "lines" in the play determines the nature of the role that we "play" in the "play."

The third meaning of play for Derrida and the deconstructionists is as behavior that is spontaneous or unorganized. It is a child's "play," that activity which has neither beginning nor end, no pre-set outcomes, and hence no particular pattern or predictability. It is activity that no one directs for someone else. It is measured by its own sense of enjoyment. Moreover, this play has a strong comic element to it; nothing is deadly serious. Here the connec-

---

28 Ibid., 190.

tion can readily be made to the third quality of the "trace" in our previous discussion of language. Here is "spacing," detachment, and difference. Here things can be whatever they are called; they are meant to be "played with." Here, things do not belong together unless one chooses for them to belong together. "Spacing" allows that. Here, detachment destroys logic, and *"différence"/"différance"* obliterates continuity.

Here play can be given its freest reign. At this point Derrida lays hold of the Greek concept of the pharmakon, the "drug, medicine" or, by extension perhaps, the "drug store." The metaphor arises from the meaning of the Greek term itself, since it sets up a playful paradox.[29] A drug, for example, can be either "a remedy or a poison, either the cure of an illness or its cause." In play something can be both good and bad at the same time; it can be both negative and positive. If there are differences in concepts, it is a play of differences. Differences can emerge as part of an activity of play, since terms can always be played off each other. What exists in the pharmakon is this essential playfulness with words. Nothing is hooked down. Words are for playing; so let's go out and play. One cannot read Derrida without understanding this fundamental motivation behind virtually all of his most serious literary work.

One of the ways the concept of play is incorporated in contemporary biblical interpretation is in the use of puns. Deconstruction interpreters love to play with language and recreate new language with words that sound like the origin but are vastly different. Stephen D. Moore, a prominent deconstructionist biblical scholar, says that punning is the result of the fact that meaning is not pinned down in a text. Language is meant to be heard, so that sound-alike words are fair play. Reading then, is inventive and irreverant. "For the serious scholars, puns and anagrams are jest a joke. Language should be heard and not seen."[30]

Homiletical Implications of Play

When we think about applying this dimension of Derrida's deconstruction to biblical texts and sermon preparation, we can easily come up short. It is not simple, and certainly there are no "methods" just sitting there waiting for us to use. We can talk about the first kind of play as "give," and remind ourselves that when we deal with the intricacies of trying to understand

---

[29] See the section in *Reader* (113 and following) on "Plato's Pharmacy" from *Dissemination*.

[30] Stephen D. Moore, "Deconstructive Criticism: The Gospel of Mark" in *Mark and Method: New Approaches in Biblical Studies* (ed., Janice Capel Anderson and Stephen D. Moore; Minneapolis: Fortress, 1992), 99.

complicated texts, we should give ourselves some "play." We need to leave ourselves some room to be wrong, for we do not "know it all" nor are we able to figure everything out. If we think of play as "performing," as being, in a sense, "on stage," then it would remind us to take on the various "roles" that a text gives us, even those with which we may not be comfortable. If we think about the play as in the glorious playground of the child, guided by spontaneity and a sense of the carefree—well, yes, let us go "play" in our texts.

In all of this, though, what we realize is that we do not have any interpretative methods as such. Rather, what we have is a profoundly simple and straightforward attitude toward the processes involved in interpretation and sermon making. We are to be playful, with places to fall down and get up again, places to try on new clothes and costumes, and places to just do whatever we want to do. However, this is not an "anything goes" attitude toward the serious business of biblical interpretation. It is anything, but that. Biblical interpretation is as serious and disciplined as it can be. It is as disciplined as one wants children on a playground to be: here are the rules; you must follow them; they are designed to ensure that you do not injure yourselves or those around you. But, within those rules, see how creative and robustly unpredictable you can be. There is, frankly, no way to deal with these "play" matters without conjuring up Jesus' dictum that "unless you become like children, you cannot enter the Kingdom of Heaven" (Matt 18:3–5). Whatever else that means, it signifies an attitude toward life and work that is filled with that innocent and playful outlook of children—filled, that is, with fun and wonder, with reverence and joy.[31]

A SAMPLE SERMON

The following sermon is an example of interpretation premised on a deconstruction theory. It demonstrates an approach to the book of Hebrews guided by Derrida's basic principles. Note the tension between the "one hand" and the "other hand," as well as the fluidity of the message in relationship to Judaism today. The preacher takes a good deal of liberty in interpreting the metaphors of sacrifice. Most important, the preacher has "played" with this passage and produced a sermon "from the heart."

---

[31] For a collection of articles written from different perspectives related to deconstruction, see ed., David Jobling and Stephen D. Moore, *Poststructuralism as Exegesis* (Semeia 54; Atlanta: Scholars Press, 1992).

"Living Together as Christians and Jews"

Hebrews 9:24–28; read
Hebrews 11:1–10

REMEMBER TEVYE, THE LONG-SUFFERING FATHER IN "FIDDLER ON THE ROOF"? HE had a way of handling things. It began with his looking longingly up at the sky and discussing things with God. It was always, "On the one hand . . . ," when he would talk though one side of whatever the matter was, and "but on the other hand . . ." There was always "on the other hand." On the one hand . . . on the other hand; on the one hand . . . on the other hand. I raise that because I cannot work in the New Testament's book of Hebrews without experiencing an "on the one hand . . . on the other hand" feeling.

For me it begins with discovering what the book of Hebrews itself actually is, a matter that we must grasp before we are ready to turn to the text that was read from Hebrews chapter 9. On the one hand, as Tevye would say, the book of Hebrews is clearly a grand celebration of Jewish history and faithfulness. The celebration reaches its high point in the glorious chapter 11 recitation of Jewish heroes. Everybody knows the list. By faith, Abel. By faith, Enoch. By faith, Noah. By faith, Abraham. "When Abraham was called," the text says, "he obeyed to go out unto a place which he was to receive for an inheritance; and he went out, not knowing whither he went." By faith, Moses. By faith, the children of Israel. By faith, Rahab. And we are told that time does not even allow the writer to describe the faith of Gideon, Barak, David, Samuel, and that grand unnamed host of those "who through faith"—again quoting chapter 11, this time from verse 33—"subdued kingdoms, wrought righteousness, obtained promises, stopped the mouths of lions . . ." Well, you know the stories, too—don't you?

It is an incredible testament to faithfulness to God on the part of Jewish giants of faith. "They were stoned," the Hebrews text says in chapter 11, verses 37 and 38, "they were sawn asunder, they were tempted, they were slain with the sword. They went about in sheepskins, in goatskins, being destitute, afflicted, illtreated, wandering in deserts and mountains and caves, and the holes of the earth—people of whom the world was not worthy." Do you hear that?

But there is even more to it. Those Jewish heroes are now the ones who make up the "great cloud of witnesses." You know the phrase with which chapter 12 begins; they keep their eyes on *us*. We are encompassed by this great cloud of witnesses. They are watching us from their celebrated places in the stands now that it is us—we—who are "running the race" of faith. But, oh, those great saints of the past—those great Jewish, Hebrew, saints. Our brothers and sisters who have gone before us, watching us, encouraging and teaching us, cheering us on . . .

On the one hand, on the one hand, the New Testament book of Hebrews is a great testament to Jewish faith—to the Jewish religion.

Then, as Tevye would have it, on the other hand, in these times in which we live, the book of Hebrews is a strikingly *anti-Jewish* document. On the other hand—and that is where the rub of it all comes in.

2

What we must not forget is that we stand, all of us now, in the long, dark shadow of the Holocaust of World War II—Hitler's unimaginable massacre of millions upon millions (how many millions we will probably never know) of Jewish men, women, and children. It is particularly striking to read the last few verses of chapter 11 (as we just did), the verses that speak so vividly of Jewish persecution and massacre, to read them in light of the twentieth century's Holocaust. And what we Christians everywhere are gradually, if finally, trying to come to terms with is the degree to which Christian theology itself provided a pretext, a rationale, an excuse—one doesn't know what to call it—not just for Hitler's Holocaust, but for the numerous holocausts, large and small, against the Jews over the past two thousand years. We have no choice, as Christians, but to try to deal with this. At, or near, the heart of that theology is a long-standing doctrine which asserts that the coming of Christianity trumped, or overcame, or wiped out, or did away with, or superceded—how shall we say it?—Judaism, or the Jewish religion. Make of it what you will, this has become a profound issue in these post-Holocaust times, even more than a half century later. To read the verse that ends the great chapter 11—the "by faith" chapter—is to see the problem in a nutshell. It says that all these, the great heroes of the Jewish faith as verse 40 puts it, "having obtained a good report through faith, received not the promise, God having provided some better thing for us, that they without us should not be made perfect." That they *without us* should *not* be made perfect.

The theology of Hebrews asserts that Christianity is a superior religion to Judaism—that Judaism was meant to be "perfected" by the coming of Christ and Christianity. That word perfected means "completed, or finished," like a beautiful butterfly that finally emerges from the caterpillar's cocoon. That's the picture in the doctrine of Christianity's "triumph" over Judaism. This doctrine, of course, is no surprise to anyone at all familiar with the New Testament thinking or its texts. What also comes as no surprise to anyone familiar with religious history is that that theology of superiority of Christianity over Judaism has been used repeatedly down through the ages to justify Christian and neo-Christian violence against, even death to, the Jewish people. That theology of superiority includes the particular branch of Christian ideology that undergirded the Nazi massacres of Jews in the mid-twentieth century. Everywhere one looks in Hebrews one finds this assumption of the superiority of Christianity, however subtle the statement.

So the question is an urgent, and profound, one: What shall we do with the book of Hebrews? It is, without question, an "on the one hand . . . on the other hand" question.

3

Let's think for a moment.

First, we need both to understand and affirm that Christianity did, in fact, arise from Judaism, that those who became the earliest Christians were first Jews. This is not only true of Jesus Himself but also of all of his disciples and even Paul the Apostle, to say nothing of that vast number of common people who gathered around them in those formative years. These Jews sought a Messiah, a promised one, and for many—and their numbers grew quickly—Jesus was that promised Messianic figure. As such, for them, Jesus was recognized and heralded as both Son of Man and Son of God. But since not all Jews understood Jesus as the fulfillment of their expectations, it meant that a break with Judaism was inevitable. A breach. A cutting apart. A division, deep and painful. Judaism was not about to disappear merely because some Jews, joined by gentiles, were learning, or finding, something new, something messianic, something even miraculous, emerging from their own Jewish ranks. Christianity was catching on; it was not going to go away.

But neither was Judaism going to go away, despite a very early first century "holocaust" against it. Indeed, that massacre by the Romans, which lasted from 68 to 70 C.E., was followed in various ways by intense political persecution of both Christians and Jews for the next fifty to sixty years. The point is that history has been dotted with numerous holocausts and pogroms against the Jews, culminating in the failed "final solution" by the Nazis within the lifetime of many of us here. But even back in the first century, large numbers of the scattered faithful Jews held onto what they had. So a break was inevitable; and out of that break two religions would stand where only one had stood before. That was the reality, regardless of who was right or wrong—and both the Christians and the Jews believed they were.

So how should those who embraced the "new" religion treat those who resisted and clung to the "old"?—with those two terms used in a chronological, rather than an evaluative or even a comparative way. Should the Christians seek the destruction of the older religion, the one that they were moving *from* in order to embrace their "new truth"? There is no question at all but that there would be great tension, even animosity, between an existing religion and one that presumed to create a different religious understanding in place of the existing one. Of course it would not be smooth and easy. Of course there would be disagreements, even bitter ones. Of course there would be recriminations on both sides, as each argued with former colleagues and groups for its own legitimacy. As was understood from the beginning, Christianity would forever be connected with Judaism because of its origins there. And Judaism, like it or not, would always be related to Christianity—regardless of how different the two religions would ultimately end up being.

Let's acknowledge that. Let's get that out in the open. Christianity arose from Judaism. Judaism spawned Christianity.

4

Let's acknowledge one other thing as we lay a background for moving toward our Hebrews 9 text. Let's acknowledge that what we find in the book of Hebrews in the New Testament represents a clear affirmation of what some Christians, having broken away from Judaism, believed—and, by and large, still believe. This is not intended to be a statement about any other religion, not even about Judaism itself.

Rather, it is to indicate what we believe about Christ and the role of Christ in our lives, and even, to some extent, *why* we believe it. We can affirm Christian belief, even setting it apart from Jewish belief, without denigrating Judaism. We can do that. And, in the context of these post-Holocaust times, that is what we Christians are called to do. We do not have to wish an end to Judaism, just because our Christianity arose from it. We do not have to contend that Judaism has to pass away in order for our Christianity to thrive. We do not have to live with hubris, certain that Christianity is better than Judaism just because it is what we embrace and affirm. Those things are simply not necessary. We can, in short, give full voice to our faith, our beliefs—beliefs expressed in various ways throughout the book of Hebrews. We can share our beliefs with others, at least those who are willing to listen to us or watch us. And what we find in our text is a succinct statement of some of those seminal beliefs of ours.

For example, in Hebrews 9, verses 24 through 28, our text for today, we encounter a series of our fundamental beliefs.

We believe, as Christians, that human sin, our sin, is what separates us from God. We do believe that, like all human beings, we have a deep need to be cleansed from our sins.

We believe that someone or something has to act on our behalf so that our sins can be taken away from us.

We believe that Christ's coming into the world was a seminal part of God's plan for the taking away of our sin.

We believe that it was in the shedding of Christ's blood in his crucifixion that the removal of our sins was made possible.

We believe that as a result of Christ's bearing our sins away in the shedding of his blood that we shall be admitted to heavenly places carrying no sins upon ourselves.

There is a lot more to the Christian faith than that—and there are even different ways in which all of this is articulated among the various Christian denominations and fellowships—but these statements come close to a common core of our belief about Christ's work on earth on our behalf.

And all of these things are found implicitly in the Hebrews text before us today.

But note that I said "implicitly" in our text. Because, as you heard the text read, there is more to it than just a recitation of Christian beliefs, as familiar as they are. There is something peculiar about the text's construction. Did you hear it? There is what we might call a veneer over the text which slightly veils those important Christian affirmations about the work of Christ on earth. The veneer is the Jewish language and theology for the remission of sins. And this is what we somehow need to understand in order to make the text useful to us.

5

Look at it like this. In order to "explain" the new Christian belief system— our system of understanding the meaning and significance of Christ's work in taking away our sins—in order to explain that, a metaphor can be most useful. A metaphor. A comparison. This is like that; or, here is how this is like that. Or, if you understand this, I will draw parallels so that you will know what I am talking about. That kind of metaphor.

What this Hebrews text gives us is the new Christian belief system—but then, for explanatory purposes, it is overlaid with a metaphor, and the metaphor is the Jewish belief system. So the writer, whoever he is, is able to say: Just as the High Priest entered into God's presence in the temple's Holy of Holies, so Christ—Christians believe—has entered into God's presence in heaven. Just as the High Priest used blood for the sending away of Jewish sins, so Christ—Christians believe—has taken away sin by the shedding of his own blood. Just as the Jews waited for the Messiah to bring their salvation, so Christ—Christians believe—will someday appear from heaven as well in order to bring salvation to those who, as the Hebrews text says, "are eagerly waiting for him."

It is a powerful explanation of Christian theology as it was emerging in the first century; it is an explanation made all the more powerful because it was pictured metaphorically with the use of the theology that was already so well known within Judaism.

This text is not a proscription for the relationship between Christians and Jews, and it does not have to be understood that way. It does not have to be turned into an anti-Jewish theology in order to be a Christian one. Christianity does not have to swallow up Judaism. It does not have to be seen as burying Judaism in order for Christianity to go happily along as the replacement religion for the Jewish faith. For those who choose Judaism, let them live with the richness of that ancient faith—and its great heroes of God. For us who are Christians, we can celebrate Judaism, and our Jewish roots, as well. But we have to do so in a way that does not demonstrate a haughty pride that we are the religion that put Judaism, well, in its place. The fact is that we can understand our Christianity better through a Jewish lens, as the metaphorical overlay of Hebrews makes clear.

On the one hand, as Tevye would tell us, we affirm our faith in Christ as Christians; and we affirm the work of Christ on our behalf. On the other hand, we must value and even learn from the affirmations of redemption that still come from those who are Jews—even today—the ones who still remain our *brothers and sisters,* as well as our ancestors in faith.

Chapter 6

What Difference Does the Nature of Meaning Make?

It is appropriate that we move from a survey of deconstruction to this final chapter on the nature of meaning. Deconstruction revolutionized our understanding of meaning. One might even say that the deconstructionists found too much meaning in words, so that meaning has become unstable and unreliable. Meaning is so elusive that efforts to pin it down are hopeless. Every text undoes whatever meaning it may seem to suggest. Each one of the critical methods we have discussed, nevertheless, presupposes some view of the nature of meaning. For these interpreters there is no meaning apart from practice and action. The historical-critical approach, for example, proposes that readers derive meaning from the historical context out of which the author wrote, as well as the author's original intention. Literary criticism credits the reader with discerning meaning, sometimes in the text and sometimes in the reading experience itself. Liberation interpretations understand meaning to involve the particular social and political struggles in which interpreters are engaged.

As a way of concluding our brief survey of the variety of critical methods available to preachers, we discuss here the issue of meaning. In effect, we return to the discussion of interpretation we began in the introduction. We do so because the issue of meaning lies buried deep within each of the methods we have explored and provides each with its primary presuppositions.

QUESTIONING MEANING

We once took for granted that we knew exactly what we meant when we said, "The meaning of this text is. . . ." As we begin the twenty-first century, for better or for worse, that is no longer the case. The erosion of certainty about meaning has been a long process, but in the last several decades post-modernism has accelerated it. The result is that we are no longer so confident that we can discover meaning in the text, or even that we know what it is we are searching for.

As postmodern criticism has progressed, the location of, or the encounter with, meaning has shifted steadily toward the present reader and away from the past. It has moved from the origin of a passage in the past toward the text and its readers. To some degree, it has moved from the notion that the author encoded meaning in the text's language. The text as text has meaning, without resorting to an understanding of its origin, as in literary criticism. The search for a text's meaning entails the examination of the reader's social, political, and economic situation as with liberation criticism. This "relocation" of meaning has been further complicated by the notion of a "true meaning" in the text. If we surrender the idea that the author's intended meaning is the true meaning, we must ask whether there is such as thing as one true meaning? Or do readers create meaning, and there may be as many meanings to a text as there are readers? Generally, we now recognize that meaning may not have any ontological, universal, or objective status.[1]

At the start of the twenty-first century, the post-modern world now asks what is meaning, what is the nature of meaning, or simply what is the meaning of meaning? Nothing takes us to the deepest level of the process of interpretation as quickly as asking and wrestling with these questions. All interpretation, whether of the Bible or of the weather forecast, presupposes some view of meaning—unfortunately we often cannot clearly articulate such views. To inquire about meaning is eventually to chase the question of what human life is about!

Earlier we said that *hermeneutic* refers to the process of interpretation of the biblical text but also has to do with all human interpretation. We are told the survivors of the Holocaust do not generally suffer from anger and the desire for revenge. Rather they battle to overcome the sense of guilt that comes when one survives while so many others died. What, indeed, is the meaning of such an event? Many of the survivors of the horrific events of

---

[1] See the discussion of meaning in G. B. Caird, *The Language and Imagery of the Bible* (Philadelphia, Penn.: Westminster, 1980), 37–84. Writing while we stood on the brink of a revolution in language, Caird identifies the different kinds of meaning which were at the time taken for granted. For instance, the meaning of words could be that to which they *refer,* or their *sense* (the contribution a word makes to a sentence), to meaning as *value* (the expression of preference), or their meaning as what the author/speaker *intended* to communicate (37–39). He does, however, acknowledge a new recognition of ambiguity in meaning (85–108).

September 11, 2001 found themselves asking a similar question: Why was I saved, while so many others perished? What is the meaning of this? Many of these survivors may still be at a loss to explain why they were spared while others were killed. Not surprisingly, some have been compelled to attribute their escape to "an act of God"—an expression that unfortunately continues in our modern world to confer legal status on the inexplicable. When we question the nature of meaning, we cut to the core of human life and not just to the world of biblical interpretation.

For now, our interests are narrower. To prepare to preach a text, we must ask what the text means. What sense does it convey? Reference may be involved in determining meaning, so we ask, to what does the language of the text refer or point? The meaning of the sermon for the members of the congregation to whom we preach is yet another matter. We preachers must ask what this text means for this particular congregation at this particular time. In both the interpretation of the text and in the preparation of the sermon, meaning is at the core of our endeavor.

All of this leads us to ask the question: What happens when a text *means?* Today any answer to that question entails the complexities of hermeneutics.

HERMENEUTICS AND MEANING

Before we pursue the meaning of meaning any further, we need to acknowledge the role of hermeneutics in the search for meaning in a text. In this discussion, we mean by the label *hermeneutics* the study of the process of interpretation, the theory behind the act of interpretation. (It seems that the word hermeneutics is fashioned on the basis of the ancient god, Hermes, who in ancient Greek mythology is often the messenger of other gods and the one who interprets the will of the gods to humans. The etymology of the word is, however, uncertain.)[2] The field of hermeneutics became a major preoccupation of both biblical interpreters and theologians in the latter half of the twentieth century, and the books written on the subject comprise a seemingly endless series of tomes, many of which are highly philosophical and theological. Our discussion will offer a very brief understanding of the discipline and how contemporary hermeneutics has shaped our understanding of meaning.

---

[2] For introductions, we recommend the articles on hermeneutics in both the *ABD* and *Dictionary of Biblical Interpretation:* B. C. Lategan, "Hermeneutics," *ABD* 3:149–54; D. E. Klemn, *Dictionary of Biblical Interpretation* 1:497–502.

Contemporary hermeneutics is best understood by means of the meta-phor of *horizons*. That is, the meaning of a text is one horizon, and the inter-preter (with his or her presuppositions, cultural setting, and ideologies) is the other horizon. Each of these boundaries is conditioned by a historical situa-tion different from the other. The reader's horizon (or view) is comprised of her or his pre-understanding on the basis of which the text is interpreted. In the process of interpretation these two horizons meet. Some propose the two *boundaries* merge into one to create meaning, or, as Hans-Georg Gadamer puts it, the "fusion" of the horizons produces understanding.[3] For others, these horizons stand separated and in tension with one another. Walter Wink speaks of "a communion of horizons." In that communion "the transmitted text lights up one's own horizon and leads to self-disclosure and self-under-standing, while at the same time one's own horizon lights up lost elements of the text and brings them forward with new relevance for life today."[4]

Anthony C. Thiselton offers a concise definition of hermeneutics, at least as the discipline has developed in recent decades:

> [H]ermeneutics in the more recent sense of the term begins with the recogni-tion that historical conditioning is two-sided: *the modern interpreter, no less than the text, stands in a given historical context and tradition. . . .* The nature of the hermeneutical problem is shaped by the fact that both the text and inter-pretation are conditioned by their given place in history. For understanding to take place, two sets of variables must be brought into relationship with each other.[5]

Meaning, then, arises out of the relationship between these two hori-zons, these two points of view. Contemporary hermeneutics almost univer-sally maintains, however, that the original author's meaning when the text was written does not limit its possibilities of other meanings at later times (see Chapter Three). Moreover, the history of hermeneutics in the modern age is saturated with philosophical views, so that in the course of trying to understand what is involved in the process of interpretation one becomes en-snared with both epistemological and ontological questions. Some of those issues involve the historical distance between the text and interpreter, the un-derstanding of language, the role of faith and the Holy Spirit in interpreta-tion, and even the nature of religious truth.

---

[3] Hans-Georg Gadamer, *Truth and Method* (London: Sheed and Ward, 1975), 273.

[4] Walter Wink, *The Bible in Human Transformation: Toward a New Paradigm for Biblical Study* (Minneapolis: Fortress, 1973), 66–67.

[5] Anthony C. Thiselton, *The Two Horizons: New Testament Hermeneutics and Philosophical Description* (Grand Rapids: Eerdmans, 1980), 11, 16. Italics original.

Another common expression arising out of hermeneutics is the allusive "hermeneutical circle." It usually refers to the fact that the text reinterprets our questions or assertions, and we are then challenged to respond to them. That is, there is a sense in which readers are engaged in a dynamic give and take with the text. While we initiate interpretation, the text responds. The meeting of the two horizons (text and interpreters) entails an exchange between the two.

Another and less common meaning of the hermeneutical circle is the circular dynamic between individual parts of a text and the whole text. The individual parts, on the one hand, make up the whole, but the whole shapes what the individual parts mean. In the discussion of narrative criticism we suggested that the whole of the document determined the meaning of the parts, but the parts contribute to the meaning of the whole. We will return later to this second understanding of the hermeneutical circle in the section, "What is 'meaning'?"

Contemporary hermeneutics has brought into focus the historical conditioning of the interpreter (i.e., pre-understanding) and how that conditioning influences the reading of a text. The vital question is whether or not humans are capable of suspending our entrenchment in our culture long enough to allow the text to speak on its own. The whole of the historical-critical method stands on the assumption that readers can achieve a degree of objectivity that allows them to understand the text. That assumption has been challenged, as we have seen, from several sources. What, then, is the option? If we cannot escape our own pre-understanding, are we then locked out of the meaning of a text? Can the meaning of the text be anything other than what we want it to be?

One simple way of taking the challenge of hermeneutics seriously may be suggested by another metaphor for reading. Suppose we think of the encounter with a text as comparable to meeting a stranger and getting acquainted. The key to such a process is asking questions about the stranger, as well as allowing the stranger to question us. We become acquainted with another by virtue of questions, and the better the questions we ask of the other person the more productive the encounter becomes. If we ask the wrong questions, we get nowhere.[6]

---

[6] The practice of asking questions of a text in order to understand it is inherent in the two (somewhat different) proposals for how we read a biblical passage found in Robert Kysar and Robert G. Hughes, *Preaching Doctrine for the Twenty-First Century* (Fortress Resources for Preaching; Minneapolis: Fortress, 1997), 36–53 and Robert Kysar, *Opening the Bible: What It Is, Where It Came From, What It Means for You* (Minneapolis; Augsburg, 1999), 69–84. Bultmann claims that there must be a correspondence between the questions we raise to the text and the interests of the text itself. See "The Problem of Hermeneutics," in *Essays: Philosophical and Theological* (London: SCM, 1955), 258.

However, it takes only a modicum of wisdom to realize that we are liable to ask the stranger questions and hear the answers in terms of our own situation. Suppose the stranger is from a region you once visited; you are likely to ask questions influenced by your knowledge of the region. But in a similar manner we can project our own problems and interests onto the stranger. Prejudice comes into play in the dialogue, as does self-interest. In other words, we may impose our issues on the stranger. If we are uncomfortable with older women because of the influence of our mother, the process of getting to know an older woman may be slow or difficult.

We ask questions of the text which help us to come to understand it, but our questions may be shaded with our own interests. An excessive honoring of Scripture, for instance, might prevent our being critical of a text. Somehow it may not occur to us to ask why a text seems to oppress women by giving them only traditional roles. We may be so committed to a point of view that we impose it on the text. If there is any truth in this concept of reading texts, then a prerequisite for understanding a text is *self-understanding*. Criticism of a biblical passage requires self-critical study.

The hermeneutical question is how we bridge the gap between ourselves and the Bible. How do we facilitate an engagement of the two horizons? So, the question of meaning in a text is rooted in the relationship between the reader and text, and the better we can understand that relationship, the more valuable our reading becomes.

Our exploration of the meaning of meaning now leads us to pose three questions: Where do we look for meaning? What does meaning mean (including what does language mean)? What, if anything, is unique about pastoral or homiletical meaning? By considering these questions in this order, we will move closer to one of the most disturbing issues before us today.

WHERE DO WE LOOK FOR MEANING?

Where is meaning? Do texts themselves mean? Or, is it only readers who make texts mean? Contemporary responses widely differ, but they may be summarized around the locus of meaning. In our interpretative efforts with a text, are we to assume that its meaning resides (1) behind the text in its historical origin, (2) in the text itself, (3) in front of the text,[7] or (4) in the

---

[7]This is a standard distinction by which many discuss the question of interpretation. For two such discussions, see the books by David L. Bartlett, *Between the Bible and the Church: New Methods for Biblical Preaching* (Nashville, Tenn.: Abingdon, 1999) and W. Randolf Tate, *Biblical Interpretation: An Integrated Approach* (rev. ed.; Peabody, Mass.: Hendrickson, 1997).

context in which it is read? Exploring these four alternatives for the location of meaning allows us to summarize much of what has been discussed in the previous chapters.

Meaning Behind, In, or In Front of the Text

Meaning behind the text. As we saw in chapter one, the historical-critical method leads us to believe that the meaning of the text is found within its original historical setting. Hence, we ask questions regarding what is behind this text. In other words, we look through the text to seen its origin. The text gives us evidence for what lies behind it, and we bring all our historical and linguistic knowledge to aid us in that search.

What is going on, for instance, in Jer 31:15, when the prophet declares, "Thus says the LORD: 'A voice is heard in Ramah, lamentation and bitter weeping. Rachel is weeping for her children; she refuses to be comforted for her children, because they are no more' "? Interpreters try to set this passage down in a particular point in history. From various sources (including the whole of Jeremiah) they construct a historical setting at a particular time and place in which the words of the text originated. With it set in that context, they then try to determine what the prophet originally meant by these words. In the case of Jer 31:15, the investigation supposes that the words are spoken to the people of Judah in exile in 722–721 B.C.E.—a time contemporaneous with the prophet when the words were part of his effort to reassure the people that God would restore their nation.[8]

To use another example, what does Paul mean by declaring in 1 Cor 11:4–5, "Any man who prays or prophesies with something on his head disgraces his head, but any woman who prays or prophesies with her head unveiled disgraces her head—it is one and the same thing as having her head shaved"? In search of the meaning of Paul's declaration, historical critics have tried to understand the social practices of women in Corinth in the middle of the first century C.E. One of the common assertions is that prostitutes or priestesses of certain cults wore their hair short, and by removing their veils, Christian women were liable to be identified with them.[9] Another interpretation sets the passage in the context of Christian women who unveiled themselves as a symbol of Christ's annihilation of all social differences, including

---

[8] See Patrick D. Miller, "The Book of Jeremiah: Introduction, Commentary, and Reflections," *NIB* 6:810–11.

[9] For example, F. W. Grosheide, *Commentary on the First Epistle to the Corinthians* (NICNT; Grand Rapids: Eerdmans, 1953), 254.

gender (Gal 3:28).[10] In both cases, Paul's words garner meaning by virtue of the setting in which they were written. Meaning arises from the historical references implied in the words of the text.

This understanding of meaning, therefore, values historical setting and also authorial intention. Such a hermeneutic assumes that a human mind lies behind the text and that a human being encoded meaning in the text in a manner appropriate to his or her day. Therefore, to ask about the meaning of text entails asking, What did the author want to say with these words? The assumption that meanings lie behind a passage in the mind of the author in a particular historical context continues to influence a good deal of biblical interpretation. The interpreter can identify the original intent of the author and communicate that "intended meaning" to others. While the view's dominance in biblical studies is weakening, it will likely continue to be an option for understanding the location of meaning for some time to come.

Meaning in the text. That we can discern a text's meaning simply by attending to what is in the text itself (without reference to its origin) seems an almost commonsense assumption, but in fact such a view was revolutionary in biblical studies around the middle of the twentieth century. The interpretation of Rom 5:12, 17 is one example.

> Therefore, just as sin came into the world through one man, and death came through sin, and so death spread to all because all have sinned. . . . If, because of the one man's trespass, death exercised dominion through that one, much more surely will those who receive the abundance of grace and the free gift of righteousness exercise dominion in life through the one man, Jesus Christ.

Traditional historical criticism (in its history of religions mode) interpreted this passage by means of what was thought to have been an early Jewish mythological understanding of Adam and sin (such as those expressed in Ecclesiasticus [Wisdom of Jesus the Son of Sirach] 25:24 and the Syriac Apocalypse of Baruch 54:15).[11] Karl Barth, however, was content to explicate this text as it stands without reference to its historical setting.[12] In doing so, he launched a movement in biblical interpretation that reached far beyond his own critical method.

---

[10] For example, Archibald Robertson and Alfred Plummer, *A Critical and Exegetical Commentary on the First Epistle of St. Paul to the Corinthians* (2d ed. ICC; Edinburgh: T&T Clark, 1914), 230.

[11] See for instance James D. G. Dunn, *Romans 1–8* (WBC 38a; Dallas: Word Books, 1988), 289. See also, Luke Timothy Johnson, *Reading Romans: A Literary and Theological Commentary* (New York: Crossroads Publishing, 1997), 86–87.

[12] Karl Barth, *The Epistle to the Romans* (trans. E. C. Hoskyns; Oxford: Oxford University Press, 1933), 164–72.

As we saw in Chapter Three, in contemporary scholarship the revolt against the historical-critical method appeals to the claim that, apart from its historical origin, a text carries meaning within itself. That meaning may or may not have something to do with what the author of the text intended. Some will argue that the author's intention is in no way relevant to the text's meaning. Once written, the text takes on its own meaning, independent of authorial intention. Whatever poets originally meant by their words does not limit what their poems can mean today.

For instance, since alchemy is hardly contemporary, George Herbert's "The Elixir" seems fatally dated. The poet compares God to the "famous stone" that transforms rock into gold and concludes:

For that which God doth touch and own
Cannot for less be told.[13]

God continues to transform human life, and we need to know little or nothing about elixir to discover that meaning. Herbert's words *mean* today in new and fresh ways each time they are read.

Among those who operate out of a literary rather than a historical paradigm for interpretation, Mark Allan Powell maintains that the narrative critic assumes that meaning lies within the text.[14] Even a difficult text such as 1 Cor 11:4–5, which we mentioned earlier, holds its own meaning, as Antoinette Clark Wire's rhetorical study of 1 Corinthians has so clearly shown. She argues that in 11:2–16, "head" (*kephalē*) functions metaphorically for authority, and the issue is Christ's authority. Paul's "pun" really has to do with the appropriate authority implicit in the actions of men as well as women.[15]

The supposition that meaning is *in* the text usually gets worked out in terms of the notion that, regardless of the author's intention, the text as it stands communicates ascertainable meaning. How one construes the idea that meaning is in the text varies among interpreters. A recent discussion of "meaning in a text" proposes that authorial intent is discernible and important. The biblical texts were created as deliberate efforts to communicate with the reader, so it is a communication between or among persons. The

---

[13] George Herbert, "The Elixir," in *Seventeenth-Century Prose and Poetry* (ed. R. P. Tristram Coffin and A. M. Witherspoon; New York: Harcourt, Brace and Company, 1929), 121.

[14] Mark Allan Powell, *What is Narrative Criticism?* (BSNT; Minneapolis: Fortress, 1990), 16.

[15] Antoinette Clark Wire, *The Corinthian Women Prophets: A Reconstruction Through Paul's Rhetoric* (Minneapolis: Fortress, 1990), 118–20.

meaning in that communication is, therefore, *presence*—the presence of the person of the author.[16]

In any case, when meaning is thought to be in the text itself, an interpreter's task is to "mine" that text for its meaning, not by appealing to the text's origin, but to the text's present content and structure. Does a text's meaning depend in any significant way on its origin? Or, is it the case that meaning is latent in the text itself without necessary reference to its origin? There is still another option.

Meaning in front of the text. In the swirl of contemporary biblical hermeneutics, the claim that the text has meaning in and of itself without recourse to its origin is a middle and moderate position. To the "left" of this middle position is one which claims that meaning for a text is created entirely by the reader "in front of the text." Meaning is not found behind the text or even in the text itself. It is found in the reader's mind. The text is not a "window" through which we look to discover its meaning. Rather, the text is a "mirror" that occasions a creation of its meaning.[17]

For clarity, we might distinguish two general positions among those who claim that meaning is found in front of the text. On the one side are those who would claim that *the reader enlivens—brings to life—the meaning resident in the text.* There is no meaning in a written text until it is read. That is, it is discerned only "in front of the text" in the act of reading. It takes a reader to make the text mean, and without a reader its meaning is dormant.[18]

Paul Ricoeur, the French philosopher and linguist, contends that meaning is found in front of the text. He insists that readers must "construct the meaning of a text." "The construction," he writes, "takes the form of a wager or a guess." Moreover,

> the construction rests upon "clues" contained in the text itself. A clue serves as guide for a specific construction . . . it excludes unsuitable constructions and allows those which give more meaning to the same words . . . in both cases, one construction can be said to be more probable than another, but not more truthful.[19]

---

[16] Kevin J. Vanhoozer, *Is There a Meaning in This Text? The Bible, the Reader, and the Morality of Literary Knowledge* (Grand Rapids: Zondervan, 1998). For a good review of this book see the one by Fred W. Burnett in the *JBL* 120 (2001): 594–95.

[17] See Chapter Three, note 19. See also Norman R. Petersen, *Literary Criticism for New Testament Critics* (GBS/NT; Philadelphia: Fortress, 1978), 19.

[18] Mark Allen Powell summarizes this view: "The relationship of reader and text is dialectical, so meaning should not be viewed as something a reader creates out of a text but rather as the dynamic product of the reader's interaction *with* the text." *What is Narrative Criticism?*, 17–18.

[19] Paul Ricoeur, *Hermeneutics and the Human Sciences* (ed. and trans. J. B. Thompson; Cambridge: Cambridge University Press, 1981), 175, 177.

Ricoeur's is typical of the views that hold meaning is found in front of the text and is a construction by the reader that uses the text's "clues" to decipher meaning.

Something of the same view has been called "hermeneutical creativity." In this case the interpreter follows an intuition and comes to a conclusion about a text's meaning. One critic summarizes this view with these words:

> It is only by some such imaginative leap, based on our own whole experience of reality as much as our attention to the text that we can sense what a religious text might mean. Subjectivity is a necessity for grasping religious truth. Some means of objectivity and critical distance follows.[20]

Before turning to the second of the views of meaning in front of the text, we need to digress slightly to note the combined importance of several interpretative movements and methods that arise as a result of admitting that meaning is in front of the text. Some feminist and ideological interpretations exemplify the first of those movements. The feminist movement has demonstrated how important gender is in the construction of meaning. It led the way in forcing biblical interpretation to become honest with regard to the construction of meaning. To be sure, feminist biblical interpretation has demonstrated the gender interests of the text itself. But beyond that, female interpreters have helped us see that we construct meaning out of our place in a society.[21] Gender positions us in culture, and that position is liable to determine the meaning we formulate from a text. Aided by scholars from different cultures and sub-cultures in North America, feminist interpreters left no place to turn than to the second movement.

This movement, which is far more radical, is the claim of some interpreters that *meaning is only a construct in the reader's mind without clues from the text.* Meaning does not lie awaiting us in the printed words. The printed words only "occasion" the creation of meaning. According to this view, what actually happens in the process of reading is that readers invent meaning from exposure to a text. So, readers themselves are responsibility for the production of meaning.[22] In the last chapter, we saw examples of how the reader alone assumes responsibility for a text's meaning.

---

[20] Robert Morgan and John Barton, *Biblical Interpretation* (The Oxford Bible Series; Oxford: Oxford University Press, 1988), 183.

[21] In her presidential address for the Society of Biblical Literature, Elisabeth Schüssler Fiorenza argued that this fact involves an ethical issue for interpreters. See "The Ethics of Biblical Interpretation" *JBL* 107 (1988): 3–17.

[22] See Edgar V. McKnight, *Postmodern Use of the Bible: The Emergence of Reader-Oriented Criticism* (Nashville: Abingdon, 1988).

Bernard Brandon Scott provides a provocative understanding of meaning in language. He supposes a communication scheme that forms a square with "message" set at one corner, "sender" at another, "receiver" at the third, and "world" at the fourth corner.

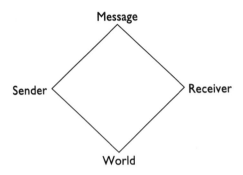

With this diagram Scott proceeds to set aside "two common misconceptions about the 'where' of language." The first is the notion that meaning is in the sender's mind and hidden in a message. The second is that a message has a single meaning. His conclusion is instructive:

> Meaning therefore is an imaginative interaction between receiver (reader) and message (text). The "more than" of meaning is the reader restoring a text to life, for without the reader's imaginative engagement a text would remain only paper and ink. *Meaning is an act of relation or association that takes place in our imagination.*[23]

Scott's emphasis on the reader's imaginative construction of meaning is one way to recognize how readers generate meaning in front of the text.

When readers are made entirely responsible for meaning, several subsequent emphases emerge, all of which we have mentioned earlier in this book. First of all, there is no such thing as a text's meaning. What we once called "the meaning of a text" becomes the reader's meaning associated with a text. Second, there are then a multitude of meanings possible for any text. The "true meaning" has nothing to do directly with a text but with the process by which a reader constructs meaning, much as we might fashion meaning from

---

[23] Bernard Brandon Scott, *The Word of God in Words: Reading and Preaching* (Fortress Resources for Preaching; Philadelphia: Fortress, 1985), 16–17. The quotation is from p. 17 and the italics ours. Later in his book, Scott summarizes by stating, "God hides in language's surplus. We encounter God in languages more than in metaphor" (75).

reading Herbert's poem. The issues of "true meaning" turn on the reader. Is the meaning you create from reading a text true to yourself?[24] Finally, this position can be interpreted as a radical form of individualism, unless it is somehow related to a community of readers. While there are indeed dangers in this sort of understanding of meaning, there may be advantages as well. The possibility of a plurality of meanings "allows scripture to illuminate the great diversity of human experience."[25] We will need to say more about meaning in social contexts, but for now note that readers' constructions of meaning may in some cases take place within a community and in relationship with those of that community. In such cases, then, we really should speak of a community's construction of meaning.

While debate rages among the proponents of these three positions, some eclectic blending of the three seems very desirable. The truth may not be confined exclusively to only one of the three options.[26] At this point, we should recognize the possibilities of some sort of synthesis of the three views of the locus of meaning. Such a possibility is pursued by W. Randolph Tate. Tate carefully reviews the three views—"the world behind the text," "the world within the text," and "the world in front of the text"—but then refuses to contend that one of these three perspectives is true without the other two. He constructs a model for communication which allows him to bring these three together into one hermeneutic.

> If the interpreter takes any of these interpretative thrusts in isolation (i.e., author-centered, text-centered, or reader-centered), consciously or unconsciously excluding the other two hermeneutics becomes an unbalanced discipline. . . . Hermeneutics is a dialogue between the text, and the reader, and the text and reader enter into in a conversational covenant *informed by the world of the author.* . . . This approach rests upon a modified communication model in

---

[24] It is interesting that Jeffrey L. Staley, a reader-response critic, responded to criticism of his work by writing an autobiographical book on the Gospel of John: *Reading with a Passion: Rhetoric, Autobiography, and the American West in the Gospel of John* (New York: Continuum, 1995) (see Chapter Three). Equally interesting is the appreciative review of Staley's book written by Stephen D. Moore, a deconstructive critic in *JBL* 117 (1998): 366–67. Staley is honest enough to recognize that reader-response criticism is a form of reader construction of meaning in front of the text, which always occurs in the context of the interpreter's own history.

[25] Morgan and Barton, *Biblical Interpretation,* 198.

[26] An effort at a synthesis is found in Vernon K. Robbins, *Exploring the Texture of Texts: A Guide to Socio-Rhetorical Interpretation* (Valley Forge, Pa.: Trinity International, 1996). Robbins attempts to construe socio-rhetorical as a kind of hub around which the concerns of the other approaches to interpretation can be attached.

which the text and reader dialogue, and in which the world of the author offers preparatory, foundational information for the dialogue.[27]

Tate contends that the concepts of meaning in the text and in front of the text are central to interpretation, while meaning behind the text provides information for the exchange. However, he also goes on to say, "Meaning takes place somewhere within this conversation and can never exist apart from the interpretative context of the reader."[28] His proposal is worthy of consideration, although the synthesis may not be as easy as he presents it.

The question of whether meaning is located behind the text, in the text itself, or in the reader in front of the text is destined to be discussed for several decades to come and will, in all likelihood, entail some radical changes in biblical interpretation. However, the movement in the last quarter of the twentieth century can clearly be traced from "behind the text" and "through the text" to lead us to the readers of the text themselves, who are the "meaning agents" in the process of the interpretation of Scripture, but who as agents always operate within a specific context.

Meaning in Context

Consequently, another view of the location of meaning might be summarized this way: the meaning of a text arises as a result of the particular context in which it is read. There is as of yet no consensus among scholars on the importance of the context of the reader in the process of discerning meaning. The issue entails deciding if the contextual reading of a text clarifies the meaning that is already in the text or whether the contextual reading actually creates the text's meaning—the same issue we encounter between meaning in and meaning in front of the text. Begging that delicate question, we want simply to say that another view of the location of meaning emphasizes the reader's context—sometimes understood to be the definitive influence on the reader and sometimes to be but one among many influences.

We have examined liberation methods of interpretation which stress that the Bible must be read in the social, political, and economic context of people and their struggles. In this type of interpretation, context produces meaning. It illumines a passage so that we can suddenly see meaning that would otherwise evade us. The basic premise is that there is no such thing as a reading that occurs outside of any context. The question is which context best illumines a passage.[29]

---

[27] Tate, *Biblical Interpretation*, 255. Italics ours.

[28] Ibid., 256–57.

[29] Paul Ricoeur is among those who claim that words really do not have meaning in and of themselves but are always contextual. Context determines meaning.

For example, Matt 2:18 quotes Jer 31:15 and interprets it outside of its context in Israel's history as found in the Hebrew Scriptures. Rather, it understands Jer 31:15 to mean something entirely different than the text might have meant in its supposed original sense. Herod's drastic and insane act to protect himself from one whom he thought threatened his throne happened, according to Matthew, in order "to fulfill" (*plēroō*) Jeremiah's words. The first evangelist seemed, by his use of this text, to believe that meaning results from the reader's context. The contemporary context in which the text is read is more important than the context in which the text was written. (See the sermon at the conclusion of Chapter One.)

As we said earlier, the first Christians, like their Jewish contemporaries, assumed—and did not find it necessary to argue in support of their view— that texts were fluid. Hence, their meaning could be discerned in the light of what reference we, the readers (at any given point in history), give the text. Christian readers of the Hebrew Scriptures clearly shared this view of texts with the rabbinic movement, which took it for granted that the meaning of the text is never fully exhausted. It may be interpreted over and over again in different contexts, and its meaning is never fully depleted. The new reference we assign to the words of the text, as it were, uncovers a meaning within the text. It appears the ancients never assumed (perhaps never considered the possibility) that the meaning of a text was fixed by its original setting.

We preachers are especially experienced with reading texts in new contexts and finding new meaning. We may do our historical-critical research and learn what meaning scholars think the text might have had in its historical origin. But we never stop there. We claim that texts have meanings that exceed their original intention, just as George Herbert's poetry does. So, we preach the meaning the text has for another time, another place, and another community of readers. In effect, we recontextualize the text, placing it in the midst of our congregation at a specific time.[30] We ask what the text means in a particular context. (See the discussion in the last part of this chapter.) Whatever those using historical-critical methods may say was the original meaning of a passage, we venture to say that the text still "means" in another and different historical context. Sometimes we call this "the living Word" of Scripture. Its meaning is never exhausted merely by pinning down what we think the original authors meant by writing it.

See *The Rule of Metaphor: Multi-disciplinary Studies of the Creation of Meaning* (trans. Robert Czerny et al.; Toronto: University of Toronto Press, 1977), 291.

[30] Robert Kysar, "Preaching As Biblical Theology: A Proposal for a Homiletic Method," in *The Promise and Practice of Biblical Theology* (ed. John Reumann; Minneapolis: Fortress, 1991), 143–56.

All of the discussion concerned with the location of meaning pushes us deeper in order to sort out more clearly what we mean when we use the word "meaning."

WHAT MEANING MEANS

What happens when a text "means"? What must take place to allow us to say, "This text means . . ."? Or, "The meaning I construct from my encounter with this text is . . . ?" Any honest answer to such questions is terribly complex, and we do not pretend to offer conclusive answers. However, in our search for a way of understanding what meaning "means," we need first of all to say something about language and its role in meaning.

Does Language "Mean"?

The last chapter nailed this question to the wall of deconstruction, and for good reason. We may need to repeat a few things about the meaning of language which we encountered in the previous chapter. Actually the three traditional understandings of meaning in language are not very helpful for our purposes, but they provide a place to begin. The *referential theory* assumes that meaning is comprised of that to which language (or gesture) refers. The meaning of chair is its reference to that object on which it is suitable for a person to sit. In this case, meaning is essentially little more than naming. The *ideational theory* assumes that all meaning is comprised of ideas and entails the communication of a thought from one mind to another. The meaning of chair, in this case, is the idea (or concept) of an object on which it is suitable for a person to sit.[31]

A dissatisfaction with both of these formulations gave rise to the *stimulus-response theory.* This view builds on the fact that the meaning of much language depends on public consensus. It is a public situation in which the meaning of language is observable. We look for meaning in "regularities of connection between utterances and publicly observable features of the communication situation." Hence, the meaning of chair is determined first of all by public consensus but more importantly by the situation in which it is used. In certain situations "have a chair" means to be

---

[31] See Scott, *The Word of God in Words,* 17. He calls the referential function of language "pointer" and the ideational function "idea." Later he argues that meaning is not a thing in a container but is an "interaction" (76).

seated, while "chair the meeting" means something quite different in certain other situations.[32]

Since there is no agreement on any of these traditional theories of meaning, we need to go further in our investigation of how (if at all) language "means." We have already discussed the change in the way we think of language and how it works, so we refer you to that discussion in Chapter Three. However, language no longer "means" as once we supposed it did. The major shifts in the understanding of language are implicit in the question of the meaning of meaning. The shift in the understanding of language entails three stages, which, when taken together, challenge our assumptions that interpreters can discern meaning in a text's language.

First, language was once thought to be tightly bound to reality beyond itself, much as the referential theory supposes. Hence, language referred us to extra-linguistic (or non-linguistic) reality. Language is now seldom understood to have non-linguistic reference (that is, reference to some objective reality other than language).

Second, then, the reference of language is not extra-linguistic but linguistic. Many would have us understand that the reference of language is always other language, or linguistic structures of some sort. If it is true that self-consciousness is itself linguistic (that is, it is constructed with linguistic symbols), the final reference of language is always to human self-consciousness.[33]

Third, assumptions about the precision of language have been nullified. The weaknesses of language have become much clearer to us and have had far-reaching impact. We now acknowledge that all language is limited in its ability both to speak of reality and to stimulate meaning. Language is culturally bound—enchained by its user's own finitude. Our language is always a mirror of who we are both socially and personally. It is always biased on both ends—biased by both the user's and the interpreter's cultural settings. Moreover, as we Christians can surely understand, language is gorged with human sin. As interpreters, we filter all language through our vested interests, our prejudices, and our brokenness, just as ideological criticism claims (see Chapter Four). As preachers, our language carries within it all of our sinfulness and limitations.[34] As a consequence of these shifts in our conception of

---

[32] William P. Alston, "Meaning," *The Encyclopedia of Philosophy* (ed. Paul Edwards; 8 vols.; New York: Macmillan, 1967), 5:233–36. The quotation is from p. 5:236.

[33] Lucy Atkinson Rose, *Sharing the Word: Preaching in the Roundtable Church* (Louisville: Westminster John Knox, 1997), 17–18, 44, 67.

[34] However, Scott asserts that the instability of language "allows for the possibility of God's appearance." *The Word of God in Words*, 18.

language, we have to ask how language can "mean" at all—at least beyond very narrow boundaries.

Finally, it follows from these shifts that the recognition of the multivalence of all language has refashioned its function. We have been forced to acknowledge that all language is filled with ambiguity and almost endless possibilities of meaning, as the deconstructionists have been saying for nearly half a century. Once we thought that precise language could limit meaning, and we relegated polyvalence to the poets. Increasingly, however, we have found that even the most precise and careful language "means" beyond the intention of its user. Once spoken or written, language is free to communicate a vast range of meaning beyond what might have been its "intended meaning." Language always has a "surplus of meaning" or a "more than." Language is always and inherently unstable. It is relational, entailing both the originator and the recipients. Consequently, Bernard Brandon Scott concludes that a passage such as John 1:14 is drenched with ambiguity: "The Word became flesh and pitched its tent among us . . . is suggestive of meaning(s). It has no single, simple meaning. It asks the reader to play imaginatively with its possibilities."[35]

Does language "mean"? Yes, obviously it does, but it has both strict limitations and almost boundless possibilities for conveying meaning. As readers we stand in front of the text, using our imaginations to construct meaning from the inherently ambiguous language we find there. We are always and inevitably construing meaning that may or may not have anything to do with the meaning intended by the author or even the supposed "sense" of the text. Words can "mean" as differently as the differences among those who read the same words.

All this comes as no surprise to preachers. Most of us, at least, have had the experience of hearing the words of our sermons construed in ways we could never have imagined. This is the case in spite of the fact that we assume we speak with some precision and with a community of believers who share a common vocabulary.[36] Of course, the instability or undecidability of our language sometimes has positive results. Not infrequently, after a sermon we thought was a lead balloon, a parishioner will tell us how in our feeble words they heard the precise message they needed at the time, regardless of whether or not that was the message we had intended to communicate! Listeners construct their own meanings from the language we use, no matter how precise we try to make it.

---

[35] Scott, *The Word of God in Words*, 25–27, 75.
[36] See Joseph M. Webb, *Preaching and the Challenge of Pluralism* (St. Louis: Chalice, 1998).

At this final level of our probe, our confidence in our ability to read a text and interpret its meaning is fatally shaken. So radical is this earthquake that we have to wonder if language "means" at all, or whether it is only we humans—we language users—who mean. This takes us to the next logical question.

What Is Meaning?

The philosophical and psychological dimensions of the question of meaning are intimidating. Nonetheless, we would like to sketch two somewhat different perspectives on meaning and then explore a possible synthesis of the two.

An existential-phenomenological perspective. One way of comprehending the essence of meaning returns to the second use of the hermeneutical circle mentioned above in the section on hermeneutics and meaning. One scholar asserts that there must be some "common ground between" the interpreter and the text if we are going to understand the text. At the very least, we find the text has to do with some human situation "in which we can imaginatively participate." Hence, the act of interpretation depends on the pre-understanding of readers—their interests, their issues, etc. "Interpretation is made possible by a certain community of interest between the text and the person who is seeking to understand it."[37]

The insistence that we must share some categories of experience with the text if it is going to have any meaning, finds its roots in the early work of Martin Heidegger. He suggested that meaning arises when we attempt to resolve the unfamiliar (*vorhanden*) by means of the familiar (*zuhanden*).[38] In a sense, this is what we mean when we say that the text examines us. It asks that we look into our experience and pre-understanding for the meaning the text offers.[39]

One interpreter of Heidegger has summarized the point with regard to biblical interpretation this way: "we rationalize the text into a world of familiar concepts and entities. . . . And in this sense, all interpretation is allegorical

---

[37] John Macquarrie, *The Scope of Demythologizing: Bultmann and His Critics* (New York: Harper & Row, 1960), 43–44. See also Thiselton, *Two Horizons*, 104–5.

[38] Martin Heidegger, *Being and Time* (trans. John Macquarrie and Edward Robinson; New York: Harper & Row, 1962), 242.

[39] Bultmann writes, "it is valid in the investigation of the text to allow oneself to be examined by the text, and to hear the claim it makes." "The Problem of Hermeneutics," 254.

interpretation."[40] It is "allegorical" insofar as the meaning we think we discern is comprehended in terms of another meaning. In this use, allegory means to speak (or understand) one thing by means of the image of another thing.[41]

In other words, we interpret all experience through, and in the light of, what we already think we know. We employ concepts, images, and propositions we have available to us, that is, the familiar. In its simplest sense, interpretation is the process of fitting some experience (such as the reading of a text) into the system or complex of ideas and images we assume to be true in one sense or another. Hence, allegory is used insofar as we recognize or construe something in the text so that we can relate it to something already in place within our system of thought. An alien text then must somehow be forced into a structure of meaning that we already assume to be true. Failure to make these connections, failure at least to posit a relationship between the text and our system of thought, renders a text meaningless. In that case, it appears to us as gibberish—a foreign and unknown tongue. If this proposal for understanding meaning is true, we construct meaning out of the raw materials we already have at hand within our view of reality. To use Bernard Brandon Scott's proposal, we imagine ways by which we can relate to the message and do so on the basis of what we already are or think we know.

Heidegger's thought contributed to the rise of a philosophical movement called *phenomenology.* One of the themes of that movement is the human effort to make sense of experience and do so by "bracketing" opinions about the human world so that one can understand directly how some phenomenon is actually lived by people.[42] It is exploration of the lived world (at the level of bare existence) so as to discover meaningful reality. In the simplest sense, meaning is the result of a careful consideration of what one actually experiences, apart from preconceived notions about the world.[43] To know in a

---

[40] A. K. M. Adam, *Making Sense of New Testament Theology: "Modern" Problems and Prospects* (StABH 11; Macon, Ga.: Mercer University Press, 1995), 175.

[41] Allegory is comprised of two Greek words: *allos* which means "other" and *agoreuein,* which means "to speak in assembly or in the market place" (*agora*).

[42] For example, see the now famous discussion of "The Look" in Jean-Paul Sartre, *Being and Nothingness: An Essay on Phenomenological Ontology* (trans. Hazel E. Barenes; New York: Philosophical Library, 1956), 252–302. Sartre analyzes the experience of the "other's gaze."

[43] See the work of John Wild, an interpreter of phenomenology. *Existence and the World of Freedom* (Englewood Cliffs, N.J.: Prentice-Hall, 1963), 34–38, and *The Challenge of Existentialism* (Bloomington, Ind.: Indiana University Press, 1959), 188–94.

phenomenological sense is to experience directly without the filters of both private and social presuppositions.

If you think this view of meaning sounds circular, you are correct. However, the method proposed by phenomenology assumes that our systems of meaning are not absolutely closed and unchangeable. Experiences challenge systems of thought and views of reality, but the human mind can enter into those experiences as others know them and find meaning. Perhaps, like us, you yourself can easily identify experiences you had that threw your system of thought, your worldview, into chaos. Reading texts can disrupt the easy maintenance of a worldview. Some of Jesus' parables seem to be designed to do just that—to subvert the dominant worldview and hint at another possibility.[44] But even the change in our systems of meaning takes place in a double relationship: on the one hand, with what we already think we know to be true and, and on the other hand, with the new phenomenon that seems to challenge our confidence.

So, for instance, when we read the parable of the unjust manager in Luke 16, the reading may disrupt our systems of meaning. But we may negotiate that disruption through means of a concept already in place in our consciousness, namely, justice.[45] To say this in different words, the relationship between the disruptive experience and our worldview or system of thought may be one of contradiction, of opposition. Even then, however, meaning arises from allegorical construal or interpretation of the text using our worldview—a construal of opposition. Opposition, moreover, is most productive when we try to suspend our own views to comprehend the experience in itself and as others live it. Meaning always arises from the relationship of an experience (in this case, the reading of a text) with the worldviews by which we live our daily lives.

---

[44]The parable of the workers in the vineyard in Matt 20 is surely a good example. John R. Donahue, S.J. comments, "Hardly any parable in the Gospels seems to upset the basic structure of an orderly society as does this one." *The Gospel in the Parables: Metaphor, Narrative, and Theology in the Synoptic Gospels* (Minneapolis: Fortress, 1988), 81–82. See also Scott, who speaks of Jesus' parables as "anti-myth." He does so "[b]ecause they disorder the mythical world; they are world-shattering" *Hear Then the Parable: A Commentary on the Parables of Jesus* (Minneapolis: Fortress, 1989), 39. Another analysis of the way Jesus' parables deconstruct the readers' or hearers' worlds is found in William R. Herzog II, *Parables as Subversive Speech: Jesus as Pedagogue of the Oppressed* (Louisville: Westminster John Knox, 1994).

[45]See, for example, Joseph A. Fitzmyer, *The Gospel According to Luke X–XXIV: A New Translation with Introduction and Commentary* (AB 28A; Garden City, N.J.: Doubleday, 1985), 1095–96.

A symbolic interaction perspective. The perspective sketched above can be interpreted in radically individualistic terms (although that would be a misinterpretation). The truth is that we know our systems of thought are socially constructed and dependent on our experience within a particular culture over a period of time. For that reason, among others, the perspective based on *symbolic interaction theory* provides a helpful corrective and perhaps a clearer picture of how we construct meaning.

The symbolic interaction perspective is best understood by starting with symbols and their role in human life. Joseph Webb defines symbol in this way:

> a symbol is, or becomes, *anything*—literally anything—into which a human being *places any meaning and/or feeling:* that is its communicative, or sociological, definition. The symbol is an arbitrary human construct, arising from an innate constructive ability within every human being.[46]

Having bestowed meaning on something (making it a symbol for ourselves), we proceed to use it in communication. A human develops an entire system of symbols, that is, an assemblage of such arbitrarily defined symbols that account for the world as we know it. Therefore, reality exists only within the human mind and in the form of these symbols, and human consciousness is erected out of our symbols. The relationship between our own symbolic realities and the objective reality (i.e., the world as it is) may vary.

Ultimately, then, meaning resides in the human act of bestowing significance of both a cognitive and emotional kind when we create our own symbols.

> Meaning is a complex blend of cognition and feeling, either positive or negative, and it is conferred on "things"—on anything—by people and cultures that use those "things." . . . We are, by nature, the creators of meaning, symbolic meaning.[47]

Moreover, humans feel a necessity to fashion for themselves a unified system of symbols, and how we do that varies from individual to individual. There is nothing inherent in the symbols we create that makes them harmonious with one another, but we create that harmony for the sake of our perspective on the world. The creation of that harmony is done allegorically; things are assigned meaning in accord with the particular symbolic system we have al-

---

[46] Webb, *Preaching and the Challenge of Pluralism*, 18. The whole of our discussion of the symbolic interaction understanding of meaning is drawn from Webb's book.

[47] Ibid., 29.

ready created for ourselves. Symbolic interaction shares with the existential/ phenomenological view an appreciation for allegorically creating meaning from that which we already think we know. According to symbolic inter-actionism, *hub symbols* are central to the unity we humans fashion for ourselves. These are special symbols which "provide the key to human behavior" of all kinds. These central symbols are especially laden with emotional importance for us, and, the more emotional importance symbols have, the more central to a person's system of meaning they become. Most of us have experienced this in ourselves or others. Certain issues seem to arouse far more intense feeling than what might seem justified. Clearly, homosexuality touches the emotionally packed hub symbols of some people in our society in very different ways.

Hub symbols have a number of important features. First, they are often the "sacred" center of our lives. They are endowed with meaning that transcends all other meaning. Second, they are the source of our values. Third, our lives are rooted in the presuppositions of these symbols, and finally, they constitute our identity as persons.[48] The sharing of hub symbols, at least in a general way, provides the basis for social alignment and group formation. While we inherit many of our symbols and especially our hub symbols from family and culture, they are also the source of our sense of belonging to a group or even our family.

When such a view of meaning is brought to the task of interpreting a biblical text, the first result is to view language for what it truly is, namely, emotionally packed and loaded with significance. There are only occasional cases of the neutral or unbiased use of language, for example, specialized languages such as found in mathematics. Reading and understanding a text involves, among other things, recognizing the emotionally charged words and sentences and then playing them against one another. The result is a kind of conversation with the text that is not unlike the conversation one might have with other people as we encounter them and their symbol systems. When, for instance, we encounter a text like Jesus' radical declaration, "Whoever comes to me and does not hate father and mother, wife and children, brothers and sisters, yes, and even life itself, cannot be my disciple" (Luke 14:26). Struggling with that text takes the form of a conversation comparable to the one many of us North Americans might have when we encounter the hub symbols of an Arabic Moslem. We converse with the text to understand its symbols. As our symbol systems clash and exchange with those of a text, a number of different "meanings" of the text may arise, just as interpreters bring a number of different symbol systems to the text. With this approach,

---

[48] Ibid., 48–52. The quotation is from p. 49.

however, we are more likely to comprehend what a text "means" in the sense of its effect on us.[49]

A proposed synthesis. Note what these two understandings of meaning— the existential-phenomenological and the symbolic interaction—share in common.

First, they both assume that we develop and live with some sort of complex of meaning or symbols which provide a unity to our lives. That unity is important, since the inclusion of "new meaning" in both cases entails relating it to our existing systems of meaning.

Second, both the perspectives we have discussed here contend that meaning is a creation of the human mind. Meaning is not an ontological reality given to us in some revelatory experience. Rather, it is our own construal of experience and the "other" whom we meet in the world. This allows for a multitude of meaning systems and accounts for both pluralism and the conflict that results from the clash among systems of meaning.

Third, both views suggest that learning is a conversation between our meaning systems and other meaning systems out of which may come (but not easily) the understanding of others and even the modification of our meaning systems.

Finally, as we have already observed, the effort to understand another claim to meaning entails an allegorical relationship between it and our own precious hub (or basic, foundational) symbols.

Needless to say, such views of meaning as we have explored here can be disturbing. To be sure, meaning may be found in reference, for example, reference among symbols or reference between an experience and one's system of meaning. However, the reference is not to some body of eternal truths somewhere in the ontological heavens. It is in reference only to what we believe we already know and cherish. In this sense, we can say that language refers us to something else, but that referral goes on within the context of our own consciousness (both individual and social) and not beyond it. Reference is, if you will, internal. Moreover, it is always linguistic or symbolic, since consciousness is linguistic or symbolic. If the consciousness to which language or symbol refers is not purely individualistic, but also social, then that linguistic reference is to social consciousness as well as to the way in which that social consciousness has been internalized by an individual.

Do such understandings of meaning leave any room for the transcendent? If there is a category of transcendence or a hub symbol for transcendence in the reader's consciousness, yes; if there is not, then, no. If we have been socially conditioned to understand some experiences in terms of a tran-

---

[49] Ibid., 84–98.

scendent reality, a text may well "mean" by being taken as a reference to that "reality." If our hub symbols entail the concept of a reality that is beyond our immediate world, then a text's reference to God may make sense. The experience of transcendence may also be, however, the process of relating an opposing reality to reality as our culture conceives it. It may be a clash between one's hub symbol and another—a clash of the "gods" as it were, since we give our hub symbols a sacred quality.

Imagination and Meaning

Another factor enters the picture here. Human consciousness has an enormous capacity for imagination. We have already reported Scott's insistence that the construction of the meaning of a message from another is accomplished through imagination.[50] Indeed, it is by imagination that we grasp the relationships (or discern allegories) between a new experience and our systems of thought. Imagination allows us the possibility of comprehending what it might be like to live another person's or group's symbol system. It is our means of empathy, of entering into another, and possibly alien, symbolic meaning system. Imagination enables us to ask the "what if" questions.

Meaning may arise, therefore, by virtue of our asking, if such and such *were* the case, what would this text mean? When Moses catches a glimpse of God's back (Exod 33:23), we try to imagine God's backside in order to experience what Moses is experiencing! In other words, if new meaning is incorporated within our systems of thought and life, it is by virtue of imagination.

The text might, then, stimulate us to imagine the transcendent, to suppose, at least for the moment, that there is another dimension of reality. This is not unlike the way the "Matrix" trilogy of movies stimulates us to imagine another dimension of reality. Whether or not we incorporate that imagined dimension into our worldview is another question entirely. It is conceivable, on the one hand, that another element of a symbol system invades consciousness in a powerful and irresistible way and with such force that we feel compelled to adopt it and assign it significant meaning, as, for instance, might be the case with a traumatic experience. On the other hand, are human systems of meaning so tightly constructed and firmly in place that we may not be able even to comprehend other systems no matter how we might imagine ourselves embracing them? Probably any generalized answer to that question is faulty but answer it we must—at least for ourselves.

---

[50] Scott, *The Word of God in Words*, 25–27, 75.

Social Location and Meaning

We need to confront another question before concluding this discussion of the meaning of meaning. It is a question related to the contextual location of meaning we described earlier and has much in common with the symbolic interaction we have just discussed. In its most radical formulation, it is the notion that meaning is nothing more or less that the projection of a particular social conditioning on another reality. Is the comprehension of meaning due entirely to the social location of readers?[51] As we have already mentioned, scholarly attention to the impact of social location has brought us to a new level of candor with regard to our interpretative efforts. We read a text out of and in the light of our own place within a particular culture at a particular time. The meaning we construct as the result of reading a passage betrays who we are and in particular what culture has made us. Our vested interests, positions of power or powerlessness, gender, ethnicity—all these figure into what meaning we construct from a text. Meaning, then, is preeminently a social construction, not a purely individualistic one, and is dependent on social systems and the interests of a particular reading community. Whether we think of meaning as experiences or symbols allegorically similar to our belief system, we dare not deny that culture and background have influenced us.

This social understanding of meaning is inevitably the case if for no other reason than that language and symbols are social constructs which contain within themselves the prevailing social systems of any culture. We have increasingly recognized, through the course of the last four decades, that language has social roots and social ramifications. Words used in the dominant culture of the West, for instance, to name persons of other ethnic backgrounds betray a Euro-centric posture. Words used for females betray the patriarchal nature of our culture. Our language not only expresses culture, but perpetuates it. For example, as George Lakoff and Mark Johnson suggest, the phrase, "we *won* her over," demonstrates the way in which warfare functions as the basic metaphor for much of our common daily language, uncovering the competitive system of North American culture.[52] Readers' constructions of meaning, therefore, involve their social setting as much as their individual personalities.

---

[51] See Fernando F. Segovia and Mary Ann Tolbert, eds., *Reading from This Place* (2 vols., Minneapolis: Fortress, 1994–1995).

[52] George Lakoff and Mark Johnson, *Metaphors We Live By* (Chicago: University of Chicago Press, 1980). See also Michel Bal, "Metaphors He Lives By," in *Women, War and Metaphor: Language and Society in the Study of the Hebrew Bible* (ed. Claudia V. Camp and Carole R. Fontaine; *Semeia* 61; Atlanta: Scholars, 1993), 185–207.

Joseph Webb asks where we acquire hub symbols and claims that we are born with a "symbol-using ability" (including hub symbols). We collect our symbol systems from the culture and the people we encounter in growing up. Moreover, we "learn" our hub symbols from our "primary or familial group," our "reference groups" (groups to which we become attached and those to which we avoid becoming attached), and finally from "the traumatic episodes of one's maturation." In each case, our histories account for our systems of thought and feeling from which we create meaning.[53]

Thus when we read a passage, we are bound to construct its meaning in terms of our culture, our particular place in that culture, and all of the peculiar interests we have. We may read it as white, affluent, Western, and empowered men. We will doubtless find some esoteric reason for believing that our interpretations are the result of an informed reading and somehow more valuable than others. We feel we need to protect the power we have as trained biblical interpreters (as either pastors or professors)—protect it against the intrusions of those who are without comparable credentials. Our employment, prestige, and power are often all at stake in this kind of construction of meaning. If, for instance, an untrained lay person should prove her or himself as a gifted biblical interpreter, our status as formally trained pastors and teachers is sorely threatened.

Different social locations produce different readings, all of which may have legitimacy given the context in which the reading is done. If meaning is a reader's construct in response to the text, and if that construction is shaped by social and cultural conditioning, meaning arises from a construal of the text on the basis of the formative powers in our histories.

The recognition of the importance of social location in the interpretation of the Bible has had some marvelous results in professional biblical studies groups. We have realized that we must, if at all possible, entertain the insights of as many as possible from drastically different social locations than our own. So, scholarly meetings and literature are newly populated with readers from the so-called "third world," of different ethnic backgrounds, gender, political persuasion, and sexual preference. Those who sit around our table are wonderfully diverse.

Notwithstanding the reality of the social conditioning of meaning, perhaps we should beware of reductionism. Biblical studies, not to mention human knowledge in general, has in the past readily fallen victim to what seems to be a viable view by making it into an instant cure-all for our questions and issues. Your authors want to leave this issue unresolved because we believe all of us need to wrestle with the degree to which the construction

---

[53] Webb, *Preaching and the Challenge of Pluralism,* 53–57.

of meaning is entirely a result of social conditioning. Having done so, we venture one additional perspective on the meaning of meaning.

PASTORAL/HOMILETICAL MEANING

Many homileticians are uncomfortable with the proposal that readers construct meaning "in front of the text"—that meaning is entirely the result of readers' efforts and that those constructions of meaning depend on social conditioning. Many would be much more comfortable with the supposition that meaning arises from the external reference of the language of the text, and in particular reference to a body of objective truth. Basic to our traditional understanding of Christian doctrine, language refers to such an external body of truth, one that does not really change over the centuries. Certainly, the understanding of meaning as a human construct is only one option among many, and the jury is still out on this thorny question. The "jury" may never settle the matter, and, furthermore, chances are it will prove to be a "hung jury," unable to come to a decision.[54]

We preachers, of all people, should recognize something very familiar in the construal of meaning as the result of an internal reference of the hearer or reader, rather than meaning behind the text, or in the text. We know, for instance (as we have already mentioned), that our listeners attach their own meanings to our sermons, in spite of all our best efforts to convey our intended, authorial meaning clearly and accurately. If we can transfer that experience of the dangers inherent in communication back onto our experience of reading biblical texts, we may see the reading experience more clearly. It may just be the case that meaning occurs when we interpret an experience like reading a text or hearing a sermon in terms of its allegorical relationship with what we already think we know, or in the light of our hub symbols and the whole of our symbol system.

Preachers will undoubtedly pick up on the mention of imagination in this discussion. We know that it is in evoking the imaginary "what if" questions that people are most often changed by preaching. We know that sometimes the best we can do when "dancing the edge of mystery"[55] is to facilitate

---

[54] For a helpful collection of essays on different approaches to interpreting Scripture for preaching see Raymond Bailey, ed., *Hermeneutics for Preaching: Approaches to Contemporary Interpretations of Scripture* (Nashville: Broadman, 1992).

[55] Eugene L. Lowry, *The Sermon: Dancing the Edge of Mystery* (Nashville: Abingdon, 1997), 6. Lowry credits David Buttrick, *Homiletic* (Philadelphia: Fortress Press, 1987), 189, with the origin of this phrase in his title.

the congregation's imaginative pondering of possibilities for their lives. When we have done our work well, our parishioners go away with new images of, and for, their lives and worlds. They go away with a mental vision of what the kingdom might be like, should we ever encounter it.

Community Meaning

We have a hunch that something like finding meaning in front of the text happens for a lot of preachers as we prepare a sermon. If we are responsible pastoral preachers, we try to bring the congregation to the text with us, so that, as we are interpreting the text, our congregation plays a significant role in the meaning we find or assign to the text.[56] In other words, the text means as it is placed in the context of a particular congregation. You may not be willing for now to admit that experiencing a text's meaning in this way is entirely our own doing—that we create meaning quite apart from what the text itself means. But certainly the four-way dialogue among the text, the interpreter, the doctrinal tradition we embrace, and the congregation is crucial to interpretation for preaching. (Furthermore, if a fifth dialogue participant is the Holy Spirit, so much the better.)

What if we were to conceive meaning as a construct facilitated by a community in our consciousness and not simply by our individual preferences? What if we were to say that the meaning we finally assign to a text is a peculiar reading *for the sake of a group of people in this time and place of which we are members?* In other words, the special quality of a homiletic understanding of meaning may be first, and foremost, the fact that we ask the text to "mean" for a particular congregation at one single point in time and located in a specific place. This suggests that homiletical meaning entails substituting a congregation's consciousness for our own consciousness. Meaning then is less the result of our own individual symbol systems as it is the result of using a group's symbol system in reading the text.

A couple of things arise from this proposal. First, pastoral interpretation is a form of community interpretation in the place of individual interpretation. Our proposal is somewhat similar to the way communities function in Latin American liberation interpretation, where a group shapes the sense of a biblical passage in terms of their own struggles (see Chapter Four). When a community attempts to read and understand a text, individual systems of thought and feeling are in dialogue with one another. If none is repressed, if all are given voice, what we have is an eclectic, pluralistic

---

[56] See Thomas G. Long, *The Witness of Preaching* (Louisville: Westminster John Knox, 1989), 77.

system of meaning. Can we find allegorical relationships between this multifarious system and the claims of the text? Can we faithfully represent an entire congregation in a four-way (or five-way) dialogue among the text, the reader, and the congregation?

Second, assuming that the congregation becomes a determining agent in the construction of the meaning of a text, the congregation's needs, in effect, should take over the preacher's own consciousness. However, being realists about this matter forces us to ask whether we want a congregation's value system, for instance, to determine our reading of a text. We are aware that congregations invariably represent prejudices and egocentricity, and we do not want to cave in to that kind of value system. Still, what we may consider to be the shortcomings of a congregation may, in fact, be an attribute and not a detriment to the fashioning of meaning. If we bring the congregation's system of meaning to our reading of text, we are more likely to find that the text poses a serious and even fatal challenge to that congregation. A congregational reading does not necessarily mean that the text will be molded into the likeness of the congregation. Just the opposite may be the case. It may speak against the congregational consciousness. Moreover, the attempt to read for a congregation may also lessen our slavery to our own prejudices and presuppositions.

Third, are we capable of this sort of reading strategy? How can we possibly fairly and fully represent the congregation in front of the text? Our own symbol systems will surely get in the way, and we will only be fooling ourselves if we think we can entirely suspend them to represent the congregation's. Doubtless, this is correct, and yet it may be that we can represent the congregation more accurately than we think. If as pastors we immerse ourselves in the congregation as best we can, if we try to develop as complete as possible an empathy for their conditions, and if we dedicate ourselves as fully as possible to their welfare, we may—just may—sometimes be able to bracket, at least in part, our own symbol systems in favor of their collective values, especially given the fact that we ourselves are part of that congregation. Or, better, might the congregation become one of our hub symbols? If this homiletical reading is possible, it requires that we all be pastors first and preachers second and that we practice trying to be a complex model of someone who represents them.

Any sermon is a sermon for a particular community at a particular time, that is, if it is a worthy sermon. We know very well that sermons taken out of their congregational context lose something. Generic sermons written to address humanity in general are emphatically dull. A good sermon has in mind one community of faith in one place and time. Haven't we all interpreted a particular text in a somewhat special way because of what it meant when set alongside the congregation we serve? This is most obvious when there has been or is about to be some significant event in the congregation's life (say, a groundbreaking, a move to a new site, or the death of a leader). Such particularity is not a weakness but the very strength of preaching. God did not become incarnate as some amorphous human who was just like everyone in the world. When the Word became flesh, it was the flesh of a Galilean living in the first century C.E. who was subjected to all of the historical limitations of any person living at the time. So, when God becomes incarnate in a sermon, it is a proclamation for a particular group at a particular time.

A Biblical Model and Precedent

The biblical tradition provides both a precedent and a model for the kind of community reading we have advocated.[57] Scholars in the historical-critical arena have long recognized that biblical authors were often dependent on and utilized traditions that preceded them and that, in this case, the authors' task was to reinterpret the tradition for the community to which they were writing. There is considerable evidence of this sort of preservation and reinterpretation in portions of the Old Testament, but it may be easier to illustrate what we mean by use of New Testament material.[58]

As we have already mentioned, many scholars assume that Matthew and Luke both availed themselves of the Gospel of Mark (or at least an early form of that document). It is clear that, if the theory of the priority of Mark is sound, Matthew and Luke both reinterpreted the tradition they found in Mark and did so, in all likelihood, to address their own, contemporary communities. For example, the attention given to poverty and riches in the Gospel of Luke makes clear to many that this evangelist wanted the Jesus story to address explicitly a community or communities in which wealth and poverty were problems. The parables of the rich fool (Luke 12:16–21) and of Lazarus and the rich man (16:19–31) are unique to the third Gospel. Luke reports Jesus' beatitude as "blessed are the poor" (Luke 6:20), and not "blessed are the poor in spirit" as Matthew has it (Matt 5:3). Moreover, following Jesus' beatitudes, Luke reports a series of "woes" which single out the rich (Luke 6:24). Among the other teachings of Jesus, Luke includes the warning against

---

[57] Most of this section comes from Kysar's article, "Preaching as Biblical Theology," 143–56.

[58] For an introduction, see Douglas A. Knight, "Tradition History," *ABD* 6:633–38.

avarice found in Luke 12:11–12, and Mary's "Magnificat" (Luke 2:46–55) clearly expresses God's continuing favor of the poor and lowly.[59]

It is needless and unnecessary to speculate whether Luke was trying to motivate the rich to share their wealth with the poor or to strengthen the poor with the assurance of God's special concern for them, or perhaps both. The impact of the Lukan text itself, without historical speculation, is both to exhort the rich to share and to dignify the poor. Luke interprets the Jesus tradition with special emphasis on this relationship.

Other examples of how authors have reinterpreted traditions, even while passing those traditions on, abound. Paul reports Jesus' prohibition against divorce (1 Cor 7:10) but then goes on to endorse divorce for Corinthian Christians who found themselves in marriages to non-believers who wish to separate (7:15). Matthew also demonstrates a willingness to reinterpret Jesus' words on divorce, which is clear from a comparison of Matt 5:32 and 19:9, Mark 10:11–12, and Luke 16:18. Even the traditions of Jesus' sayings were not so sacred that they could not be reinterpreted for new situations!

The biblical traditions have often been *recontextualized,* so that they speak a new and needed word to those in other situations. The traditions were not absolute and unchangeable, rather just the opposite. They were flexible and even required reinterpretation for new situations.

We preachers do much the same thing in our use of Scripture in contemporary sermons. The tradition that comes to us is the Bible itself, and our task is to enliven it, so that it speaks a new word to congregations in very different situations. We recontextualize biblical passages. Of course, the tradition we receive has been declared canon by the ancient church—which means that there are some boundaries of interpretation that perhaps we ought not cross—but these boundaries depend almost entirely on your view of canon and what the church intended by it. There is, however, what we might call "a homiletic freedom" in the treatment of biblical passages for the sake of the proclamation of the Word. Note that this freedom is not meant to soften or bleed Scripture of its impact, but just the opposite, to enable its relevance for a contemporary congregation. We suggest that today preachers follow in the footsteps of the biblical authors who practiced their freedom to empower the tradition to speak anew to their readers.

Another way in which the preacher's interpretation for preaching and the biblical authors' use of tradition are connected is through their modes of transmitting Scripture. In some (but not all) cases, the biblical writers may have

---

[59] See Halvor Moxnes, *The Economy of the Kingdom: Social Conflict and Economic Relations in Luke's Gospel* (OBT; Philadelphia: Fortress, 1988).

been interpreting oral tradition and passing it on in writing. That is probably true of the Pentateuch of the Old Testament and of the first written forms of the Gospels. In the latter case, Jesus' ministry was transmitted orally until the evangelists or their predecessors committed the tradition to writing (see the discussion of form criticism in Chapter One).[60] Paul's use of tradition probably entailed setting in writing what had come to him orally (for example, 1 Cor 15:3–7). Freezing the oral tradition in writing robbed it of at least some of its flexibility. In oral form, a story could be interpreted to address an audience in new ways.[61] In written form, the author had to be more deliberate in changing the tradition to accommodate the needs of the readers.[62]

Preachers, on the other hand, take written documents composed in large part from oral tradition and turn them back into oral form. That is, we reverse the writing process for the sake of restoring flexibility to the written word, in the hope that in doing so we can more effectively allow it to speak of the contemporary situation.

To summarize, we contend that the Christian tradition from its origin in Jesus was reinterpreted time and again in order that it might continue to speak with relevance and power in countless new situations. Moreover, the early Christians followed Jewish tradition in freely reinterpreting Hebrew Scriptures for the same purpose. Preachers turn the written word back into oral form when we reinterpret biblical passages for the sake of the proclamation of the Gospel in a new age, and we do so utilizing a certain freedom that comes with the task of recontextualizing Scripture. Far from a tool we invent for preaching, recontextualizing and reinterpreting Scripture are rooted in the earliest traditions of both Judaism and Christianity. This does not mean that the process is made any easier by recognizing its roots. Instead, it is likely to be more difficult when we realize we walk in the footsteps of the biblical writers.

---

[60] An important book on what it meant for the early church to move from oral to written transmission is Werner H. Kelber, *The Oral and the Written Gospel: The Hermeneutics of Speaking and Writing in the Synoptic Tradition, Mark, Paul, and Q* (Philadelphia: Fortress, 1983).

[61] Bernard Brandon Scott speaks of the "performances" of a parable in the oral tradition ("[t]he dynamic process that produces an extant text"), and argues that the parables exhibit the characteristics of an orality which was creative and changing. They were gradually "scrubbed clean" and left "with few if any useless details." *Hear Then the Parable*, 35–42, 428. The quotations are from pp. 428 and 36 respectively.

[62] The Jewish tradition is set in writing but still remains flexible in its interpretation, which, in turn, is written and passed on in the form of the Talmud and the Mishnah. Rabbis continue to read both Scripture and Talmud and debate their meaning.

What of our responsibility to be "true to the text?" Does the proposal that preachers recontextualize a passage for the sake of their congregations not give them right to depart radically from the passage's message? True, recontextualizers must preserve what might be called the "spirit of the text" if they are to claim that there is a living word in their message. The goal, however, is not simply to repeat the biblical message but to try to do today what a biblical text has done before. So, for instance, our faithfulness is not determined by any kind of one-to-one correlation between the passage and our sermon but on how the purpose, role, function of the passage is reinterpreted for our congregation. If, for example, the purpose of the beatitudes is to bring insight and confidence to a community, then those beatitudes should target the very people today who need insight and confidence.

AN EXAMPLE

The example of a sermon must, in this case, be accompanied with a sufficient description of the congregation for which the sermon was prepared, so that it becomes clear how the preacher's interpretation of the text for the sermon involved the conscious presence and power of a congregation. We hope to show how a preacher discovered (or constructed) a certain meaning from a biblical text because of his or her consciousness of the needs of the congregation. Therefore, we first describe the congregation and how it impacted the preacher's biblical interpretation before we present the sermon that was written for the situation.

The Congregation's Situation. The situation we present here is fictional, at least so far as we know. However, the description is based on a composite constructed from several congregational situations we have known.

St. Timothy's was a relatively small congregation with an average worship attendance of seventy-five. It was a rural congregation, with the building itself set between a cornfield on one side and a pasture in which cattle grazed on the other. Congregants were, for the most part, in the economic lower or lower-middle classes and most were homemakers, farmers, and "blue collar" workers. The highest educational level was a high school diploma, and a good many men (in particular) had little more than a junior high education. The average age was forty-five, and most of the young people were eager to finish high school and move away to find a better life for themselves. At one time, parishioners belonged to a rather close and tightly knit community beyond the church, but that community was dissolved when, first, the local school was closed and students were assigned to larger schools farther away from the area and, second, when the rural post office closed. Now these people saw one another only at church and church events.

With few exceptions, the congregants of St. Timothy were generally devout and dedicated Christians, although there were a few who were members of the church for social reasons alone. While the majority were sincere seekers, they had been discouraged at every turn. The church had experienced a regular turnover of pastors, because it could only afford to pay for recent seminary graduates, who were eager to move quickly into a less desolate location once one became available. The church was "dying," as more and more young people moved away and as its older members died. The building was in desperate need of repair. All repairs had to be done by church members themselves since no maintenance funds were available.

The discouragement was wider than the issues related to their church. Most of the members believed their community was as good as dead, and they had little hope for the future. The older people were resigned to spend their final years on the old family farm, knowing that after their deaths their beloved farm would be sold to one of the corporate farming enterprises moving into the county. The depression was social, economical, and personal, and it ate away at any confidence in religious faith.

The congregation's discouragement was a challenge for its pastor. What could be done to help these people understand their value and dignity in God's eyes? The obvious wealth and influence of television preachers had a profound effect on most of the members, with the result that the members thought their faith was inferior and weak. The newest pastor was convinced that this congregation did not need to be "beaten over the head with law." They needed most of all to hear and appropriate the Gospel's message of love and acceptance. The pastor struggled to make her sermons empowering and affirming events. The more she came to know the members of the congregation, the more she realized how deep and debilitating the social depression was.

The Sermon. On this Sunday the assigned lectionary Gospel reading was Luke 17:5–10 (Proper 22, series C). The pastor saw that the disciples' request, "Increase our faith" (v. 5), fit her congregation like a glove, for none of them felt their faith was even significant, much less, powerful. The pastor recognized that to stress this part of the lesson and emphasize how Christians need to increase their faith in God and Christ would directly feed the congregation's already low self-esteem. It would likely fit their state of depression to be chastised for their lack of faith, because they keenly felt their lack of success suggested they needed such a scolding. The second half of the reading (vv. 7–10) was equally troublesome. Jesus compares the disciples to servants who deserve no credit for doing what they do, and should say only, "We are worthless slaves; we have done only what we ought to have done!" (v. 10b).

The pastor wanted something more out of the lesson and worked hard at reading the text again and again with this particular congregation in mind. Her dialogue among herself, the text, and the congregation produced what seemed to her a new "twist" on the passage—a different perspective. The community-based interpretation of the Gospel lesson resulted in the following sermon.[63] The first part attempts to articulate for the congregation their general sense of inadequacy. In the second part, the preacher shares the good news of the passage. The first part of the sermon seeks to give expression to the congregation's feelings, and the in the second part the preacher announces the good news of the passage.

---

[63] Portions of this sermon are published in Kysar's article, "Preaching the Lesson" (Proper 22), *Lectionary Homiletics,* IX (1998): 7–8.

"Enough Faith"

Proper 22, series C
Luke 17:5–10

AT SOME TIME OR ANOTHER, MOST OF US HAVE SAID WITH THE DISCIPLES, "INCREASE our faith!" There are so many times when our faith seems inadequate. Inadequate to face the onslaught of troubles and uncertainties. Inadequate to empower faithfulness in a difficult world.

The disciples seem to sense that Jesus has just spoken of such an occasion. In the verses just before our lesson for today, he urges them, "Be on your guard!" Then Jesus admonishes them to forgive the same person seven times in a single day (Luke 17:3–4). Now whose faith is sufficient for such endless forgiveness? The disciples recognize their inadequacies for such boundless forgiveness. So, they beg for more faith. Surely, just an increase in their faith would be an easy answer—a quick fix for our tiny morsel of faith—so that we could freely forgive others. God can recharge our faith. Boost its capacity to forgive, to believe through life's storm, to remain secure when faith is threatened. So, today many of us pray with the disciples: "Increase our faith!"

When was the last time you asked God to increase your faith? Certainly that was my prayer on the days immediately after the events of September 11, 2001. Or, maybe a time of illness brought this prayer out of you. Or, the illness or death of a loved one. On one occasion, I was desperately trying to forgive a person who had offended me time and again. So, I had to ask God for enough faith to change my attitude toward this person. Many of us pray with the disciples: "Increase our faith!"

We feel so inadequate in our efforts to serve Christ. Who are we, after all? We can't believe that without greater faith we can be of any use to Christ, much less to ourselves! And we hear a great deal these days about "having faith" and having "more faith." Some television preachers are endlessly haranguing us for not having enough faith. It sounds like we are doomed to failure, since most of us haven't enough faith—at least by the measurement of some of these media preachers. The result of the whole emphasis on "having more faith" is that it makes us feel so worthless. Our tiny portion of faith is far too weak to please God.

Jesus, however, surprises us. His response to the disciples' request isn't what we might expect. At first, it doesn't seem very compassionate—not very understanding of the disciples' plea.

Jesus says a morsel of faith is enough! A tiny grain of faith the size of a mustard seed is enough to move a tree! With this suggestion, Jesus jolted the disciples and continues to jolt us. You really don't need more faith than a single seed! Your morsel is enough to change things! We think we need quantity. But Jesus says a seed is enough.

Mustard seeds are used for seasoning. They are like garlic. A little goes a long way. Some of us have eaten food spiced with just a touch of garlic and tasted it the rest of the day! Just so, Jesus claims, a morsel of faith seasons our whole lives.

But our culture specializes in abundance. It trains us to think more is better—more of anything is better than less. Two televisions are better than one. The more cars and trucks the better. How many pairs of shoes have accumulated in your closet? Our culture specializes in abundance. Hence, many of us are inclined to value quantity when it comes to religious faith. Our society trains us to think that *more faith* would be better.

Jesus, however, upsets that applecart. Faith has a peculiar quality, much like the seasonings we use in our food. A little does a lot. Abundance in this case is measured not with a scale but with a meter that detects potency. Like a mustard seed, faith measures high in power. Some things cannot be measured in terms of quantity. Can we measure the amount of love we have for another? The quantity of generosity we possess? Or hope? Faith is not a substance that is valued by its plenty. It cannot be measured like a thing.

A tiny seed of faith is enough! The faith you have is enough. You and I don't need to apologize for our quantity of faith. It only takes a tiny morsel.

Let's call her Ann. Somewhere in her life Ann swallowed a mustard seed of faith. When the winds of a divorce blew through her life, she was sure her faith was too little. Her husband simply walked out. She was left with no income, bills to pay, kids to raise all on her own. "Increase my faith!" she prayed. She is not at all sure her prayer was ever answered. But she is sure that somewhere within herself she found courage to go on. Her tiny mustard seed seasoned her life. It uprooted a mighty oak of distress, hopelessness, and despair, threw it in the sea of nothingness. In its place, her tiny tidbit of faith planted a new tree—a tree of determination, decisiveness, and strength. A mustard seed of faith proved ample for the occasion.

But there is something more about our faith we should remember! We may be tempted to think we are responsible for having faith. Yet that seems a bit self-centered, doesn't it? That is, everything depends on our ability to produce faith! Like, if we just grit our teeth and try hard enough, we'll have more faith.

Here the disciples get it right. They know that only Christ can increase their faith, so they make their request: "Increase our faith!"

We can't increase our own faith by our own efforts. I suppose it is a bit like enjoyment or fun. Have you ever set out to "have fun?" My husband and I used to do that almost every Friday. Friday was our day off, and we would begin the day determined to have fun. We would plot the day's activities in order to have fun. From time to time during the day we would look at one another and ask, "*Are we having fun yet?*"

Fun seldom results from seeking it. You set out to do something else and are surprised when you realize you are having fun! Faith is much the same. It is not likely to come when we are determined we are going to have faith. It comes when we are occupied with service to others. It comes as a result of service. As a result of proclaiming the news of God's love.

Yet we may still be missing the point here! It is not our faith that finally matters!

If we have faith, it is only because we are strengthened to do so. What finally matters is not our own faith, but the God to whom the faith is directed.

Are you a fan of the late Charles Schlutz' cartoon strip, "Peanuts"? I most certainly am and have been for many years. Do you remember that recurring annual series in which Charlie Brown tries to kick the football? Every fall it's the same: Lucy holds the ball and promises (again!) not to move it. Charlie thinks, "Well, maybe this time I can trust her." So, he runs to kick it, and, of course, at the last second Lucy pulls it back, and poor Charlie sails up in the air and ends up on his back. There on the ground he utters, "Good Grief!"

What's funny about those strips? It's almost the same every fall. What's funny, of course, is that Charlie seems never to learn. He is a pitiful case of trying again and again when he ought to know better. He has every reason not to have faith in Lucy, and not a single reason to trust her promise.

Our faith originates for the exactly the opposite reason. Our faith depends finally on God's faithfulness. Because God's promise is faithful. God can be trusted. We *are faithful only because God is faithful!*

So we don't have to go around with a dip stick by which we measure our faith. Thanks to God, we have enough faith!

Selected Bibliography

The authors have gathered these works from those cited throughout the book. We think that each of them might prove helpful to preachers. Many are, of course, general reference books which are important for any student of the Bible.

Adam, A. K. M. *Making Sense of New Testament Theology: "Modern" Problems and Prospects*. Studies in American Biblical Hermeneutics 11. Macon: Mercer University Press, 1995.

————. *What Is Postmodern Biblical Criticism?* Guides to Biblical Scholarship. New Testament Series. Edited by Dan O. Via Jr. Minneapolis: Fortress, 1995.

Adam, A. K. M., ed. *Handbook of Postmodern Biblical Interpretation*. St. Louis: Chalice, 2000.

Aichele, George et al., eds. *The Postmodern Bible: The Bible and Culture Collective*. New Haven: Yale University Press, 1995.

Anderson, Janice Capel and Stephen D. Moore, eds. *Mark and Method: New Approaches in Biblical Studies*. Minneapolis: Fortress, 1992.

Aune, David E. *Revelation 1–5*. Word Biblical Commentary 52a. Dallas: Word, 1997.

Bailey, James L. and Lyle D. Vander Broek. *Literary Forms in the New Testament: A Handbook*. Louisville: Westminster John Knox, 1992.

Bailey, Raymond, ed. *Hermeneutics for Preaching: Approaches to Contemporary Interpretations of Scripture*. Nashville: Broadman, 1992.

Bal, Michel. "Metaphors He Lives By." Pages 185–207 in *Women, War and Metaphor: Language and Society in the Study of the Hebrew Bible*. Edited by Claudia V. Camp and Carole R. Fontaine. *Semeia* 61. Atlanta: Scholars Press, 1993.

Barrett, C. K. *The New Testament Background: Selected Documents.* Rev. and exp. ed. New York: Harper and Row, 1987.

Barth, Karl. *The Epistle to the Romans.* Translated by E. C. Hoskyns. London: Oxford, 1963.

Bartlett, David L. *Between the Bible and the Church: New Methods for Biblical Preaching.* Nashville: Abingdon, 1999.

Beardslee, William A. *Literary Criticism of the New Testament.* Guides to Biblical Scholarship. New Testament Series. Philadelphia: Fortress, 1970.

Beck, David R. *The Discipleship Paradigm: Readers and Anonymous Characters in the Fourth Gospel.* Biblical Interpretation 27. Leiden, New York, Cologne: Brill, 1997.

Belo, Fernando. *A Materialist Reading of the Gospel of Mark.* Translated by Matthew J. O'Connell. Maryknoll: Orbis, 1981.

Berger, Peter L. and Thomas Luckmann. *The Social Construction of Reality: A Treatise in the Sociology of Knowledge.* Anchor Books ed. Garden City: Doubleday, 1967.

Best, Ernest. *From Text to Sermon: Responsible Use of the New Testament in Preaching.* Atlanta: John Knox, 1978.

Betz, Hans-Dieter. *Galatians.* Hermeneia. Philadelphia: Fortress, 1979.

Boerma, Conrad. *The Rich, the Poor, and the Bible.* Translated by John Bowden. Philadelphia: Westminster, 1978.

Boring, M. Eugene, Klaus Berger, and Carston Colpe, eds. *Hellenistic Commentary to the New Testament.* Nashville: Abingdon, 1995.

Brawley, Robert L. *Centering on God: Method and Message in Luke-Acts.* Literary Currents in Biblical Interpretation. Louisville: Westminster/John Knox, 1990.

Brown, Raymond E. *The Epistles of John: Translated with Introduction, Notes, and Commentary.* The Anchor Bible 30. Garden City: Doubleday, 1982.

———. *An Introduction to the Gospel of John.* Edited by Francis J. Moloney. New York: Doubleday, 2003.

Brown, Robert McAfee. *Unexpected News: Reading the Bible with Third World Eyes.* Philadelphia: Westminster, 1984.

Brueggemann, Walter. *Hopeful Imagination: Prophetic Voices in Exile.* Philadelphia: Fortress, 1986.

Bultmann, Rudolf. *Essays: Philosophical and Theological.* Translated by James C. G. Greig. London: SCM, 1955.

———. *Existence and Faith: Shorter Writings of Rudolf Bultmann.* Edited and translated by Schubert M. Ogden. New York: Meridian Books, 1960.

———. *The History of the Synoptic Tradition.* Translated by John Marsh. Oxford: Basil Blackwell, 1963.

————. *Primitive Christianity in Its Contemporary Setting.* Translated by R. H. Fuller. New York: Meridian Books, 1957.

————. *Theology of the New Testament. 2 vols. Translated by Kendrick Grobel. New York: Charles Scribner's Sons, 1951.*

Buttrick, George Arthur et al., eds. *The Interpreter's Dictionary of the Bible.* 4 vols. New York: Abingdon Press, 1962.

Caird, G. B. *The Language and Imagery of the Bible.* Philadelphia: Westminster, 1980.

Cannon, Katie Geneva and Elisabeth Schüssler Fiorenza, eds. *Interpretation for Liberation.* Semeia 47. Atlanta: Scholars Press, 1989.

Childs, Brevard S. *Introduction to the Old Testament as Scripture.* Philadelphia: Fortress, 1979.

Chopp, Rebecca S. *The Power to Speak: Feminism, Language, God.* New York: Crossroad, 1991.

Clements, R. E. *Isaiah 1–39.* The New Century Bible Commentary. Grand Rapids: Eerdmans, 1980.

Clévenot, Michel. *Materialist Approaches to the Bible.* Maryknoll: Orbis, 1985.

Collins Adela Yarbro. *Crisis and Catharsis: The Power of the Apocalypse.* Philadelphia: Westminster, 1984.

Cone, James H. *Black Theology and Black Power.* New York: Seabury, 1969.

————. *God of the Oppressed.* San Francisco: Harper, 1997.

Conzelmann, Hans. *The Theology of St. Luke.* Translated by Geoffrey Buswell. New York: Harper and Row, 1961.

Culpepper, R. Alan. *Anatomy of the Fourth Gospel: A Study in Literary Design.* Foundations and Facets: New Testament. Philadelphia: Fortress, 1983.

Davis, Robert Con. *Contemporary Literary Criticism: Modernism through Post-Structuralism.* New York: Longman, 1986.

Derrida, Jacques. *"Différance."* Pages 1–28 in *Margins of Philosophy.* Translated by Alan Bass. Chicago: University of Chicago Press, 1982.

————. *Dissemination.* Translated by Barbara Johnson. Chicago: University of Chicago Press, 1981.

————. *Glas.* Translated by John P. Leavey Jr. and Richard Rand. Lincoln: University of Nebraska Press, 1986.

————. *Of Grammatology.* Translated by Gayatri Chakravorty Spivak. Baltimore: Johns Hopkins Press, 1979.

————. *The Post Card: From Socrates to Freud and Beyond.* Translated by Alan Bass. Chicago: University of Chicago Press, 1987.

Donahue, John, S.J. *The Gospel in the Parables: Metaphor, Narrative, and Theology in the Synoptic Gospels.* Minneapolis: Fortress, 1988.

Doty, William G. *Letters in Primitive Christianity.* Guides to Biblical Scholarship. New Testament Series. Philadelphia: Fortress, 1973.

Dunn, James D. G. *Romans 1–8*. Word Biblical Commentary 38a. Dallas: Word, 1988.

Eissfeldt, Otto. *The Old Testament: An Introduction*. New York: Harper & Row, 1965.

Ellingsen, Mark. *The Integrity of Biblical Narrative: Story in Theology and Proclamation*. Philadelphia: Fortress, 1990.

Elliot, John H. *A Home for the Homeless: A Sociological Exegesis of 1 Peter, Its Situation and Strategy*. Philadelphia: Fortress, 1981.

Elliott, John H., ed. *Social-Scientific Criticism of the New Testament and Its Social World*. Semeia 35. Atlanta: Scholars Press, 1986.

Esler, Philip Francis. *Community and Gospel in Luke-Acts: The Social and Political Motivations of Lucan Theology*. Society for New Testament Studies Monograph Series 57. Cambridge: Cambridge University Press, 1987.

Farmer, William. *Jesus and the Gospel*. Philadelphia: Fortress, 1982.

————. *The Synoptic Problem: A Critical Review of the Problem of the Literary Relationships between Matthew, Mark, and Luke*. New York: Macmillan Company, 1964.

Farris, Stephen. *Preaching that Matters: The Bible and Our Lives*. Louisville: Westminster John Knox, 1998.

Fee, Gordon D. *The First Epistle to the Corinthians*. The New International Commentary on the New Testament. Grand Rapids: Eerdmans, 1987.

Felder, Cain Hope, ed. *Stony the Road We Trod: African American Biblical Interpretation*. Minneapolis: Fortress, 1991.

Festinger, Leon, Henry W. Riecken, and Stanley Schacter. *When Prophecy Fails: A Social and Psychological Study of a Modern Group that Predicted the Destruction of the World*. New York: Harper & Row, 1956.

Fiorenza, Elisabeth Schüssler. *Bread Not Stone: The Challenge of Feminist Biblical Interpretation*. Boston: Beacon, 1984.

————. *In Memory of Her: A Feminist Theological Reconstruction of Christian Origins*. New York: Crossroad, 1984.

————, ed. *Searching the Scriptures: A Feminist Introduction*. New York: Crossroad, 1993.

————, ed. *Searching the Scriptures: A Feminist Commentary*. New York: Crossroad, 1994.

Fitzmyer, Joseph A. *The Gospel According to Luke X–XXIV: A New Translation with Introduction and Commentary*. The Anchor Bible 28a. Garden City: Doubleday, 1985.

Freedman, David Noel, ed. *The Anchor Bible Dictionary*. 6 vols. New York: Doubleday, 1992.

Frei, Hans. *The Eclipse of Biblical Narrative: A Study in Eighteenth and Nineteenth Century Hermeneutics*. New Haven: Yale University Press, 1974.

Furnish, Victor Paul. *II Corinthians: A New Translation with Introduction and Commentary.* The Anchor Bible 32A. Garden City, N.Y.: Doubleday, 1984.

Gadamer, Hans-Georg. *Truth and Method.* London: Sheed & Ward, 1975.

Gager, John G. *Kingdom and Community: The Social World of Early Christianity.* Prentice-Hall Studies in Religion Series. Englewood Cliffs, N.J.: Prentice-Hall, 1975.

Gottwald, Norman K. *The Tribes of Israel: A Sociology of the Religion of Liberated Israel, 1250–1050 B.C.E.* Maryknoll: Orbis, 1979.

———, ed. *The Bible and Liberation: Political and Social Hermeneutics.* Maryknoll: Orbis, 1993.

Grant, Robert M. *A Short History of the Interpretation of the Bible: An Introduction to the History of the Methods Used to Interpret Scripture.* Rev. ed. New York: Macmillan, 1963.

Grosheide, F. W. *Commentary on the First Epistle to the Corinthians.* New International Commentary on the New Testament. Grand Rapids: Eerdmans, 1953.

Hahn, Ferdinand. *Historical Investigation and New Testament Faith: Two Essays.* Philadelphia: Fortress, 1983.

Hahn, Herbert F. *The Old Testament in Modern Research: With a Survey of Recent Literature by Horace D. Hummel.* Exp. ed. Philadelphia: Fortress, 1966.

Harrelson, Walter. *From Fertility Cult to Worship.* Anchor Books. Garden City, N.J.: Doubleday, 1970.

Hayes, John H., ed. *Dictionary of Biblical Interpretation.* 2 vols. Nashville Abingdon, 1992.

Heidegger, Martin. *Being and Time.* Translated by John Macquarrie and Edward Robinson. New York: Harper & Row, 1962.

Heil, John Paul. *The Gospel of Mark as a Model for Action: A Reader-Response Commentary.* New York: Paulist, 1992.

Herzog, William R. II. *Parables as Subversive Speech: Jesus as Pedagogue of the Oppressed.* Louisville: Westminster John Knox, 1994.

Holladay, William L. *Jeremiah 2.* Hermeneia. Minneapolis: Fortress, 1989.

Holmberg, Bengt. *Paul and Power: The Structure of Authority in the Primitive Church as Reflected in the Pauline Letters.* Philadelphia: Fortress, 1978.

Hughes, Robert G. and Robert Kysar. *Preaching Doctrine for the Twenty-First Century.* Fortress Resources for Preaching. Minneapolis: Fortress, 1997.

Hultgren, Arland J. *The Parables of Jesus: A Commentary.* Grand Rapids: Eerdmans, 2000.

Jobling, David and Stephen D. Moore, eds. *Poststructuralism as Exegesis.* Semeia 54. Atlanta: Scholars Press, 1992.

226 PREACHING TO POSTMODERNS

Jobling, David and Tina Pippin, eds. *Ideological Criticism of Biblical Texts.* Semeia 59. Atlanta: Scholars Press, 1992.

Johnson, Luke Timothy. *Reading Romans: A Literary and Theological Commentary.* New York: Crossroad, 1997.

Kamuf, Peggy, ed. *A Derrida Reader: Between the Blinds.* New York: Columbia University Press, 1991.

Keck, Leander, ed. *The New Interpreter's Bible.* 12 vols. Nashville: Abingdon, 1994–1999.

Kee, Howard Clark. *Knowing the Truth: A Sociological Approach to the New Testament.* Minneapolis: Fortress, 1989.

———. *Miracle in the Early Christian World: A Study in Sociohistorical Method.* New Haven: Yale University Press, 1983.

Kelber, Werner H. *The Oral and the Written Gospel: The Hermeneutics of Speaking and Writing in the Synoptic Tradition, Mark, Paul, and Q.* Philadelphia: Fortress, 1983.

Kennedy, George A. *New Testament Interpretation through Rhetorical Criticism.* Chapel Hill: University of North Carolina Press, 1984.

Kingsbury, Jack Dean. *Conflict in Mark: Jesus, Authorities, Disciples.* Minneapolis: Fortress, 1989.

Knight, Douglas A. *Tradition and Theology in the Old Testament.* Philadelphia: Fortress, 1977.

———. *The Traditions of Israel.* Society of Biblical Literature Dissertation Series. Missoula: University of Montana Press, 1973.

Kysar, Robert. *I, II, and III John.* Augsburg Commentary on the New Testament. Minneapolis: Augsburg, 1986.

———. "The Dismantling of Decisional Faith: A Reading of John 6:25–71." Pages 161–82 in *Critical Readings of John 6.* Edited by R. Alan Culpepper. Biblical Interpretation 22. Leiden: Brill, 1997.

———. *The Fourth Evangelist and His Gospel: An Examination of Contemporary Scholarship.* Minneapolis: Augsburg, 1975.

———. *Opening the Bible: What It Is, Where It Came From, What It Means for You.* Minneapolis: Augsburg, 1999.

———. "Preaching As Biblical Theology: A Proposal for a Homiletic Method." Pages 143–56 in *The Promise and Practice of Biblical Theology.* Edited by John Reumann. Minneapolis: Fortress, 1991.

———. *Preaching John.* Minneapolis: Fortress, 2002.

———. *Stumbling in the Light.* St. Louis: Chalice: 1999.

Lakoff, George and Mark Johnson. *Metaphors We Live By.* Chicago: University of Chicago Press, 1980.

Long, Thomas G. *The Witness of Preaching.* Louisville: Westminster/John Knox, 1989.

Lowry, Eugene L. *The Homiletical Plot: The Sermon as Narrative Art Form.* Atlanta: John Knox, 1980.

———. *How to Preach a Parable: Designs for Narrative Sermons.* Abingdon Preacher's Library. Nashville: Abingdon, 1989.

———. *The Sermon: Dancing the Edge of Mystery.* Nashville: Abingdon, 1997.

Mack, Burton I. *Rhetoric and the New Testament.* Guides to Biblical Scholarship. New Testament Series. Minneapolis: Fortress, 1990.

Macquarrie, John. *The Scope of Demythologizing: Bultmann and His Critics.* New York: Harper & Row, 1960.

Malbon, Elizabeth Struthers. *In the Company of Jesus: Characters in Mark's Gospel.* Louisville: Westminster John Knox, 2000.

Malina, Bruce J. *The New Testament World: Insights from Cultural Anthropology.* Atlanta: John Knox, 1981.

Malina, Bruce J. and Richard L. Rohrbaugh. *Social Science Commentary on the Synoptic Gospels.* Minneapolis: Fortress, 1992.

———. *Social Science Commenary on the Gospel of John.* Minneapolis: Fortress, 1998.

Mann, C. S. *Mark: A New Translation with Introduction and Commentary.* The Anchor Bible 27. Garden City, N.J.: Doubleday, 1986.

Martyn, J. Louis. *History and Theology in the Fourth Gospel.* 3d rev. and exp. ed. The New Testament Library. Louisville: Westminster John Knox, 2003.

McKenzie, Steven L. and Stephen R. Haynes, eds. *To Each Its Own Meaning: An Introduction to Biblical Criticisms and Their Application.* Rev. and exp. ed. Louisville: Westminster John Knox Press, 1999.

McKim, Donald K., ed. *The Bible in Theology and Preaching: How Preachers Use Scripture.* Rev. ed. Nashville: Abingdon, 1994.

———, ed. *A Guide to Contemporary Hermeneutics: Major Trends in Biblical Interpretation.* Grand Rapids.: Eerdmans, 1986.

McKnight, Edgar V. *Postmodern Use of the Bible: The Emergence of Reader-Oriented Criticism.* Nashville: Abingdon, 1988.

Meeks, Wayne A. *The First Urban Christians: The Social World of the Apostle Paul.* New Haven: Yale University Press, 1983.

———. "The Man from Heaven in Johannine Sectarianism." Pages 169–206 in *The Interpretation of John.* Edited by John Ashton. Studies in New Testament Interpretation. Edinburgh: T&T Clark, 1997. First published in *The Journal of Biblical Literature* 91 (1972): 44–72.

Miles, Jack. *God: A Biography.* New York: Vintage Books, Random House, 1995.

Miranda, José. *Marx and the Bible: A Critique of the Philosophy of Liberation.* Maryknoll: Orbis, 1974.

———. *Communism in the Bible.* Maryknoll: Orbis, 1982.

Moore, Stephen D. *Literary Criticism and the Gospels: The Theoretical Challenge*. New Haven: Yale University Press, 1989.

Morgan, Robert and Jon Barton. *Biblical Interpretation*. Oxford Bible. Oxford: Oxford University Press, 1988.

Mowinckel, Sigmund. *The Psalms in Israel's Worship*. 2 vols. Translated by D. R. Ap-Thomas. Oxford: Basil Blackwell, 1962.

Moxnes, Halvor. *The Economy of the Kingdom: Social Conflict and Economic Relations in Luke's Gospel*. Overtures to Biblical Theology. Philadelphia: Fortress, 1988.

Myers, Ched. *Binding the Strong Man: A Political Reading of Mark's Story of Jesus*. Maryknoll: Orbis, 1988.

Newsom, Carol A. and Sharon H. Ringe. *The Women's Bible Commentary*. 2d ed. enl. with the Apocrypha. Louisville: Westminster John Knox, 1998.

Neyrey, Jerome H. *The Ideology of Revolt: John's Christology in Social Science Perspective*. Philadelphia: Fortress, 1988.

Nisbet, Robert A. *The Sociological Tradition*. New York: Basic Books, 1966.

Noth, Martin. *The Old Testament World*. Translated by Victor I. Gruhn. Philadelphia: Fortress, 1966.

Osiek, Carolyn, R.S.C.J. *What Are They Saying about the Social Setting of the New Testament?* Rev. ed. New York: Paulist, 1992.

Ourisman, David J. *From Gospel to Sermon: Preaching Synoptic Texts*. St. Louis: Chalice, 2000.

Patte, Daniel. *The Gospel according to Matthew: A Structural Commentary on Matthew's Faith*. Philadelphia: Fortress, 1987.

———. *Paul's Faith and the Power of the Gospel: A Structural Introduction to the Pauline Letters*. Philadelphia: Fortress, 1983.

———. *Preaching Paul*. Fortress Resources for Preaching. Philadelphia: Fortress, 1984.

———. *What is Structural Exegesis?* Guides to Biblical Scholarship. New Testament Series. Philadelphia: Fortress, 1976.

Patte, Daniel and Aline Patte. *Structural Exegesis: From Theory to Practice*. Philadelphia: Fortress, 1978.

Perrin, Norman. *Jesus and the Language of the Kingdom: Symbol and Metaphor in New Testament Interpretation*. Philadelphia: Fortress, 1976.

———. *What is Redaction Criticism?* Guides to Biblical Scholarship. New Testament Series. Philadelphia: Fortress, 1969.

Pervo, Richard I. *Luke's Story of Paul*. Minneapolis: Fortress, 1990.

———. *Profit with Delight: The Literary Genre of the Acts of the Apostles*. Philadelphia: Fortress, 1987.

Petersen, Norman R. *Literary Criticism for New Testament Critics*. Guides to Biblical Scholarship. New Testament Series. Philadelphia: Fortress, 1978.

Pilgrim, Walter E. *Good News to the Poor: Wealth and Poverty in Luke-Acts.* Minneapolis: Augsburg, 1981.

Pippin, Tina. *Death and Desire: The Rhetoric of Gender in the Apocalypse of John.* Literary Currents in Biblical Interpretation. Louisville: Westminster John Knox, 1992.

Powell, Mark Allen. *What Is Narrative Criticism?* Guides to Biblical Scholarship. New Testament Series. Fortress, 1990.

Pritchard, James B., ed. *Ancient New Eastern Texts Relating to the Old Testament.* Princeton: Princeton University Press, 1950.

Ricoeur, Paul. *Hermeneutics and the Human Sciences.* Edited and translated by John B.Thompson. Cambridge: Cambridge University Press, 1981.

―――. *The Rule of Metaphor: Multi-disciplinary Studies of the Creation of Meaning.* Translated by Robert Czerny et al. Toronto: University of Toronto Press, 1977.

Robbins, Vernon K. *Exploring the Texture of Texts: A Guide to Socio-Rhetorical Interpretation.* Valley Forge: Trinity International, 1996.

Robertson, Archibald and Alfred Plummer. *A Critical and Exegetical Commentary on the First Epistle of St. Paul to the Corinthians.* 2d ed. The International Critical Commentary. Edinburgh: Clark, 1914.

Rose, Lucy Atkinson. *Sharing the Word: Preaching in the Roundtable Church.* Louisville: Westminster John Knox, 1997.

Rosenau, Pauline Marie. *Postmodernism and the Social Sciences: Insights, Inroads, and Intrusions.* Princeton: Princeton University Press, 1992.

Rowland, Christopher and Mark Corner. *Liberating Exegesis: The Challenge of Liberation Theology to Biblical Studies.* Louisville: Westminster John Knox, 1989.

Russell, Letty M., ed. *Feminist Interpretation of the Bible.* Philadelphia: Westminster, 1985.

―――, ed. *The Liberating Word: A Guide to Nonsexist Interpretation of the Bible.* Philadelphia: Westminster, 1976.

Sanders, James A. *Canon and Community: A Guide to Canonical Criticism.* Guides to Biblical Scholarship. Old Testament Series. Philadelphia: Fortress, 1984.

―――. *From Sacred Story to Sacred Text.* Philadelphia: Fortress, 1987.

Schottroff, Luise and Wolfgang Stegemann. *Jesus and the Hope of the Poor.* Maryknoll: Orbis, 1986.

Schottroff, Willy and Wolfgang Stegemann, eds. *God of the Lowly: Socio-Historical Interpretations of the Bible.* Maryknoll: Orbis, 1984.

Scott, Bernard Brandon. *Hear Then the Parable: A Commentary on the Parables of Jesus.* Minneapolis: Fortress, 1989.

―――. *The Word of God in Words: Reading and Preaching.* Fortress Resources for Preaching. Philadelphia: Fortress, 1985.

Segal, Alan F. *Paul the Convert: The Apostolate and Apostasy of Saul the Phari-see*. New Haven: Yale University Press, 1990.

Segovia, Fernando F. *"What Is John?" Readers and Readings of the Fourth Gos-pel*. Symposium 3. Atlanta: Scholars Press, 1996.

Segovia, Fernando F. and Mary Ann Tolbert, eds. *Reading from This Place: Social Location and Biblical Interpretation in the United States*. Vol. 1. Minneapolis: Fortress, 1995.

————, eds. *Reading from This Place: Social Location and Biblical Interpreta-tion in Global Perspective*. Vol. 2. Minneapolis: Fortress, 1995.

Shuler, Philip L. *A Genre for the Gospels: The Biographical Character of Mat-thew*. Philadelphia: Fortress, 1982.

Smith, D. Moody. *John among the Gospels*. 2d rev. ed. Columbia, S.C.: Uni-versity of South Carolina Press, 2001.

Staley, Jeffrey Lloyd. *The Print's First Kiss: A Rhetorical Investigation of the Im-plied Reader in the Fourth Gospel*. Society of Biblical Literature Disserta-tion Series 82. Atlanta: Scholars Press, 1988.

————. *Reading with a Passion: Rhetoric, Autobiography and the American West in the Gospel of John*. New York: Continuum, 1995.

Stambaugh, John E. and David L. Balch. *The New Testament in Its Social En-vironment*. Vol. 1 of *Library of Early Christianity*. Edited by Wayne A. Meeks. Philadelphia: Westminster, 1986.

Stegemann, Wolfgang. *The Gospel and the Poor*. Philadelphia: Fortress, 1984.

Stendahl, Krister. "Biblical Theology: A Program." Pages 11–44 in *Meanings: The Bible as Document and as Guide*. Krister Stendahl. Philadelphia: Fortress, 1984.

Stroup, George W. *The Promise of Narrative Theology*. Atlanta: John Knox, 1981.

Stuhlmacher, Peter. *Historical Criticism and Theological Interpretation of Scripture: Toward a Hermeneutics of Consent*. Philadelphia: Fortress, 1977.

Talbert, Charles H. *The Apocalypse: A Reading of the Revelation of John*. Louis-ville: Westminster John Knox, 1994.

Tamez, Elsa. *Bible of the Oppressed*. Translated by Matthew J. O'Connell. Maryknoll: Orbis, 1982.

Tate, W. Randolf. *Biblical Interpretation: An Integrated Approach*. Rev. ed. Peabody: Hendrickson, 1997.

Taylor, Vincent. *The Formation of the Gospel Tradition*. London: Macmillan, 1957.

Theissen, Gerd. *The Miracles Stories of the Early Christian Tradition*. Philadel-phia: Fortress, 1983.

————. *Psychological Aspects of Pauline Theology*. Translated by John P. Galvin. Philadelphia: Fortress, 1987.

————. *Sociology of Early Palestinian Christianity.* Philadelphia: Fortress, 1978.

Thiselton, Anthony C. *The Two Horizons: New Testament Hermeneutics and Philosophical Description.* Grand Rapids: Eerdmans, 1980.

Thiselton, Anthony C., Roger Ludin, and Clarence Walhout, eds. *The Responsibility of Hermeneutics.* Grand Rapids: Eerdmans, 1985.

Trible, Phyllis. *God and the Rhetoric of Sexuality.* Overtures to Biblical Theology. Philadelphia: Fortress, 1978.

Tuckett, Christopher. *Reading the New Testament: Methods of Interpretation.* Philadelphia: Fortress, 1987.

Vanhoozer, Kevin J. *Is There a Meaning in This Text? The Bible, the Reader, and the Morality of Literary Knowledge.* Grand Rapids: Zondervan, 1998.

Vaux, Roland de. *Ancient Israel.* 2 vols. New York: McGraw-Hill, 1961.

Vines, Michael E. *The Problem of Markan Genre. The Gospel of Mark and the Jewish Novel.* Academia Biblica. Atlanta: Scholars Press, 2002.

von Wahlde, Urban C. *The Earliest Version of John's Gospel: Recovering the Gospel of Signs.* Wilmington: Michael Glazier, 1989.

Waetjen, Herman C. *A Reordering of Power: A Socio-Political Reading of Mark's Gospel.* Minneapolis: Fortress, 1989.

Wainwright, Arthur. *Beyond Biblical Criticism: Encountering Jesus in Scripture.* Atlanta: John Knox Press, 1982.

Webb, Joseph M. *Comedy and Preaching.* St. Louis: Chalice, 1999.

————. *Old Texts, New Sermons: The Quiet Revolution in Biblical Preaching.* St. Louis: Chalice, 2000.

————. *Preaching and the Challenge of Pluralism.* St. Louis: Chalice, 1998.

Webb, Joseph M. and Robert Kysar. *Greek for Preachers.* St. Louis: Chalice, 2001.

Westermann, Claus. *Isaiah 40–66.* The Old Testament Library. Philadelphia: Westminster, 1969.

Wicks, Robert. *Modern French Philosophy: From Existentialism to Postmodernism.* Oxford: Oneworld, 2003.

Wild, John. *The Challenge of Existentialism.* Bloomington, Ind.: Indiana University Press, 1959.

————. *Existence and the World of Freedom.* Englewood Cliffs, N.J.: Prentice-Hall, 1963.

Wilder, Amos N. *The Language of the Gospel: Early Christian Rhetoric.* New York: Harper & Row, 1964.

Williams, Delores S. *Sisters in the Wilderness: The Challenge of Womanist God-Talk.* Maryknoll: Orbis, 1993.

Wink, Walter. *The Bible in Human Transformation: Toward a New Paradigm for Biblical Study.* Philadelphia: Fortress, 1973.

————. *Engaging the Powers: Discernment and Resistance in a World of Domination.* Vol. 3 of *The Powers.* Minneapolis: Fortress, 1992.

————. *Naming the Powers: The Language of Power in the New Testament.* Vol. 1 of *The Powers.* Philadelphia: Fortress, 1984.

————. *Unmasking the Powers: The Invisible Forces That Determine Human Existence.* Vol. 2 of *The Powers.* Philadelphia: Fortress, 1986.

————. *When the Powers Fall: Reconciliation in the Healing of Nations.* Vol. 4 of *The Powers.* Minneapolis: Fortress, 1999.

Wire, Antoinette Clark. *The Corinthian Women Prophets: A Reconstruction through Paul's Rhetoric.* Minneapolis: Fortress, 1990.

Wolf, Hans Walter. *Obadiah and Jonah: A Commentary.* Translated by Margaret Kohl. Minneapolis: Augsburg, 1986.

Wright, G. Ernest. *Biblical Archaeology.* Abridged. Philadelphia: Westminster, 1960.

Index of Authors and Subjects

Index of Scripture References